GIVING YOUTH
A BETTER CHANCE

Options for Education,
Work, and Service

*A Report
with Recommendations
of the Carnegie Council
on Policy Studies
in Higher Education*

GIVING YOUTH
A BETTER CHANCE

Options for Education,
Work, and Service

DISCARD

Jossey-Bass Publishers
San Francisco • Washington • London • 1979

GIVING YOUTH A BETTER CHANCE
Options For Education, Work, and Service
    The Carnegie Council on Policy Studies in Higher Education

The Carnegie Council Series

The following publications are available from Jossey-Bass Inc., Publishers, 433 California Street, San Francisco, California 94104.

*The following technical reports are available from the Carnegie
Council on Policy Studies in Higher Education, 2150 Shattuck Avenue,
Berkeley, California 94704.*

Contents

Part II: Schooling

Preface

Most of the work of the Carnegie Council has related directly to problems of higher education, but we have become convinced that those who are concerned with the future of higher education must also give serious consideration to the severe labor market and school problems facing segments of youth, especially minority group youth in inner cities and in some rural areas. This conviction is based on several considerations:

- There are serious inequities between the increasing resources devoted by our society to young people enrolled in higher education and the much less adequate resources allocated to those who do not enroll in college.
- Talent is lost to higher education and to society because of societal circumstances that push or pull potentially talented young people out of the educational stream at too early an age.
- Society must be increasingly as concerned with the qualifications and motivation of non-college youth entering the crafts, trades, and services as those entering occupations that require college training; to paraphrase John Gardner: in the excellence of its plumbers as of its philosophers.
- The costs to society of unemployment and delinquency among youth, as well as of lifelong patterns of unemployment and criminal activity among adults who get a poor start in life, are a drain on societal resources for other purposes, including support of higher education.

- Some institutions of higher education, notably community colleges, are increasingly involved in manpower programs for non-college youth. There is also a strong case for closer linkages than now exist between occupational education and work experience programs for both secondary and post-secondary students.
- More generally, the relationships between secondary education and higher education should be a continuing concern of institutions of higher education. One of the special reports issued by the Council's predecessor, the Carnegie Commission on Higher Education, entitled *Continuity and Discontinuity* (1973a), was concerned with these relationships.
- Higher education is responsible for training teachers, and there is much evidence that necessary changes in teacher education have lagged behind changing societal needs.
- Some successful experiences in higher education may be applicable to secondary education, such as work-study programs, basic educational grants to cover the subsistence costs of needy students, cooperative education programs, occupational placement centers, and the encouragement of diversity within and among institutions.
- The fact that the size of the teenage population will be declining in the 1980s creates an opportunity for increasing the resources devoted to non-college youth, especially the disadvantaged, without increasing total expenditures (in constant dollars) on youth.
- Recent moves to expand manpower programs for youth are to be commended, but these are in large part rescue operations aimed at youth who have dropped out of school or who have gained little benefit from school. We are concerned about the need for more attention to the trade-off between adequate resources devoted to in-school youth and rescue operations for out-of-school youth.

The United States is by no means alone in facing a problem of critical proportions relating to the education and employment of youth. Rising youth unemployment has been arousing increasing concern in nearly all of the industrial democracies, while it has become more and more clear throughout the 1970s that prolongation of schooling has brought with it severe problems of adjustment for many young people who are being held in school through a combination of parental and societal pressures and are not deriving much benefit from the experience.

Because we thought that there might be valuable insights for American policy in more adequate knowledge of how these problems are being met in other countries, we decided several years ago to sponsor the preparation of a group of essays on education and youth employment in selected countries.

Several of these essays have already appeared in the form of separate volumes on individual countries, and the remaining essays are forthcoming. We will also publish a volume that includes summaries of these essays, along with a chapter by Margaret S. Gordon on comparative youth unemployment in Western industrial countries as viewed by an economist and a chapter by Martin Trow on youth problems as viewed by a sociologist, entitled *Youth Education and Unemployment Problems: An International Perspective.* We are grateful to the German Marshall Fund for its support of this international project and to the International Council for Educational Development for carrying out the responsibility of helping to identify, and negotiating with, authors of the essays on particular countries. These volumes are listed in Appendix B.

Participants and observers of the two international symposia in 1976 and 1977 on the problems of youth employment and education are listed in Appendix C.

We also wish to thank the many experts on various aspects of youth problems who have been consulted and who provided assistance in the preparation of this report. They are listed in Appendix D.

In addition, we wish to thank Bay Area youth experts who served as a special advisory committee in earlier stages of this report: Curtis Aller, Department of Economics, San Francisco State University; Bruce Fuller, Assembly Education Subcommittee on Postsecondary Education, Sacramento; Van Dusen Kennedy, School of Business Administration, University of California, Berkeley; David Kirp, Graduate School of Public Policy, University of California, Berkeley; Martin Trow, Graduate School of Public Policy, University of California, Berkeley;

David Tyack, School of Education, Stanford University; Lloyd Ulman, Institute of Industrial Relations, University of California, Berkeley; Clair Vickery, Department of Economics, University of California, Berkeley.

Finally, we wish to express our appreciation for the work of our staff on this report, especially that of Margaret S. Gordon, who was assisted by Charlotte Alhadeff and Ruth Goto.

Members of the Carnegie Council on Policy Studies in Higher Education

Nolen Ellison
President
Cuyahoga Community College

Nell Eurich
Senior Consultant
International Council for
*   Educational Development*

Daniel J. Evans
President
The Evergreen State College

E. K. Fretwell, Jr.
Chancellor
The University of North Carolina
*   at Charlotte*

Margaret L. A. MacVicar
Associate Professor of Physics
Massachusetts Institute of
*   Technology*

Frank Newman
President
University of Rhode Island

Robert M. O'Neil
Vice-President
Indiana University at Bloomington

Rosemary Park
Professor of Education Emeritus
University of California at Los
*   Angeles*

James A. Perkins
Chairman of the Board
International Council for
Educational Development

Alan Pifer
President
The Carnegie Foundation for the
*   Advancement of Teaching*

Joseph Platt
President
Claremont University Center

Lois D. Rice
Vice-President
College Entrance Examination
*   Board*

William M. Roth

Stephen H. Spurr
Professor
LBJ School of Public Affairs
University of Texas

Clark Kerr
Chairperson
Carnegie Council on Policy Studies
*   in Higher Education*

GIVING YOUTH
A BETTER CHANCE

*Options for Education,
Work, and Service*

1

Summary of Concerns and Recommendations

Essential Facts

1. The "youth problem" in the United States is not going away. Yet our society has a better opportunity to deal effectively with it in the 1980s and the 1990s than we have had in the past two decades. Instead of growing explosively as it did in the 1960s, the youth population will be declining throughout most of the period from now to 2000. This will make it possible to devote more resources to the solution of what have been intractable youth problems, within a budget of stable or even declining expenditures for youth in toto.

What are the problems that are not going away of their own accord?

- Substantial dropout rates from high school continue—23 percent overall, 35 percent for blacks, 45 percent for Hispanics. (See Figure 1 for these and other selected data.)
- Substantial numbers of high school graduates have deficiencies in language and numerical skills—estimated at 20 percent.
- High school is an alienating experience for many young people; like a prison—albeit with open doors—for some.
- A surprisingly large percentage of adults do not look back on their high school experience as rewarding. Nearly one-half of the 1960 high school students in the Project Talent survey,

Figure 1. Selected data on youth

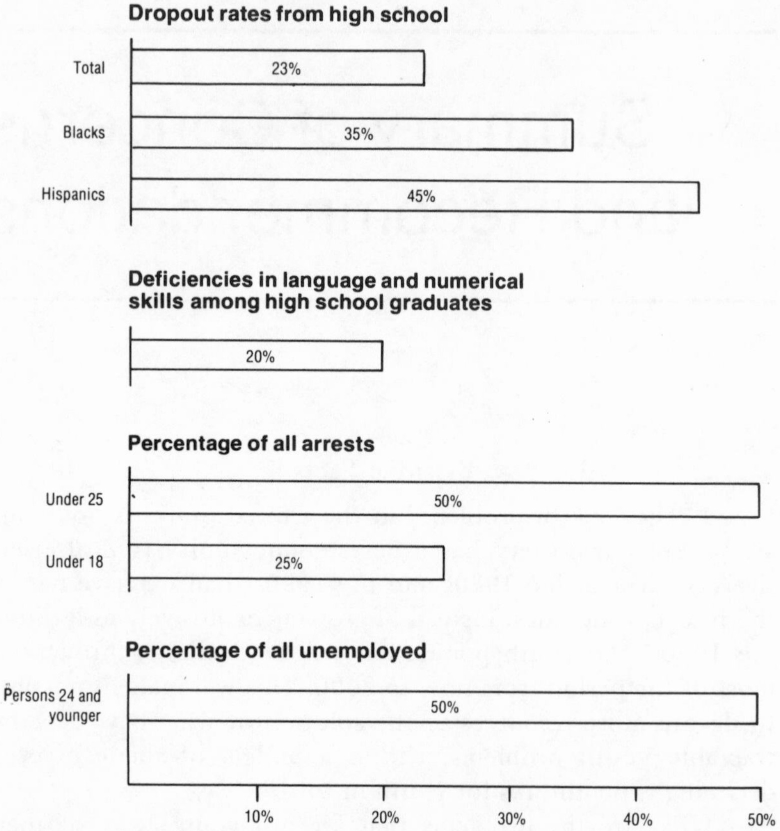

Dropout rates from high school

Total	23%
Blacks	35%
Hispanics	45%

Deficiencies in language and numerical skills among high school graduates

20%

Percentage of all arrests

Under 25	50%
Under 18	25%

Percentage of all unemployed

Persons 24 and younger	50%

10%   20%   30%   40%   50%

when questioned in a followup survey 11 years later, did not consider their high school experiences to have been "valuable" or even "fairly useful" (Wilson and Wise, 1975, p. v). By comparison, only about 15 percent of college students rate their experience as unsatisfactory.

· Nearly one-half of today's high school students do not consider the work in school hard enough (U.S. National Center for Education Statistics, 1979, p. 73).

· A general environment that would enable youth to make an effective transition into adulthood is deficient in many respects, including little early contact with the world of work and little opportunity ever for organized service to others. It is "knowledge rich" but "action poor,"[1] or, at least, action poor.

· Specifically, the transition into permanent jobs in the labor market is difficult for many youths.

· A sense of dependency is carried on too long; and, with it, a sense of rebellion against authority.

· Crime rates are high—more than 50 percent of all arrests are of youth under 25, and nearly 25 percent of those arrested are juveniles (under 18).

· Pockets of high and prolonged unemployment exist and will not be eradicated without special efforts—nearly 50 percent of all unemployment is accounted for by persons 24 and younger; and some pockets of youth have unemployment rates of 60 percent and higher, as traditionally measured.

· Nearly 6 percent of youth seem to have opted out of education, the labor market, and other customary pursuits.

· The number of nonwhite youths potentially subject to some form of inequality of opportunity will rise from 15.8 percent of the population aged 16 to 21 in 1980 to 18.7 percent in 1990 and then stabilize at about that proportion. This is a rise of nearly 20 percent in the share of the age cohort. The population of young Hispanics is also growing rapidly and will form a rising percentage of the total youth population. Counting Hispanics, the "minority" portion of youth will be at least 25 percent and possibly as high as 30 percent in 2000.

· Those who fall behind are by no means all members of disadvantaged minority groups. The unemployment rate among low-income white youths is as high as among low-income black youths, and the school dropout rate of low-income white youths is even higher than that of low-income blacks. In terms of numbers, disadvantaged white youths far exceed disadvantaged minority youths.

· As the already advantaged advance, the less advantaged tend to fall farther behind; and social cleavage widens and social

---

[1]See the discussion in *Youth: Transition to Adulthood* (1973, especially summary, introduction, and the introduction to part 3).

unrest accelerates. We are in danger of developing a permanent underclass, a self-perpetuating culture of poverty, a substantial and continuing "lumpen-proletariat" in the "home of
opportunity where every man is the equal of every other
man." We are in danger of creating a set of policies that provides a substantially free ride financially for many of the successful and permits, if it does not ensure, a bum's rush for the
unsuccessful in the race for life chances.

· Even among the most able, many young people fall behind in
the race. We estimate that about 100,000 more young people
would enter college each year if the percentage of "most
able" entrants from low-income and moderate-income families came up to that of the most affluent one-fourth of
families. We define the "most able" as the top 25 percent in
academic ability, and the loss of the talent of members of this
group is particularly costly to the nation.

As a society, we are spending a great deal more to help
low-income youth enter college than we are spending to help
low-income youth who are in high school, or who graduate
from high school but do not enter college, or who drop out of
school (see point 9 in the following discussion). Thus, there is a
problem of inequity—we need to redress the balance.

Beyond the issue of inequity, however, young people who
are failing to learn how to function effectively in a democratic
society present a problem to the entire society. We all pay a
price in terms of safety in our streets and our homes; in terms
of heavy social costs for unemployment, law enforcement, and
prisons; and in terms of the social malaise that stems in part
from the recognition that we are not meeting the problems of
many of our youth successfully.

The problems call for more than just money—although we
do recommend certain increased expenditures. They call for
mobilization within communities and for leadership on the part
of employers and unions, as well as civic and school officials.
National leadership and federal and state money can help, but
in the end the problems will be solved, if at all, mostly in local
communities and partly by private agencies. Money will help,

but by itself it will do very little. It will take a great deal of public and private initiative at the local level.

The quality and nature of the treatment of youth is an incisive commentary on a society in its entirety—on the family, the schools, the economy, the government, the culture, the beliefs of the people, their standards of conduct toward one another. In its youth a society can see itself in a huge but distorted mirror—as in a fun palace. The mirror of youth reflects back to our society a whole series of visions—some beautiful, some horrendous.

2. The number of unemployed youths is bound to go down over the next decade or more for demographic reasons; but, as we have just noted, this will not end the "youth problem." The number of 16-year-olds in 1990 as compared with 1980 (according to the Census Bureau's intermediate projection) will be as follows:

$$1980 = 100^2$$
$$1990 = 77$$

The population of 16- to 21-year-olds will reach its low point in 1994, as follows:

$$1980 = 100$$
$$1994 = 74$$

An even lower Census Bureau projection, which now appears more likely, shows the 16-year-old population reaching its low point in 1995.

Young people generally will be in high demand. Military demand for eligible males, as a percentage, will develop as follows:

$$1980 = 25 \text{ percent}$$
$$1990 = 30 \text{ percent}$$

Higher education will try very hard to retain its number of stu-

[2] Four million persons now reach age 16 each year; the number will be just over three million in 1990.

dents. This will be difficult in the face of a decline in the college-age population (18- to 24-year-olds) of 23 percent from 1978 to its low point in 1997. Private employers and government agencies will also be competing to secure employees within the reduced age cohort.

Youth will be in high demand, not in high oversupply. Two decades of surplus will be followed by nearly two decades of deficit. Many youths will never have had it so good.

3. Youth unemployment has been exaggerated in the recent past. This exaggeration has caused undue attention to unemployment as *the* problem of youth, when there are, in fact, many problems and some of them more serious and harder to handle. The reasons for this exaggeration have been two:

a. Military personnel have been excluded from the base.
b. All college and high school students who are not in the labor force have also been excluded.

The overall distribution of the age cohort is shown in Figure 2, and distribution by race and sex in Figure 3. For the age cohort as a whole, 6 percent are not in school (on a full-time basis) and not in the armed forces, but in the labor force and unemployed.

What tends to be forgotten is how many young persons (under age 25) have been added to the labor force since 1960 and absorbed into employment—over 10 million; also nearly 10 million adult women; and perhaps 5 million immigrants (legal and illegal). Higher education has also absorbed 7.6 million additional young persons since 1960. The absorptive capacity of the labor market and of higher education over the past 20 years has been enormous; without it, what has been a difficult situation (about 1.2 million youth in the 16- to 21-year-old group unemployed and not in school) would have been an intolerable one.

Unemployment for youth is often short-term due to a rapid turnover in jobs. Whereas, in 1978, 23 percent of all unemployed workers were long-term unemployed (out of work 15 weeks or more), only 15 percent of the unemployed in the 16-

Figure 2. Activity status of young people aged 16 to 21, 1978

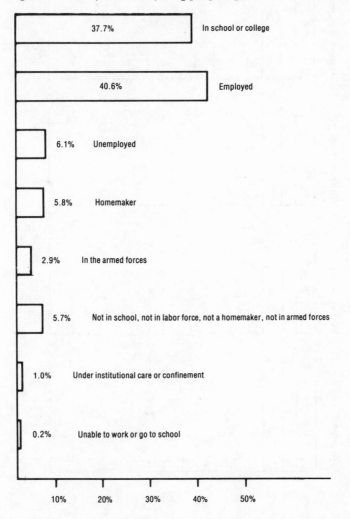

Source: Computed from data in U.S. Bureau of the Census (1979c); U.S. Bureau of Labor Statistics (1979, tables 3 and 7).

to 21-age group were long-term unemployed. As a proportion of the total age cohort, these long-term unemployed were only 1.3 percent (including both students and nonstudents). Data on duration of unemployment are not available for the two groups separately.

Figure 3. Activity status of young people aged 16 to 21, by race and sex, 1977

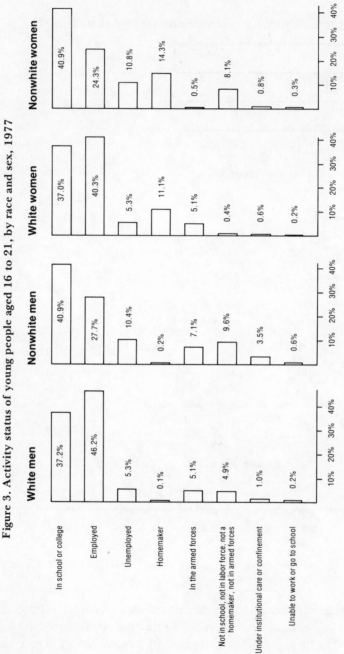

Source: Computed from data in U.S. Bureau of the Census (1979c); U.S. Bureau of Labor Statistics (1979, tables 3 and 7).

4. Pockets of high unemployment among youth are concentrated in certain groups. Particularly revealing, in view of the concern of this report with the relations between education and the labor market, are the data in Figure 4, which show unemployment rates for recent high school graduates who are not

Figure 4. Unemployment rates for recent high school graduates (not in college) and school dropouts, by race, October 1977

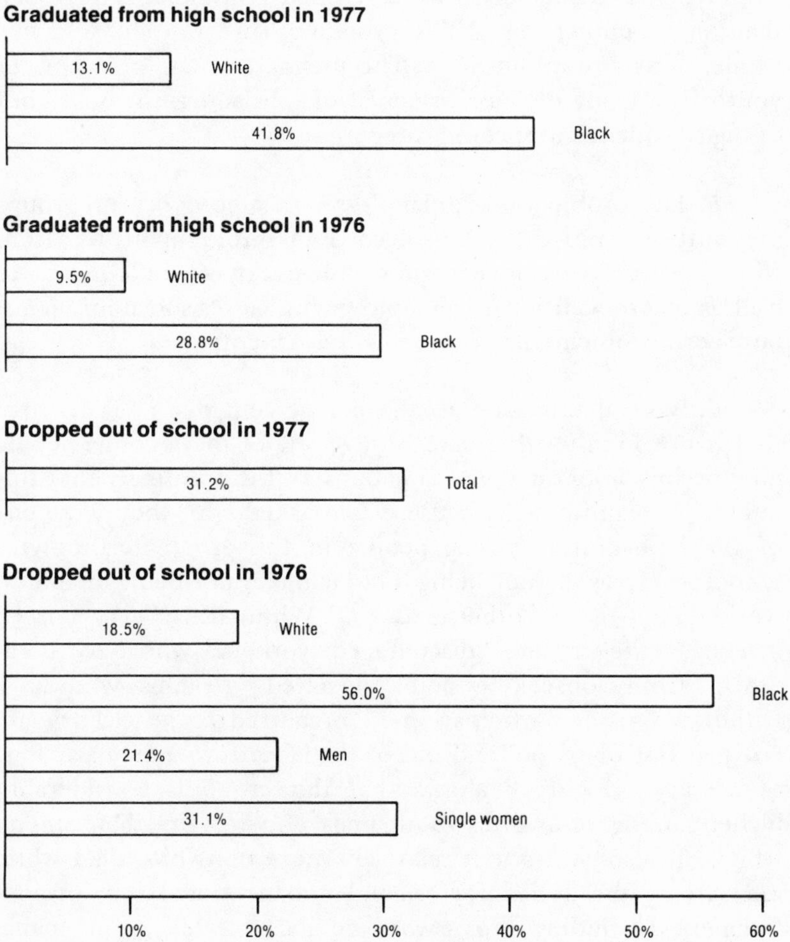

Graduated from high school in 1977

13.1%	White
41.8%	Black

Graduated from high school in 1976

9.5%	White
28.8%	Black

Dropped out of school in 1977

31.2%	Total

Dropped out of school in 1976

18.5%	White
56.0%	Black
21.4%	Men
31.1%	Single women

10%   20%   30%   40%   50%   60%

Source: U.S. Bureau of Labor Statistics (1978).

enrolled in college and for recent school dropouts. Here we use unemployment rates as generally defined (we fully recognize the many deficiencies in their standard measures), that is, the unemployed as a percentage of members of the group who are in the civilian labor force. As a percentage of the entire cohort, the rates would of course, be much lower. The far higher unemployment rates for blacks are the most striking aspect of the data, but recent white dropouts had a very high rate of unemployment, while single women fared considerably less well than men among the 1976 dropouts (the rate for married women was not published). The unemployment problem for youth is not one of massive denial of jobs across-the-board but of high incidence in specific categories.

5. The problems of unemployment among certain groups of youth will not easily be solved. Full employment, by itself, will not entirely remove their problems. It will take micro- as well as macro-solutions. Unemployment causes social problems, but social problems also cause unemployment.

6. We call attention to the 5.7 percent of the age cohort that is not in any other category. A few of these young people may be in school on a part-time basis, but it is unlikely that this number is significant, because, when asked why they were out of the labor force, young people in this group did not give school as a reason (nor being a homemaker nor being unable to work). They gave "other reasons." Within this "very miscellaneous" category are "discouraged workers" who have withdrawn from jobseeking and "alienated" persons who have withdrawn from participation in organized society. They are not just out of school and out of the labor force; they are "out of society." Figure 3 shows that this group is considerably higher among nonwhites—both male and female—than among whites. It also shows that relatively more nonwhite than white men are in the armed forces, under institutional care or confinement (including those who are incarcerated), and unable to work. Thus, it is not just unemployment that accounts for the lower proportion of nonwhite men who are employed.

The gravest problems are among the long-term unemployed (1.3 percent) and the "out-of-society" group (5.7 percent), which total about 7 percent of youth (16-21) or about 1.8 million persons, with 80 percent of this total in the "out-of-society" category. We say "among" because these are not homogeneous groups and some members may be in quite satisfactory situations, as, for example, in viable communes.

The public attention directed at unemployment has obscured the many other and more serious problems. Youth in America is not suffering from a single malady (unemployment), and no single patent medicine (full employment) will cure the many illnesses. We have instead a growth, more like a cancer in our body politic—causes not fully known, cure not fully known. But it creates great pain in the suffering of ruined lives, crime, drug addiction, lost hopes, social fears, reduced productivity, raised social expenditures, and disdain for authority.

The concentration on unemployment has largely buried from sight the deeper problems. This has been a disservice to the American people. We face a cancer, not a common cold.

The youth problem is more manageable than it has looked because the numbers are smaller than had been assumed and will become still smaller; but it is more intractable, involves more of the many facets of our society, requires more kinds of solutions—more ingenuity, more determination and devotion, more understanding.

7. We make these general points as background for our recommendations:

There are many youth problems.

Unemployment has been only one of them; and, where it has been most intense, it will not easily evaporate.

The "out-of-everything" group may constitute an even more severe problem than the unemployed—the latter at least are still trying to get a job.

8. Constructive activities by individual youths, in some situations, cost the public in expenditures per young person less than the nonconstructive use of time:[3]

[3]For an earlier effort at comparisons, see Alan Pifer (1971).

Constructive		*Nonconstructive*	
Employment	$0	Unemployment	$ 1,500

High school	$ 2,500	Juvenile incarceration	$18,000
College	2,000		
Military	10,500		
Peace Corps	15,000		
Vista volunteers	6,700		
CETA	$4,000-$8,000		

It obviously costs the public far less to have young persons in school or at work than in jail.

9. Federal government expenditures for education and employment are far higher for a low-income youth attending college than for a low-income youth who is still in high school or who has dropped out of high school, as a special report prepared by the Congressional Budget Office at the request of Senator Harrison Williams, chairman of the Senate Committee on Labor and Human Resources, shows:

Federal expenditures on education
and employment per young person

	Low-income youth[4]	All youth
In college	$1,940	$675
In high school	278	97
High school dropout	339	168
High school graduate	238	78
College dropout	51	21

The data show that the disparities are wide for all youth, but they are especially significant for low-income youth, because problems of unemployment and dropping out are particularly severe among low-income youth.

The low level of federal expenditures on low-income in-

---

[4]Low-income youth include those in the lowest one-fifth in terms of family income. The data are from a press release issued by Senator Williams, July 12, 1979.

school youth largely reflects the fact that expenditures under Title I of the Elementary and Secondary Education Act of 1965 and other child development and child care programs are heavily targeted toward prekindergarten, kindergarten, and elementary school children and not toward secondary school students:

	Estimated total expenditures (FY 1980) (thousands)	*Per participant*	*Per student*
Title I Prekindergarten and kindergarten	$ 344 (10%)	$787	n.a.
Grades 1 to 6	2,469 (71%)	782	$133
Grades 7 to 12	671 (19%)	778	35
Vocational Education Grades 7 to 12	498	199	24

Federal expenditures on vocational education go a little way toward redressing the balance between elementary and secondary education, but, as we show in Section 7, could be used more effectively.[5]

These priorities appear doubtful to us, in view of the serious problems of absenteeism and dropping out in grades 10, 11, and 12; and in view of deficits in basic skills. Federal money is not now being spent in proportions that are geared to the intensity of the problems.

Fundamental Concerns

10. We concentrate our attention on the years 16 to 21 when the problems of transition to adulthood are most intense. The most troublesome years are 16 to 17, when we are most likely to "lose the game" with and for some youth—when some

---

[5]Our estimates of the allocation of Title I funds are based on Larson and others (1977, p. 26) and assume the same number of participants as in 1973-74. However, data prepared by the Congressional Budget Office for Senator Williams indicate that only 5 percent of Title I funds nationwide are expended on secondary students.

youth clearly advance but others clearly retrogress. The most dangerous hours are weekdays 2:00 to 6:00 p.m., between the time when many, even most, students "split" from school and the time the parent or parents arrive home from work.

We also concentrate on the areas of schooling, work, and service.

We acknowledge that many problems originate before age 16 and continue after age 21. We also acknowledge that there are many problems for youth outside of schooling, work, and service—in areas of family life, urban living, temptations of drugs and alcohol, uncertainties about the future, lack of respect for the performance of many social institutions, and others.

We note, in particular, that a lot of the problems that have become endemic in many high schools have moved down into some junior high schools, including lack of discipline, absenteeism, vandalism, and use of drugs.

11. We note that a society based on industrial pursuits creates very special difficulties for young persons (as also for the aged—less engaged than in earlier societies in productive labor and less embraced by family ties). For youths, the transition from childhood to adulthood has at least four relatively new and troublesome aspects:

• The transition from school to work is very abrupt. In pre-industrial societies, as on the farm or in the family shop, school and work were more melded; there was no sharp break from 100 percent of one to 100 percent of the other. The transition is also more uncertain. Far fewer young persons follow in the footsteps of their parents. Many more possible careers are open before them, but none of them are assured.
• The transition is also very long. We have greatly prolonged youth—the period from adolescence to adulthood. We have created what might be called "compulsory youth"—a substantial time between dependence and independence, a twilight zone of uncertainty and ambiguity of status. There are some good explanations of why this period is now longer; among

them, in particular, is that biological maturity comes earlier and full acceptance by the institutions of the adult world comes later. And it does take more time than in earlier days to accumulate job skills; to try out the market to see what it wants and what the young person realistically has to offer; to make decisions about lifestyle as well as vocation; to decide on geographical location and possible life companions. We have created a new stage of young adulthood.

· No institution has a clear and fully accepted responsibility for following the welfare of persons through the stage of young adulthood. The influences of the parental family and also of the school have often declined by this stage of life, and youths have not yet established their own families and their own more or less permanent job connections. It is often particularly difficult for them to move from jobs in the insecure, unstructured, secondary labor market to the more structured, primary market.

· Youths are often left largely to the guidance, companionship, and mercy of their peers and the electronic media (Figure 5). They have not yet been embraced by the welfare employer and the welfare union; or, as for the aged, by the welfare state. In a highly organized society, this condition of comparative neglect adds to personal freedom, but it also has its grave perils for those who, for one reason or another, are unable or unwilling to make good use of that freedom.

12. Specifically, these are our major concerns:

· Reducing dropouts and absenteeism in high school.
· Improving basic skills of high school graduates.
· Giving high school students an opportunity to develop useful work habits.
· Reducing the alienating aspects of the high school experience.
· Easing the transition from high school to the labor market.
· Improving the paths into higher education.
· Improving the paths into military service.
· Creating many more opportunities for other forms of service by youth.

Figure 5. Changing patterns of influence on youth

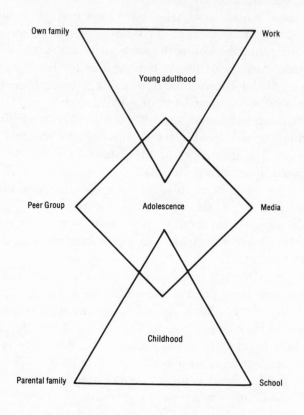

Source: Kerr (1977, p. 141).

13. We accept, for the purposes of this report, among other aspects of the environment, the following as "givens," whether we like them or not (and some of them we do not like):

· More one-parent families, and more mothers at work.
· The high attractiveness of "street life" for some young people; the high returns for participation in the "subterranean" economy, in "off-the-books" activities; the easy choice of full-time leisure.

- The difficulty the schools and jobs have in competing with the automobile, TV, the radio, drugs, the disco parlors; even with the free and "adult" life of living on Aid to Families with Dependent Children (AFDC—given to unmarried or separated young women with children).
- The temporary, dead-end nature of many of the jobs in the unstructured labor market that provide most of the openings for young persons, the unattractive aspects of many of these jobs, and their comparatively low pay.
- A standard minimum wage that applies also to youths, contrary to the situation in many other countries.
- Continuing competition for youths in the labor market from women newly entering employment and from legal and illegal immigrants.
- Heightened aspirations of youths for the types of jobs that they are willing to accept and a growing sense of the entitlements that society is thought to owe to them.
- The continuing existence of some totally alienated young persons whom our recommendations will not reach.
- The insolubility of some problems—which means that it is best to concentrate on problems that can be solved and on those that can be made more tolerable, even if not fully solved.

14. We emphasize that, just as there is no "youth problem" in the singular, there is also no single entity of "youth." We have found useful the typology of Martin Trow (discussed in more detail in Section 14). It has led us to the development of a related typology that is more quantifiable than Trow's and that bears more directly on our specific concerns:

I. *The Advantaged:* young persons from families in the top two-thirds of the income range and who finish high school.

II. *The Financially Disadvantaged:* young persons from families in the bottom one-third of the income range who finish high school but, where doing so, may impose a financial hardship on their families and where attendance in college does impose such a hardship.

III. *The Socially Deprived:* young persons who do not finish

high school for reasons of social circumstances (family and community deprivations, and social prejudices).
IV. *The Personally Deprived:* young persons who do not finish high school for reasons of personal circumstances (mental, physical, or psychological disabilities).
V. *The Opt-outs:* young persons who do not choose to participate in established educational or economic institutions of society for reasons of personal choice or philosophical orientation.

Schematically our version of the Trow typology is as follows:

	High school performance	
Family income	*Complete*	*Dropout*
Top two-thirds	Advantaged	Personally deprived
		Opt-outs
Bottom one-third	Financially disad-	Socially deprived
	vantaged	Personally deprived
		Opt-outs

We recognize that this is a crude way of categorizing a heterogeneous group of young people. We put forward this classification system, however, because:

a. It helps to make the point that we are dealing with more than a monolithic entity of "youth."
b. It makes it possible to quantify these gross classifications and thus to indicate the size of our problem (Figure 6).
c. It creates the possibility of relating some of our recommendations, to target groups, as we shall do later.

In particular, we should like to note two problems with this system of classification:

• Young persons may get through high school but not have basic skills in the handling of numbers and language, and thus they may be "internal" dropouts. The external dropout

Figure 6. Estimated distribution of population aged 16 to 21 by Carnegie typology, by race or ethnic origin

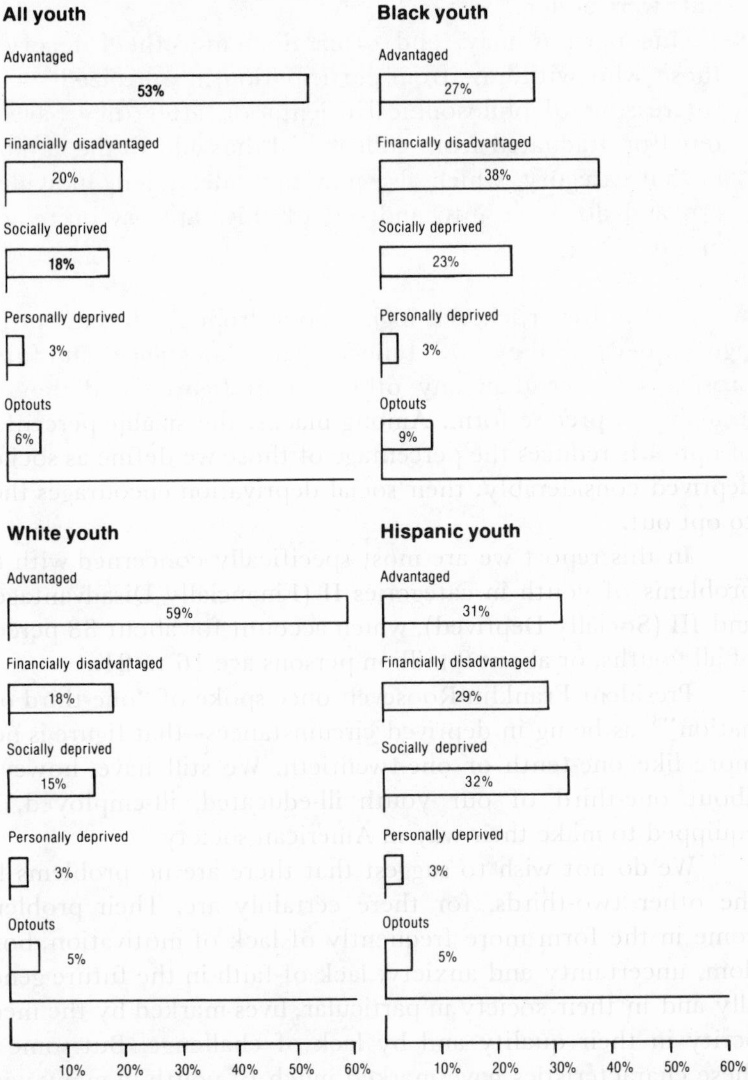

All youth

Advantaged
53%

Financially disadvantaged
20%

Socially deprived
18%

Personally deprived
3%

Optouts
6%

Black youth

Advantaged
27%

Financially disadvantaged
38%

Socially deprived
23%

Personally deprived
3%

Optouts
9%

White youth

Advantaged
59%

Financially disadvantaged
18%

Socially deprived
15%

Personally deprived
3%

Optouts
5%

10% 20% 30% 40% 50% 60%

Hispanic youth

Advantaged
31%

Financially disadvantaged
29%

Socially deprived
32%

Personally deprived
3%

Optouts
5%

10% 20% 30% 40% 50% 60%

Note: Typology is a modification of Trow's (see Section 14). The percentage shown as "personally deprived" exceeds the percentage classified as "unable to work" or "under institutional care or confinement" in Figure 2, because not all the physically or mentally handicapped are unable to work. Moreover, some of those in institutions are not disabled but are incarcerated.

Source: Carnegie Council estimates.

figures do not fully reflect the severity of the problem. Thus, Category III would be somewhat larger if these internal drop-outs were added.

· Young persons may, and often do, enter the category of those who withdraw from participation in organized society for reasons of philosophical orientation after they have entered or graduated from college and thus add to the numbers in that category, which also may be understated. Individuals can and do move into and out of this category quite commonly.

We have, however, chosen high school dropout rates as our key figures, because they both reflect past circumstances and future prospects better than any other set of figures; and they are available in precise form. Among blacks, the sizable percentage of opt-outs reduces the percentage of those we define as socially deprived considerably; their social deprivation encourages them to opt out.

In this report we are most specifically concerned with the problems of youth in categories II (Financially Disadvantaged) and III (Socially Deprived), which account for about 38 percent of all youths, or about 9 million persons age 16 to 21.

President Franklin Roosevelt once spoke of "one-third of a nation"[8] as being in deprived circumstances—that figure is now more like one-tenth or one-twentieth. We still have, however, about one-third of our youth ill-educated, ill-employed, ill-equipped to make their way in American society.

We do not wish to suggest that there are no problems for the other two-thirds, for there certainly are. Their problems come in the form more frequently of lack of motivation, boredom, uncertainty and anxiety, lack of faith in the future generally and in their society in particular, lives marked by the mediocrity in their quality and by lack of challenge. But some of these characteristics have marked much of youth in many parts of the world throughout the ages.

[6]"I see one-third of a nation ill-housed, ill-clad, ill-nourished" (Second Inaugural Address, Jan. 20, 1937).

Priority Recommendations

15. We have chosen to concentrate largely on recommendations of programs:

- that are open to all youth and not just to the more disadvantaged and deprived, although these latter may particularly benefit
- where administrative mechanisms are already in place to effectuate the program
- that are not highly vulnerable to error and abuse
- that have proven successful on trial in the United States or elsewhere
- Where the potential cost is reasonable

We are impressed with the local initiative and successful experiments around the nation and, in particular, cite projects worth emulating in:

Baltimore	Hartford	Milwaukee	Portland
Boston	Houston	New York	Seattle
Dallas	Los Angeles	Philadelphia	Syracuse

We are also impressed by the good results that have come from private actions by social welfare and church groups.

We draw on what we consider to be successful programs abroad (see Appendix A) and particularly in:

China	Germany	Sweden
France	Japan	United Kingdom

By now there is much experience here and abroad with the handling of youth problems, and we believe the time has come to draw on that rich experience in the development of an overall program of attack on these problems.

Our main goal is to present to young persons the reality that "many ways are open to them, no one sanctioned above its alternative, and that upon them and them alone lies the burden of choice" (Mead, 1961, p. 246). We also would like to see the

development of a body of youth, the members of which will
know—more so than they now do—when they need more information on which to base their choices and how to get it.

We make these recommendations with the conviction that
there has been a plentitude of criticism of youth but a paucity
of action to aid youth constructively. American society has
been criticism-rich and action-poor.

The recommendations that follow relate to social policy.
We wish to emphasize, however, that basic responsibility lies
with the family and with the individual young person. Social
policy can be greatly improved, but it cannot substitute for
good environments in families and good decisions by youths.

We regret that there are many unknowns about which we
wish we could make recommendations that we could have confidence in—particularly, how to prepare and select effective
teachers and how to prepare and select effective school administrators. These are absolutely essential ingredients in the performance of schools. It is a tragedy that so little is known about
how to ensure their high quality.

1. Make age 16 the age of free choice to leave school, take a
   job, enter the military service, enter other forms of service,
   continue in school, enter college, enter an apprenticeship. In
   particular, we see no clear need for compulsory attendance
   in school after age 16. At age 21, young persons should be
   as fully on their own as possible. Special help and the sense
   of dependency it fosters should not go on indefinitely.

High Schools

2. Change the basic structure of high schools by making them
   smaller or by creating diversity within them or both; by
   creating full-time specialty schools, particularly for the
   grades 11 and 12; by creating part-time specialty schools—
   one or two days a week per student on a rotating basis—by
   providing one or two days a week for education-related
   work and/or service. We set forth several such models in
   Figure 7 and discuss them more fully in Section 8. We must
   find ways to break up the big, monolithic high school and

Figure 7. Illustrative models of alternative school plans at the secondary level

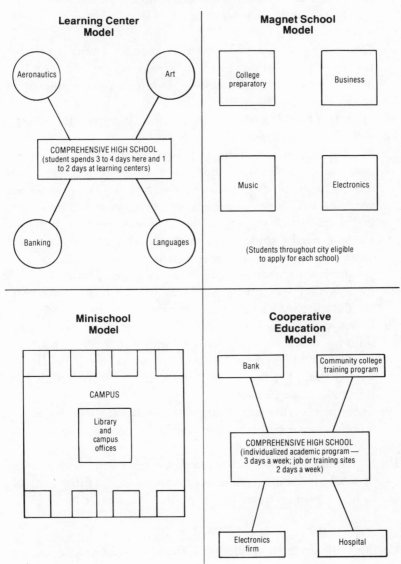

Source: Carnegie Council.

its deadly weekly routine. We believe that instruction in basic skills and general knowledge can be concentrated without loss of achievement in three effectively used days per week.

3. Create work and service opportunities for students through the facilities of the high schools, making performance part of the student record. We also favor a renewed emphasis on student out-of-class activities.

4. Stop the tracking of students; all programs should be individualized programs.

5. Put applied skill training in private shops (with the exception of clerical skills and home economics), when not moved to the postsecondary level. The basic vocational (and academic) skills for the high school to concentrate on are the skills of literacy and numeracy—and good work habits.

6. Finance needy students through work-study programs and more effective efforts to place them in jobs.

7. Create job preparation and placement centers in the high schools that will follow students for their first two years after graduation or other termination.

8. Improve the capacity of secondary schools to teach basic skills by allocating more federal funds under the Elementary and Secondary Education Act to secondary schools. We strongly support the "Push for Excellence" program led by Reverend Jesse Jackson.

9. Encourage earlier entry from high school into college and more programs combining the last year or two of high school with college.

10. Experiment with vouchers and greater freedom of choice, particularly among *public* schools. Bureaucratic controls have not assured quality; competition to survive may.

Postsecondary

11. Concentrate most applied skill training at the postsecondary level and particularly in the community colleges (in four-year comprehensive colleges where a community college is not in the locality).

12. Create programs in community colleges (and selected comprehensive colleges) where young persons can be prepared for jobs and placed in jobs on a part-time basis while attending college.

     More broadly, the community college should take on a residual responsibility for youth. This can become the sixth great role for the community college in addition to (a) academic transfer programs, (b) technical training, (c) terminal general education, (d) community service programs (instruction in nonacademic, nonvocational subjects as requested by members of the community), and (e) community-based programs (such as conferences, cultural events). It would involve being available to all youths in the community to advise on academic and occupational opportunities, to offer job preparation classes, to make job placements, to work out individual combinations of employment and classroom instruction, to develop and to make referrals to service opportunities, to make referrals to CETA employers, to make referrals to sources of legal and medical advice, to refer to and to create apprenticeship programs. Additional and specialized personnel will be required for this purpose. These might be known as "youth service functions." Youths would be given an institutional base of operation. We badly need better and more encompassing "institutions for the young" (Coleman, 1973, p. 398).

13. Revise student aid programs to target them more to low-income students (as recommended in our recent report on *Next Steps for the 1980s in Student Financial Aid,* 1979).

14. Have all colleges create offices of community services to help students find off-campus service opportunities as part of their work-study assignments or on a volunteer basis.

15. Improve teacher training programs, including workplace experience for teachers.[7]

16. Encourage colleges and universities to assist local schools in basic skills training.

[7]See recommendation of Husen (1979, p. 162).

Labor Market

17. Eliminate special "protective" legislation in the employment of youth that restricts the work they can do as compared with adults.
18. Eliminate social security taxes for teenage youth and their
employers—making it more profitable for the one to accept
employment and the other to offer it.
19. Create nonprofit "job corporations" that will prepare and
place students in jobs, and handle their pay and fringe benefits—in effect, acting as contractors for them and making it
easier for others to employ them. Care would need to be
taken that such an approach did not result in corruption
and exploitation.
20. Provide a system of retention bonuses for young persons
who have suffered long-term unemployment or heavy turnover to encourage them to stay on jobs, as part of the CETA
program and possibly after participation in prior CETA programs.
21. Augment current apprenticeship programs and create new
ones including:
   • Civil service apprenticeships
   • Military apprenticeships for 16- and 17-year-olds, and for
     persons 18 and over not eligible for service but who can
     be made eligible through such a program.
22. We do not recommend, at this time, a general program of
wage subsidies for the employment of youth. Such programs have not proved very effective and appear too open
to abuse and error. But we strongly favor training subsidies
for employers who provide on-the-job training for disadvantaged youth or who expand apprenticeship opportunities.

Service

23. Create a multifaceted voluntary youth service, with initiative for most service projects coming from the local level
and with educational benefits attached to the service program.
24. Create a National Educational Fund into which service
credits and other contributions can be paid and then drawn

upon later in life. We see a future in which students, with few exceptions, have a chance to earn the subsistence costs of their college education and some (but not always all) of their tuition; a future in which they are on a self-help basis.

25. Keep the draft voluntary. We see no current need for a compulsory draft, although there are possible circumstances when it might become necessary later. We see great problems in making the draft compulsory. We note that military policy, however it develops, will have a crucial impact on all youth policy.

Community

26. Develop in every sizable community a work-education council as proposed by Wirtz and the National Manpower Institute (1975, pp. 65ff.), which will bring together school officials and representatives of employers, unions, and public agencies to coordinate programs for youth.

We started this list of recommendations by saying that the age of free choice should be 16, but we have added that free choice should also be among more and better paths:

a. Improved high schools
b. More assurance of financial support to the needy in attending college
c. More opportunities in the labor market and better transition mechanisms into the labor market
d. Earlier and easier entry into the military service
e. A vast expansion of other service opportunities

The proposals we advance should:

• Marginally aid the Advantaged.
• End the category of the Financially Disadvantaged by providing more opportunities for earnings, work-study grants, and student assistance, particularly in high school since much has already been done at the college level.
• Substantially reduce the category of the Deprived—for rea-

sons of social circumstances, and, perhaps, over time, it can be cut in half. To wipe out this category entirely will take major renovations in living conditions in urban and rural slums, many improvements in the quality of family life, and the end of racial discrimination.
- Slightly affect, if at all, youth deprived for reasons of personal ability.
- Slightly affect, if at all, the numbers of the opt-outs—for reasons of strictly personal choice or for reasons of philosophical orientation. There is an irreduceable number of such youths in any society, and American culture as a whole seems to induce some expansion of this category.

Thus, slightly more than one-quarter of all youth would significantly benefit: the 20 percent who are financially disadvantaged and perhaps one-half of those (or 9 percent of the total) who are socially deprived. This amounts, currently, to 7.3 million persons. Problem groups would still remain, representing the impacts of the most intractable problems of all. However, potentially, nearly all of youth would be aided to some appreciable extent by the measures we support.

The net costs of our suggested programs to the federal government range from $1.4 billion to $1.9 billion in 1980-81, depending on the severity of the current recession. If unemployment rises substantially in 1980, increased expenditures for youth programs will be needed. Several of our proposals, moreover, such as the work-study program and the comprehensive youth service program, call for gradually increasing expenditures during the course of the 1980s, but these rising expenditures should be at least partially offset by reductions in the social costs associated with dropouts, juvenile delinquency, and school security measures, among others.

Against the costs of our proposals, we set greater equality of opportunity for all of our youth; the liberation of talent now lost to society; a higher average level of basic skills; a smoother transition into the world of work; more certainty that most youths will have set before them one or more acceptable choices; the prospect that more youths will reach adulthood prepared to contribute constructively to the welfare of others;

and a declaration that American society is a caring society in relation to its youth.

We need a full-participation society as much as we need a full-employment economy.

16. Should a depression come, we urge quick action on the following in particular:

Item   6—financing needy students in high school
Item 14—targeting student financial aid in college more toward low-income students
Item 21—creation of civil service and military apprenticeships
Item 23—creation of a multifaceted voluntary youth service

The energy crisis adds to the importance of trying to hold students in high school in the afternoons, as compared with "tooling around," and to reduce absenteeism:

Item 2—breaking the deadly weekly routine
Item 3—creating work and service opportunities
Item 9—creating opportunities to get an early start on college-credit studies

17. We see, overall, a better future for most youth—even a much better future—for the next two decades than the past two, barring war and depression; the most favored generation since the 1950s. The possibility, and we think the likelihood, of better social policies is one reason. The certainty of a deficit of youth—and the resultant competition to attract young persons by colleges, by employers, by the military, by the churches, and by the unions—is another reason. There should be and can be more and better choices for youth; less segregation of youth from age, of race from race, of education from work and service, of youth from employment, of opportunities for the poor from those for the rich; less sense that youths are "outsiders" in relation to the rest of society—unwanted and often uncared for. These developments can help to restore some of the largely lost challenge to youth that you "have the world before you."

Part I

Background

2

Schooling, Employment, and Community Behavior: Inseparable Problems

From a global perspective, America's record of educating its youth is a success story. Educational attainment of young people has reached very high levels by international standards, although Japan has recently moved ahead of the United States and Canada is not far behind. The American response to the challenge of educating the huge generation of postwar babies that moved through our schools and colleges in the 1950s and 1960s was an enviable achievement. We built the schools, we trained and recruited the teachers, and in the 1960s we expanded our systems of higher education so that colleges were accessible to young people—and to many adults as well— throughout the nation and in almost every community of any appreciable size.

There is, however, another more disturbing side of the situation of youth that has become increasingly apparent in the 1960s and 1970s. One manifestation of this is a very high rate of youth unemployment, and another is a critical situation in our school system. Both problems are particularly severe in the inner cities of large metropolitan areas and in some rural areas. But in certain respects, the problems of the schools are nationwide. They are found in affluent suburbs, middle-sized cities, and small towns, as well as in large cities and rural areas.

By now there is a vast literature on youth unemployment. There is also a large and growing literature on school problems. But they are generally quite separate. We propose to consider both the labor market and educational aspects, with particular attention to the relations between them. The fact that success of youth in the job market is strongly related to educational attainment is well established. It is those who have dropped out before completing high school, along with those who have graduated without having learned even the basic skills of reading and arithmetic, that have the most difficult time in the job market. This is true not only in the United States, but in all industrialized countries (see Gordon, forthcoming). At the same time, the inadequacies of the schools are at least partly responsible for the facts that many youngsters drop out and that many others learn very little. We believe that changes in our schools, especially at the secondary level, are vitally needed, and that there is a need to relate our manpower policies for youth more closely to what is happening in the schools, as we are beginning to do.

Youth Unemployment

High youth unemployment rates have been a matter of concern in the United States since at least the early 1960s, and we have developed a number of manpower programs to deal with them, without much success, although the programs have clearly helped many individual young people. But in the years since the early 1960s, we have learned a great deal about youth unemployment. One of the most important lessons is that it is not a serious problem for the great majority of young people but that it is a severe problem indeed for certain segments of American youth.

Students and Nonstudents

One of the distinctive characteristics of the youth unemployment problem in the United States is the fact that among our youthful jobseekers are many students who are looking for part-time work. Nearly one-half of all the students in the 16- to 21-age group are in the labor force—they are either working (mostly on a part-time basis) or they are seeking work. In most other industrial countries, part-time work among students is much less common, except to some extent in the summer, and students in many of these countries are not counted as part of the labor force at all.

How much difference does the inclusion of students make in the youth unemployment problem? We have noted in Section 1 that about 1.2 million persons aged 16 to 21 were not enrolled in school and were unemployed in 1977. They represented about 5 percent of the total population in the age group but 14.7 percent of the nonstudent civilian labor force—the official unemployment rate for this group. There were also 870,000 students who were unemployed in October 1977. They represented 3.4 percent of the total age group but 14.3 percent of the student civilian labor force. Thus, the official unemployment rates of students and nonstudents were very similar.

Unemployment among students is clearly a less serious social problem than unemployment among nonstudents. It is much less likely to be of long duration than unemployment among youthful nonstudents. A more important consideration, however, is that the unemployment experienced by students, while interfering with their capacity to pay for the cost of their education (usually temporarily), is not likely to have much long-term impact on their eventual careers. Prolonged unemployment among youthful nonstudents or frequent shifts from one temporary job to another may result in a lifetime pattern of poor earnings and unemployment.

It is sometimes argued that youthful students—especially those 16- to 17-year-olds—should be eliminated from labor force and unemployment data, since their unemployment is not a matter of serious social concern. In fact, the National Commission on Employment and Unemployment Statistics, which published its final report in September 1979, tentatively considered eliminating all 16- and 17-year-olds from the labor force on the grounds that most of them were only marginally attached to the labor force and nearly 90 percent were in school

(National Commission on Employment and Unemployment Statistics, 1979, pp. 35-36). The Commission's final decision, however, was to continue including them. We agree with this decision. Elimination of all 16- and 17-year-olds from labor force statistics would have reduced the overall unemployment rate in 1977 only from 7.0 to 6.5 percent and would have reduced the unemployment rate for youth (redefined from 16-21 to 18-21) only from 14.5 to 13.4 percent. Their exclusion would, therefore, make relatively little difference in unemployment rates and would create complications, because 16 is the legal minimum age under the Fair Labor Standards Act and the legal school-leaving age in most states. Moreover, we believe that 16 should be the legal school-leaving age in all states and that emphasis on opportunities for work experience for students in the 16- to 17-age group should be greatly increased.

Another possible way of redefining the labor force would be to eliminate all students aged 16 to 21. This would have reduced the overall unemployment rate in 1977 from 7.0 to 6.6 percent but would not have reduced the youthful unemployment rate at all, since unemployment rates of students were slightly lower than those of nonstudents in this age group.

Significantly, however, if we consider those students whose *major activity* is school attendance (presumably chiefly full-time students), we find that their unemployment rate is somewhat higher than that of nonstudents. This is probably because part-time students are likely to be employed. Eliminating full-time students aged 16 to 21 from the labor force would reduce both the overall unemployment rate and the youth unemployment rate slightly.

Inclusion of students in our labor force statistics does not, even so, have the effect of inflating either the overall unemployment rate or the youth unemployment rate appreciably. However, it is important to keep in mind, in formulating policies to combat youth unemployment, that there is an immeasurable difference in the social significance of the unemployment of a suburban 16-year-old who is seeking a baby-sitting job and the unemployment of a 19-year-old in Harlem who dropped out of school three years ago and has held nothing but a few temporary jobs since then.

Race and Ethnicity

The data presented in Section 1 tell part of the story about the far more serious incidence of unemployment among minority groups than among majority youths. Yet in terms of numbers most unemployed youths are white. Among those aged 16 to 21 and not enrolled in school in October 1977, three-quarters of unemployed youths, or about 900,000, were white. But the unemployment rate was far higher for blacks than for whites—36.1 compared with 12.0 percent.[1]

Comparable data for in-school and out-of-school youth in this age group are not available for Hispanics, but the more accessible figures for the 16- to 19-age group indicate that in 1978 the unemployment rate was 13.9 percent for whites, 36.6 percent for blacks, and 20.6 percent for Hispanics. Within the last group, those of Puerto Rican origin had a higher unemployment rate (29.2 percent) than those of Mexican origin (22.1 percent), while the Cuban rate—not published because of problems with sample size—was apparently considerably lower and brought down the rate for Hispanic teenagers as a whole.

There is another important respect, also, in which the situation of nonwhites is of far greater concern. There has been a decided upward trend in the unemployment rate for nonwhite teenagers since 1954, whereas the data reveal only a slight upward trend in the unemployment rate of white teenagers and no appreciable upward trend in the ratio of the unemployment rate of white teenagers to the overall adult rate (Figure 8). Thus, the unemployment problems of nonwhite teenagers appear to be structural in nature—much less closely related to fluctuations in the economy than those of white teenagers.

In an interesting recent analysis, based on unpublished data for March 1976, Feldstein and Ellwood (1979) found that more than half of the difference between the unemployment rates of white and nonwhite male teenagers who were not in school was explained by such influences as family income and

---

[1]Throughout this report we shall use data for nonwhites whenever separate data for blacks are not available; we shall use separate data for blacks when they are available. Because blacks comprise more than 90 percent of the nonwhite population, data for nonwhites do not usually differ greatly from data for blacks.

Figure 8. Unemployment rates of teenagers by race,
annual averages, 1954 to 1978

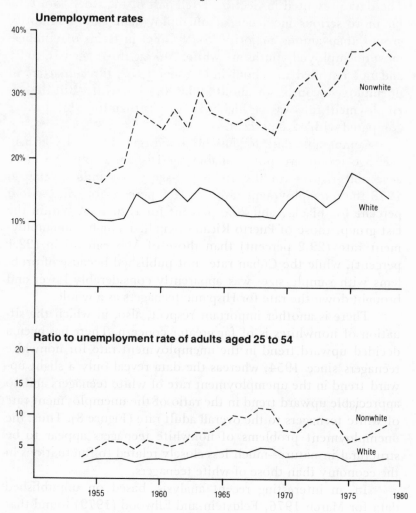

Source: The President (1978); *Employment and Earnings* (1979).

family composition. And yet, one significant and unexplained
difference remained—whereas nonwhites and whites in low-
income families had similarly high unemployment rates and
those in high-income families had similarly low rates, the nonwhites from families in a moderate income range ($10,000 to

$20,000) had a much higher unemployment rate than the whites. In this connection, however, it is important to keep in mind that more than 90 percent of Hispanics are classified as whites in Census data, and that Hispanics form a larger proportion of low-income whites than of the white population in general. We estimate, for example, that 15 percent of the white parents of teenage students with incomes of less than $10,000 in 1977 were Hispanics, compared with only 6.5 percent of all white parents of such students, regardless of income, who were Hispanic.[2] Thus, the presence of Hispanics in the low-income white youth population probably raises the unemployment rate of white low-income youth somewhat.

The Floundering Period

Much of the unemployment of young people is associated with their tendency to move into and out of the labor force while still in school and to change jobs frequently when they are in the labor force. They go through a "floundering period" as they try out jobs until they find one that suits them. Thus, the unemployment of young people tends to be shorter in duration than that of adults, and for many youths the experience of the floundering period ends in a relatively stable, secure job, whereas first jobs are often temporary and low paid.

This successful movement from less desirable to more desirable jobs is, however, much more easily accomplished by whites than by blacks. A recent analysis of longitudinal data has shown that white youth who experienced unemployment generally improved their labor market position as a result, whereas the reverse was true for blacks. The analysis was based on a comparison of the employment status and wages in 1975 of young persons whose earlier labor market experiences as teenagers had been surveyed from 1967 on in the National Longitudinal Surveys (Becker and Hills, 1979, p. 71).

The Role of Education

It is the least educated young people who are particularly likely to experience unemployment, but here again the contrast be-

[2]Estimated from data in U.S. Bureau of the Census (1979b, table 14).

tween blacks and whites is striking (Figure 9). Within the out-of-school population of 16- to 24-year-olds, unemployment rates decline almost steadily with rising educational attainment. Among blacks, however, those with only eight years of education have a somewhat lower rate than those with one to three years of high school (undoubtedly reflecting longer labor market experience). Among the whites, those with one to three years of college have a slightly lower unemployment rate than those with four years of college. But, regardless of educational attainment, the rates are much higher for blacks.[3]

Particularly significant in the context of our concerns with the relationship between education and employment is the fact that the unemployment rate of black high school graduates in 1977 was nearly three times that of white high school graduates. If we consider only recent high school graduates rather than all of those in the 16 to 24 group, the situation is even more alarming, as Figure 4 shows.

These high rates of unemployment among recent black high school graduates are a matter of concern not only for those directly affected but also for their impact on the motivation of nonwhites still in high school. It would hardly be surprising to find a good many black students discouraged from staying on and graduating if the value of a high school diploma in the labor market appeared to be so uncertain.

The Inner City

The employment situation of nonwhite youth is particularly difficult in the inner city, where a very large proportion of teenage blacks live. In the poverty sections of metropolitan areas, the unemployment rate of nonwhite teenagers was 43 percent in 1978, while rates in other parts of metropolitan areas and in nonmetropolitan areas were somewhat lower (Figure 10).

---

[3]Until 1977, these data were provided for nonwhites rather than for blacks, and in 1976 the unemployment rate of nonwhite college graduates was actually lower than that of whites. This apparently reflected the very low unemployment rates of Chinese- and Japanese-American graduates who not only are unlikely to be unemployed but also have a very high rate of college graduation. Thus, for certain subgroups, the differences between nonwhites and blacks may be substantial.

Figure 9. Percentage of civilian labor force unemployed,
by educational attainment and race, persons aged 16 to 24
not enrolled in school, October 1977

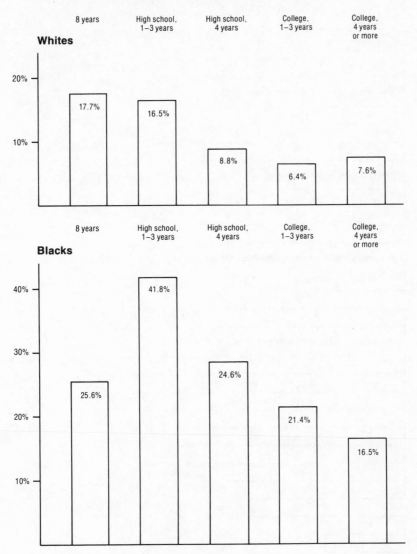

Source: U.S. Bureau of Labor Statistics (1978, table I).

Figure 10. Unemployment rates of young people aged 16 to 19, by race, selected areas, 1976 or 1978

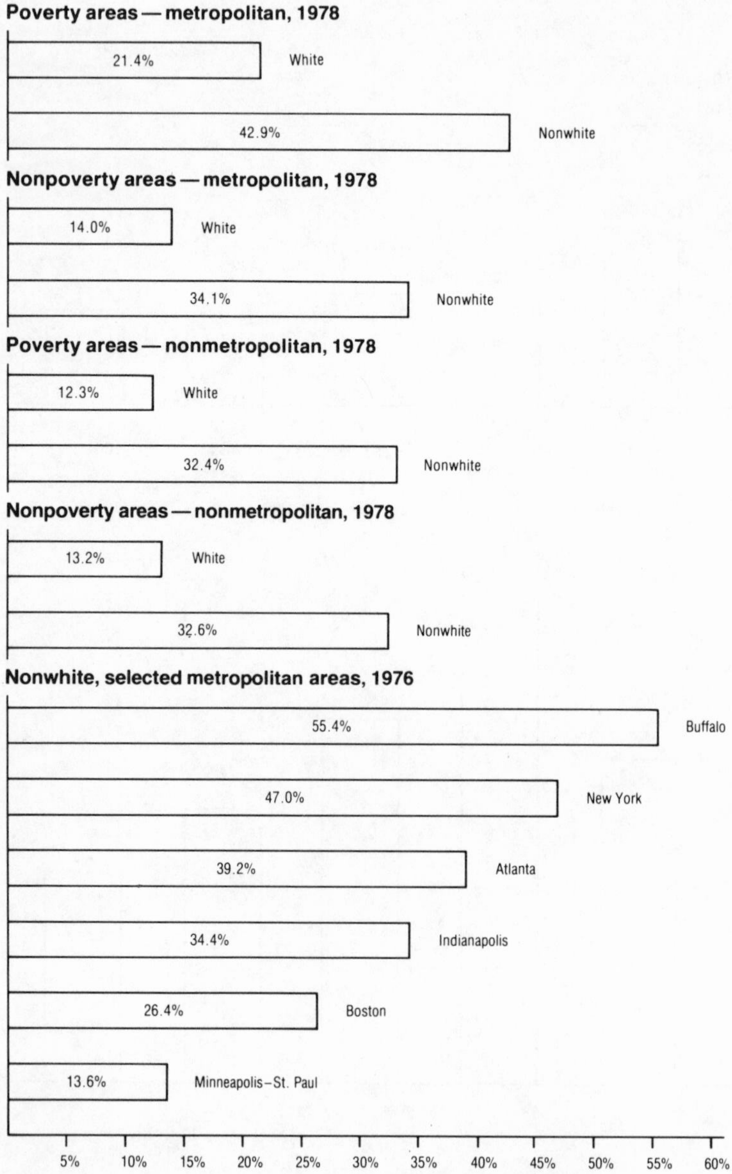

Poverty areas — metropolitan, 1978

21.4% White

42.9% Nonwhite

Nonpoverty areas — metropolitan, 1978

14.0% White

34.1% Nonwhite

Poverty areas — nonmetropolitan, 1978

12.3% White

32.4% Nonwhite

Nonpoverty areas — nonmetropolitan, 1978

13.2% White

32.6% Nonwhite

Nonwhite, selected metropolitan areas, 1976

55.4% Buffalo

47.0% New York

39.2% Atlanta

34.4% Indianapolis

26.4% Boston

13.6% Minneapolis–St. Paul

5%   10%   15%   20%   25%   30%   35%   40%   45%   50%   55%   60%

Source: U.S. Bureau of Labor Statistics (1979, table 55; 1977).

Among white teenagers, the unemployment rate was considerably higher in the inner city areas than elsewhere, but even so it was only about one half that of the nonwhites in the same areas.

As Mangum and Walsh (1978, pp. 28-29) point out, "more than 60 percent of all unemployed black teenagers were located in central cities, in contrast to 23 percent of all unemployed white teens, during the second quarter of 1977."[4] The increasing concentration of minority groups in the population of central cities reflects the net result of the out-migration of whites to the suburbs, the continuing in-migration of minority groups, and the relatively higher birth rate among minority groups. Meanwhile, various forces—especially availability of low-cost land and access to the newer modes of transportation—have encouraged out-migration of industry to suburban and to nonmetropolitan areas. As a result, there has been not only a tendency for the number of blue-collar jobs in central cities to decline but also a tendency for the tax base to erode. Hence, the fiscal crisis of the central cities, of which New York is simply the best-known example.

The out-migration of blue-collar jobs means that job opportunities for youth within the central cities tend to be heavily concentrated in trade and service occupations, where jobs are frequently low paid, temporary, and part time. Moreover, dual labor market theorists argue that the urban labor market tends to be divided into two segments: the primary and the secondary. Ghetto workers tend to get jobs in the secondary labor market, which is characterized by low wages and low fringe benefits, debilitating production speeds, low-status work, unpleasant working conditions, unsympathetic supervision, inequitable industrial relations arrangements, low promotional opportunities, and unstable employment (U.S. Manpower Administration, 1972, p. 9).

---

[4]Expressing the data in a different way, Feldstein and Ellwood (1979) show that whites constituted 64 percent of unemployed male teenagers in central cities in 1976, but even so, the black unemployed teenagers were much more concentrated in central cities.

In spite of a general tendency for the nonwhite youth unemployment rate to be high in inner-city areas, there are wide variations among cities in the severity of the problem. A special analysis of unemployment of nonwhites aged 16 to 19 in 30 large metropolitan areas in 1976 shows that the rate ranged from a low of 13.6 percent in Minneapolis to 55.4 percent in Buffalo. We have included six of these areas in Figure 10. In a search for factors accounting for the differences among the 30 areas, we found a significant relationship between the nonwhite teenage unemployment rate and two other variables: the overall unemployment rate in the area and the percentage of minority group members in the population of the area. But we also found that the relative position of individual areas shifted from year to year—primarily because of changes in the comparative severity of overall unemployment in the area.[5]

Particularly illuminating as to the barriers to employment of certain groups of inner-city youth are the conclusions of Vocational Foundation, Inc. (n.d.), a New York City agency specializing in counseling and placement services for young people with correctional backgrounds:

1. Widespread requirement of the high school diploma—which they do not have—as a "passport to the job market."
2. Use of written tests for job qualification that closely resemble schoolroom exams—with which they cannot cope.
3. Child labor laws and workmen's compensation rules that bar them from night shifts, from working where liquor is sold, and from using heavy machine tools, construction equipment, forklifts, and other tools common in today's work place.
4. Worksite insurance rates, associated with the workmen's compensation system, that are prohibitively high for those who might employ them and that in many instances raise the cost of employing them to a level substantially above the minimum wage.
5. Arbitrary age limits pertaining to drivers licenses and other

[5]For a much more extensive analysis of intercity differences, see Friedlander (1972).

licenses that exclude most of them from a wide range of jobs, from beautician to taxi driver.

6. Arrest records and correctional histories that bar them from employment, together with polygraph tests based on these data.
7. Age and education requirements that exclude them from apprenticeships.
8. Minimum wage laws that price them out of the job market.
9. Regulations relating to welfare, food stamps, Medicaid, housing allowances, and legal assistance programs that tie benefits to joblessness and discourage them from working.
10. Just plain race and age discrimination.

At the same time, the jobs that Vocational Foundation is able to get for its clients are frequently temporary and low paid (see Section 14).

Will Youth Unemployment Go Away?

The view is rather widespread that the youth unemployment problem will become much less serious in the 1980s when the teenage population declines. Those who hold this view tend to believe that the rise in youth unemployment in the 1960s and early 1970s was largely attributable to the bulge in the teenage population, creating a supply of young jobseekers that the labor market simply could not absorb.

We are less optimistic about the outlook for several reasons:

1. The rise in the ratio of the teenage to the adult unemployment rate that occurred in the 1960s was almost entirely attributable to the rise in the nonwhite teenage unemployment rate, as Figure 8 shows. The ratio of the white teenage unemployment rate to the adult rate rose very little. This suggests that it was not the overall rise in the youthful population that created the problem, but rather factors that especially affected the job market for youthful nonwhites.
2. Even though the rise in the youthful population per se does not appear to explain the youth unemployment problem, this

does not mean that there is no problem on the supply side of the labor market. The pronounced rise in the labor force participation rate of married women has meant increased competition for the types of relatively unskilled jobs for which youth qualify,[6] as has the influx of aliens, legal and illegal. The relatively unfavorable job market for college graduates that developed early in the 1970s also meant that college graduates were often competing successfully for the types of jobs that would have gone to high school graduates in the past. These influences on the supply side can be expected to continue, although we expect the job market for college graduates to improve from about the mid-1980s on when the number of college graduates can be expected to decline or level off.

3. Although the youthful population as a whole will decline in the 1980s, the youthful black population will tend to level off rather than decline, and the youthful Hispanic population will probably increase. Thus, as we noted in Section 1, minority groups will form a rising proportion of the youthful population in the next two decades.

4. There are good reasons for believing that barriers to the employment of youth, especially poorly educated and minority group youth, on the demand side of the labor market are the principal reason for high unemployment rates among the young. This view is reinforced by an analysis of the situation in other industrial democracies (Gordon, forthcoming).

The barriers to youth employment listed by the Vocational Foundation are especially relevant for high school dropouts and youths with correctional backgrounds, but there are also impor-

---

[6]A special analysis of detailed occupational changes from 1960 to 1970, however, showed that, on the whole, the occupations in which job opportunities were favorable for women were also those in which opportunities were favorable for teenagers, while women and teenagers were similarly adversely affected by poor job opportunities in certain other occupations (notably semiskilled manufacturing jobs), but that women were clearly taking jobs involving driving away from teenagers, probably because of lower insurance rates and greater confidence of employers in the reliability of women as drivers (Gordon, forthcoming).

tant obstacles to employment of youth that apply much more generally:

• *Long-run structural changes in the labor market,* including the decline of employment in agriculture and in nonagricultural small business, have greatly reduced family employment opportunities for youth. The downward trend in employment in relatively unskilled jobs in manufacturing, construction, and utilities has also played a major role. While this decline has been accompanied by a rise in employment in relatively unskilled trade and service jobs, there are fewer opportunities in trade and service industries for the acquisition of skills that qualify workers for movement up the occupational ladder. Trade and service jobs, moreover, are often casual or intermittent.

In an interesting recent analysis, Freeman (1979, p. 27) reaches the following conclusions:

> As far as can be told, much of the relatively high rate of youth joblessness can be attributed to turnover and mobility patterns that are normal in the U.S. economy, but much is also directly related to a dearth of jobs. Demand forces, which have come to be neglected in favor of supply in much popular discussion of youth joblessness, are major determinants of variation in youth employment over time and among areas. For groups facing the most severe joblessness problems, however, the difficulty due to lack of jobs appears to be compounded by problems of employability related to deleterious social patterns.

In a sense, then, the problem *is* partly a supply problem, not so much in terms of numbers as in terms of quality. Youngsters who have dropped out of school or graduated without basic skills or learned poor work habits from getting jobs only in the secondary labor market are shunned by employers. At the same time, this is not to deny that part of the problem is attributable to discrimination on the basis of race.

• *Growing rigidities in the labor market* make it more difficult for young people to enter the labor force at low pay and gradually improve their position. These include (1) protective labor legislation, (2) seniority and other provisions of collective bargaining agreements that protect the jobs of adults to the detriment of the young, and (3) rising costs of employing the young. As a factor in rising costs, the minimum wage has received the lion's share of the attention, but high entry rates under collective bargaining agreements (which often greatly exceed the minimum wage) are also an important factor, as are rising fringe benefits, which, on the average, added about 35 percent of wages to employer costs in 1975 and probably are even higher today (Chamber of Commerce, 1976, p. 5).

• *The geographical decentralization of industry* has already been mentioned as a factor that has limited job opportunities for youth in inner-city areas.

• *Widespread reluctance of employers to hire young people* exists partly for reasons already mentioned (high costs, for example) but partly also because employers believe (often with some justification) that young workers cannot be trusted to show up on time or that too many of them, even among high school graduates, lack basic skills. One employer survey conducted in eight cities indicated that a majority of employers would not hire persons under 20 for full-time jobs (Gavett and others, 1970), while another study indicated that employers rarely cited high wages as a reason for not hiring youth, but tended rather to mention such factors as "uncertainty over legal restrictions," "high turnover," and the like (National Committee on Employment of Youth, 1975, p. VII-32).

The Schools

Adults who look back on their own school experience as reasonably peaceful, if not inspiring, have been reading with alarm about violence in the schools, widespread absenteeism, and declining test scores. In fact, the problems, at least in some school systems, are at least as disturbing as high minority group youth unemployment rates and may be even more difficult to overcome. Absenteeism and violence appear to be considerably more serious in ghetto schools than in suburban schools, but the problem of declining test scores is found in all types of schools and among all types of students, although not necessarily to the same degree.

Dropouts

When James B. Conant wrote his penetrating book on the contrasts between ghetto and suburban high schools, *Slums and Suburbs* (1961), the far higher dropout rates in ghetto schools represented one of the most significant contrasts. This difference persists.

In the first half of the 1960s, the long-run upward trend in the high school graduation rate accelerated, dropout rates of both whites and nonwhites declined, and the difference between the dropout rates of the two races narrowed somewhat. Since around 1965, however, the high school graduation rate has leveled off at about 75 percent, implying a dropout rate of 25 percent. This is higher than the 17 percent dropout rate mentioned in Section 1, which refers to the percentage of the 18- to 19-year-old population neither enrolled in school nor holding a high school diploma (shown in the bottom part of Figure 11 for whites, blacks, and Hispanics separately). The high school graduation rate is computed differently from the other rates shown in Figure 11. It represents the number of high school graduates, as reported by schools, divided by the total 17-year-old population. The other measures are based on household surveys of the civilian noninstitutional population. A very small part of the difference, but not more than about 1 percent, is explained by young people in institutions. Probably the major explanation of the lower dropout rate indicated by the household survey data is reluctance of respondents to admit that youthful members of the household (either in the 18- to 19-year-old population or among those aged 18 or more in the 16- to 24-year-old population) are not high school graduates.[7]

---

[7]The fact that high school graduation does not occur until age 18 or 19 for a good many young people is not a significant factor in explaining the differing results, be-

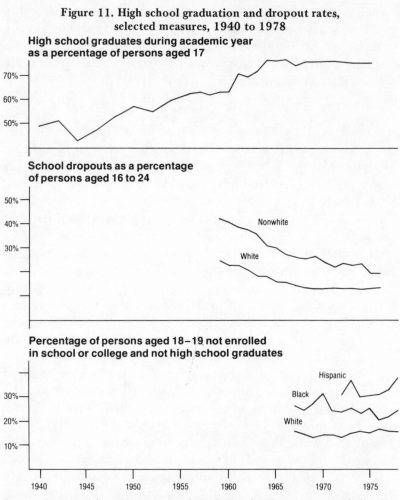

Figure 11. High school graduation and dropout rates,
selected measures, 1940 to 1978

Source: Computed from U.S. Bureau of the Census (1975, part 1, p. 379); U.S. National Center for Education Statistics (1978a, p. 60); U.S. Bureau of Labor Statistics, *Special Labor Force Reports,* appropriate years; U.S. Bureau of the Census, *Current Population Reports,* appropriate years.

cause we would get almost the same high school graduation rate if we were to divide high school graduates by the average population of 17- to 19-year-olds, since adjacent single-age cohorts of young people do not differ appreciably in size. Small portions of the difference are probably explained by the facts that some 18 to 19-year-olds have obtained high school equivalency certificates and that some are enrolled in two-year colleges without having graduated from high school. A small portion of the difference is explained by a somewhat higher proportion of dropouts in the armed forces (30 to 31 percent) than in the civilian population, in spite of the preference of the armed forces for high school graduates (Comptroller General of the United States, 1978).

The important point is that no progress has been made in reducing the overall dropout rate since the mid-1960s. Moreover, the rates continue to be considerably higher for blacks and Hispanics than for whites, and these minority groups are a rising proportion of the youthful population, as we have seen. It is true that there has been a slight downward trend in the proportion of school dropouts among nonwhites aged 16 to 24 and also among blacks aged 18 to 19 (as indicated by the middle and bottom sections of Figure 11), but this may be more a reflection of declining school standards than of a real gain in educational attainment, as we shall see when we consider declining test scores. Moreover, dropout rates are much higher in inner-city areas than nationwide figures indicate.

Despite the lower dropout rate in the white population, we find that in low-income families the dropout rate of whites is higher than that of blacks, though slightly below that of Hispanics.[8] Thus, the lower overall dropout rate of whites is explained by the higher income level of the white population. But, among those from families with incomes under $10,000 in 1977, the percentage of whites aged 14 to 17 who were not enrolled in school was 13.2 percent, compared with 6.7 percent for blacks and 13.7 percent for Hispanics. Eliminating Hispanics from whites does not alter the dropout rate for whites significantly. In terms of numbers, moreover, the whites in this age group who drop out far exceed the numbers of either blacks or Hispanics—about 304,000 whites (other than Hispanics), 81,000 blacks, and 59,000 Hispanics in this age group were not enrolled in 1977. The numbers who ultimately drop out are considerably larger, because some students, especially in minority groups, leave school at age 18 or 19 without graduating. Approximately one million students in the relevant age group do not graduate from high school each year.

During the 1960s, the federal government, the states, and the media placed a great deal of emphasis on the importance of reducing the dropout rate. More recently, there has been some shift in emphasis to the problems of students who graduate

---

[8]This finding is based on data showing the enrollment status of persons aged 14 to 17 by family income in U.S. Bureau of the Census (1979b, table 14).

from high school without basic competency in reading and arithmetic.

Meanwhile, experts are by no means agreed on the wisdom of programs designed specifically to reduce the dropout rate. One of the most illuminating studies of male dropouts (Bachman, Green, and Wirtanen, 1971) concludes that dropping out is overrated as a problem in its own right and is more appropriately viewed as a *symptom* of other problems, which have their origins much earlier in life. The problems "involve a serious mismatch between some individuals and the typical high school environment" (p. 171). More specifically, those prone to drop out are likely to be from families at low socioeconomic levels, and especially from large families or broken homes. They are likely to score below average on ability tests, to have poor classroom grades, and to have been held back one or more grades in school. They are also likely to have a background of delinquency, and they tend to be lower than average in self-esteem and in occupational aspiration.

Absenteeism

In recent years, it has become increasingly clear that many students who continue to be registered in school are chronic truants. In fact, it has been suggested "that 'truancy rates' constitute a better measure [than dropout rates] of the quantity of schooling that different students receive" (Gordon, 1977, p. 207). Reliable national statistics on truancy, however, are not available. Persons who are knowledgeable about the absenteeism problem point out that statistics on Average Daily Attendance (ADA) form the basis for state aid (and some federal aid) to local school districts and that school officials have a vital stake in making the statistics "look good." Thus, it is alleged that, if a student is present when the official count for the day is taken (usually in the morning), school officials may take little interest in whether that student is present for the rest of the day.

Such data as are available from scattered special studies in urban school districts suggest a shocking problem of absenteeism. A study by the Economic Development Council of New York City (1977) showed that on a typical school day in

1975-76, 111,000 children, or about 10 percent of total enrollment, were chronically truant from the city's public schools.
Another 117,000 were absent, but with valid excuses. The total
absence rate of about 20 percent was higher than the statewide
average, but similar to absence rates in five other major urban
centers in the state. Absence rates were appreciable, but lower,
in elementary schools than in junior high schools, and they were
highest in senior high schools. Puerto Rican students had the
highest rates, followed by blacks and Hispanics other than
Puerto Rican. In 15 high schools where blacks constituted a
majority of the student body, the average daily absence rate was
32 percent; and, in 5 schools dominated by Puerto Ricans, the
rate was 38 percent.

The pervasiveness of the problem of absenteeism is indicated by the fact that 35 percent of public secondary school
principals responding to a survey on serious problems in the
schools identified absenteeism (absence for an entire day) as a
"very serious" or "serious" problem (Figure 12).

A study by the Children's Defense Fund (1974) stresses
the point that truancy and dropping out were not entirely voluntary—that many children were pushed out or excluded from
schools. Also, significantly, an analysis of 1970 census data conducted as part of that study showed that the percentage of children or youth not enrolled in school was far higher in one-
parent than in two-parent households, suggesting a relationship
between growing absenteeism and the increase in the proportion
of female-headed households. The proportion of children under
18 living with mother only rose from 10.7 percent in 1970 to
17 percent in 1978. Although an increase in the percentage
occurred among both whites and blacks, the 1978 proportion
was 42 percent of black children, compared with 13 percent of
white children (U.S. Bureau of the Census, 1979a, tables H and
4).

Violence

A recent congressionally mandated study sheds a great deal of
light on the problem of violence in the schools (U.S. National
Institute of Education [NIE], 1977b). The most encouraging

**Figure 12. Serious problems in the schools: Public secondary
principals' opinions**

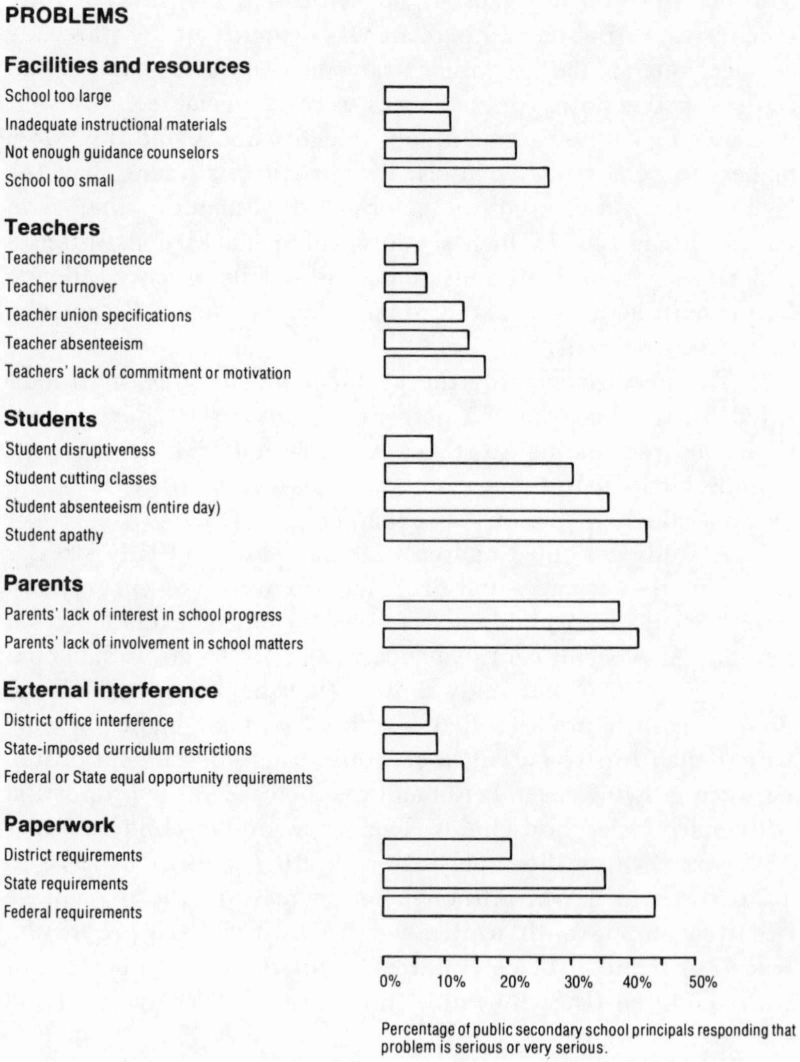

PROBLEMS

Facilities and resources

School too large
Inadequate instructional materials
Not enough guidance counselors
School too small

Teachers

Teacher incompetence
Teacher turnover
Teacher union specifications
Teacher absenteeism
Teachers' lack of commitment or motivation

Students

Student disruptiveness
Student cutting classes
Student absenteeism (entire day)
Student apathy

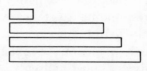

Parents

Parents' lack of interest in school progress
Parents' lack of involvement in school matters

External interference

District office interference
State-imposed curriculum restrictions
Federal or State equal opportunity requirements

Paperwork

District requirements
State requirements
Federal requirements

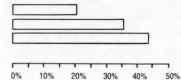

0%   10%   20%   30%   40%   50%

Percentage of public secondary school principals responding that
problem is serious or very serious.

Source: U.S. National Center for Education Statistics (1978c, figure 2.3).

finding is that the problem is not becoming more serious. Acts of violence and property destruction in the schools increased throughout the 1960s and the early 1970s but then leveled off. The study also indicated that only about 8 percent of all schools had a serious problem of violence, but that figure represented approximately 6,700 schools. Although the incidence of violence was directly related to community size, it was by no means confined to big-city schools. It was, however, much more likely to be a serious problem in secondary than in elementary schools.

Not surprisingly, the NIE study indicated that violent students were particularly likely to be those who had given up on school, did not care about grades, and found the courses irrelevant. Relatively few schools, the study showed, had regular police stationed in them, but the proportion that did was much higher in large-city secondary schools (15 percent). However, the use of school security officers was much more widespread. A central conclusion was that strong and effective school governance, particularly by the principal, could help greatly in reducing school crime and misbehavior. In fact, the leadership role of the principal appeared to be a critical factor in itself.

Declining Test Scores

After moving gradually upward for over a century, the reading, writing, and mathematical skills of American students from elementary school through college fell quite sharply from the mid-1960s until recently, and it is not entirely clear that the downward trend has been reversed. The decline involved all ethnic groups, all socioeconomic classes, both private and public school students, and all regions of the nation. It also involved students at most achievement levels. The only exception to the pattern was the reading levels of pupils in the first three grades and in knowledge of science among college entrants and college graduates (recently reported to be declining, however).

There has been a great deal of debate over the causes of the decline. Educators tend to attribute poor achievement to environmental factors, arguing that what happens in the school-

room is inconsequential in dealing with the negative consequences of disadvantaged family background, lack of jobs, poor
housing, racism, and the like. However, a study by the Hudson
Institute (Armbruster and others, 1975) lays the blame directly
on the educators. Teachers, the authors argue, no longer require
homework because it is too much work to correct it. "Rap sessions" are much easier than prepared lessons, and young teachers are particularly likely to have lax standards.

Somewhat similar, though less one-sided, are the conclusions of two education writers for the *Los Angeles Times* who
spent four months investigating the problem in 1976 (McCurdy
and Speich, 1976a, 1976b, 1976c). They place the blame
squarely on "widespread and pervasive erosion of academic
standards within the American educational system." The drop
in standards was manifested in several ways. In both schools and
colleges, there was a decline in emphasis on basic academic programs and a rising emphasis on electives that are academically
less demanding. At the same time, especially in the high schools,
"vastly greater emphasis was placed on vocational education,
further diminishing the importance of the academic curriculum." These authors also emphasize grade inflation as a major
characteristic of the erosion of standards.

In addition, McCurdy and Speich mention such factors as
the jump in the number of single-parent families, the growth of
violence and disruptions in school, and the use of drugs and
alcohol as possible influences. They tend to regard the role of
television viewing by children as inconclusive. And they argue
that the blame cannot be placed on busing since the decline in
test scores has affected all regions of the country, including the
South, where there has been extensive desegregation, and the
North and West, where there has been little. Moreover, they
argue, studies have shown no adverse effects of integration on
the achievement of white children and mixed, but largely neu-
tral, results for minority pupils.

A report by the Stanford Research Institute (Larson and
others, 1977) reached similar conclusions, but also pointed out
that (1) basic skills are not ordinarily part of the school curriculum beyond the elementary grades; (2) certification require-

ments for intermediate and secondary teachers reflect this concept, and therefore teachers feel unprepared to cope with students who arrive in their classes unable to read the standard textbooks; and (3) the fact that the decline has occurred since the early 1960s must be explained in considerable part by the increasing tendency for all levels of government to require intermediate and secondary schools to adapt their curricula to concepts of career education, ethnic history and culture, desegregation, sex and family education, and the like. Thus, new subjects have crowded the curriculum and help to explain decreasing emphasis on more traditional subjects.

A panel appointed by the College Entrance Examination Board (Willard W. Wirtz, chairman) was concerned entirely with a study of the decline in scores on Scholastic Aptitude Tests (SAT) for college entrants. The population of young people aspiring to college entrance has broadened considerably during the period of declining test scores, and the study concludes that this factor did account for a substantial part of the decline in SAT scores from 1963 to 1970, but not from 1970 on. Like the other studies we have discussed, the Wirtz panel blames a large part of the decline on such factors as acceptance of excessive student absenteeism, grade inflation, reduced homework, and automatic grade-to-grade promotion (College Entrance Examination Board, 1977).

One problem that has received relatively little attention is the mobility of the population *within* inner cities, which has a very adverse effect on a pupil's progress. In San Francisco, it has been found that it is not unusual for a pupil to be in a particular school only one semester and then move to another part of the city. Moreover, studies conducted in San Francisco high schools under the direction of Sanford Dornbusch at Stanford University indicate that low-achieving black and Chicano students are praised by their teachers and thus not challenged to improve their performance (Massey, Scott, and Dornbusch, 1975; Fernandez, Espinosa, and Dornbusch, 1975).

By the mid-1970s, it was clear that educators and the general public were becoming more concerned about the problem of declining test scores, and a strong movement got underway to require minimum competency of high school graduates. By 1978, 36 states had enacted legislation or promulgated administrative rulings calling for minimum competency testing (U.S. National Center for Education Statistics, 1979, table 2-10). Less than half of these states, however, used the tests as a requirement for high school graduation. A few states required them for grade-to-grade promotion, while the other states evidently used them for such purposes as measuring comparative performance in different school districts.[9] Reports on the results of examination requirements for high school graduation are thus far very mixed, and it is probably too early to reach conclusions about their effects.

Suburban Schools

There is no doubt that the most serious problems of violence and delinquency are found in and around big-city schools, but the suburbs have not escaped the problems of the 1970s. We have seen that test scores have dropped in all types of schools. Moreover, there is a problem of absenteeism in suburban schools, though it is less often associated with criminal activity than in the big cities. Even so, the proportion of secondary schools reporting one or more criminal offenses to police in a five-month period in 1974-1975 was about as high (81 percent) in the outer ring of metropolitan areas as in the central cities (82 percent) and considerably higher than in nonmetropolitan areas. Robberies and assaults were less frequently reported in the suburban areas, but drug abuse and alcohol abuse were somewhat more likely to be reported than in the central cities (U.S. National Center for Education Statistics, 1978c, p. 90).

There is some evidence, however, that it is in the lower-income areas of suburban school districts that problems similar to those of big-city schools are especially likely to be found. Absenteeism within the Mount Diablo Unified School District— a suburban district east of the Oakland-Berkeley area in California—which increased sharply in the early 1970s was particularly

---

[9]For a discussion of some of the issues involved in the use of different types of competency tests, see Stadtman (1977).

likely to occur in lower-income areas with mobile populations and high rates of social problems, such as marital difficulties, alcoholism, and unemployment (Campbell, 1973).

Rural Schools

Rural schools have always had their own special problems, and consolidation of school districts has not always helped. Even after consolidation, high schools in some sparsely populated areas are too small to offer a well-rounded program. Moreover, where youngsters have to travel long distances to school, dropout and absenteeism rates tend to be high. Inadequate financing also continues to remain a problem for rural schools, although increased state aid has helped in a number of states. School progress has long been a particularly acute problem for the children of migratory farm workers whose families move from place to place in response to seasonal work opportunities. This problem is especially serious among Chicano families in the Southwest and among black families in certain agricultural regions in the South. In nonmetropolitan areas, the percentage of Hispanics aged 18 to 19 who were neither in school nor high school graduates in 1977 was 45.5 percent (U.S. Bureau of the Census, 1979b, table 2).

Loss of population through out-migration has frequently exacerbated the problems of rural school districts in providing adequate education, but recent indications that migration patterns have been shifting in the 1970s toward repopulation of small towns and rural areas may change this situation.

Student Apathy and Boredom

Student apathy and boredom are problems in many of the schools. Figure 12 shows that the percentage of principals reporting that student apathy was a "serious" or a "very serious" problem (41 percent) was higher than the proportion who considered absenteeism a serious or very serious problem (35 percent). We also noted in Section 1 that nearly one-half of high school students did not think they had to work hard enough. Thus, student opinion tends to be consistent with the finding of the groups that have studied the decline in test scores—lax standards are a pervasive problem.

The Exceptions

If we have presented a gloomy view of secondary schools in the United States, we do not mean to suggest that there are not promising exceptions. In fact, the CEEB panel study (1977) identifies 60 high schools that had stable test scores from the mid-1960s to 1973 and some tendency for scores to rise from 1973 to 1976. In a special study prepared for the CEEB panel, these schools were compared with a group of schools with sharply declining test scores (Echternacht, 1977); the National Association of Secondary School Principals (NASSP, 1978) later conducted a more intensive survey of 34 of the schools with stable or rising test scores. In 1976 the schools with stable or rising scores were characterized by a student body that included only 8 percent from minority groups on the average, while the schools with the most steeply declining scores reported an average minority representation of 35 percent in 1976, compared with 20 percent in 1965.

Among the significant differences between the two groups of schools revealed by the Echternacht study (1977) were the following:

- Enrollment in advanced mathematics courses had declined to a greater extent in the schools with decreasing scores.
- Students from steady score schools reported more years of study, not only in mathematics but also in English, foreign languages, and physics.
- More than 50 percent of the schools with decreasing scores reported increases in their dropout rates since 1965, compared with only 12 percent of the schools with steady scores.
- The schools with decreasing scores were considerably more likely to be in buildings that were more than 20 years old than were the schools with steady scores.
- About one-third of the schools with decreasing scores, compared with only one-tenth of the schools with steady scores, had made major efforts to adopt' mixed-ability or heterogeneous class groupings in the previous ten years.
- Teachers in the schools with steady scores tended to have had more experience than those in schools with decreasing scores.

- Both groups of schools, however, reported that teachers used teacher aides more frequently, were less dedicated, had more formal education, had less desire to enforce high academic standards, were more permissive, spent less time outside class with their students, and placed less emphasis on classroom discipline in 1976 than did their counterparts in 1965.
- Both groups of schools also reported that their students were more often truant, involved in discipline problems, alcohol and drug abusers, and delinquent in 1976 than in 1965.
- About 77 percent of the schools with steady scores had made a major effort to adopt work-study programs since 1965, compared with 42 percent of the schools with declining scores.

The location of the schools was not revealed in the Echternacht study, but it seems probable that many of the schools with sharply declining scores were in inner-city areas. This is suggested by their rising minority enrollments and their increasing dropout rates. The 34 schools included in the NASSP study (1978) of schools with steady scores were identified and were mostly in moderate-sized communities or suburbs, although a few were in large cities. An important point brought out in the NASSP study, which was somewhat more oriented toward principals' opinions than the Echternacht study, was that high motivation on the part of both students and parents was a factor in the superior test score records.

There are success stories in some inner-city areas as well. As we shall see in Section 8, some large-city school systems have developed successful alternative school programs, including "magnet" schools that are usually distinguished by their efforts to develop a superior program in a specialized field, such as the arts or sciences, and that draw students from all over their cities. Interestingly, also, there are Catholic schools in slum areas, whose students are predominantly from minority group families and are frequently not Catholic, that are doing an outstanding job of education on budgets that look tiny compared with those of nearby public schools.

Problems for the Community

High youth unemployment and school dropout rates involve problems not only for the individuals concerned, but also for their communities. Juvenile delinquency, welfare dependency, a propensity for lifelong poverty for many, and a tendency toward lifelong criminal patterns for some are all involved. In ghetto areas of large cities, these problems are inextricably associated with the slum environment, and their solutions are clearly not to be found solely in labor market or school policies. They involve welfare reform, housing policies, health policies, law enforcement policies, and many others, but education and employment policies, with which this report is concerned, can make a difference, as experience in some communities has shown.

Juvenile Delinquency and Crime

On the supposition that "the devil makes work for idle hands," the belief is widespread that one of the most serious consequences of youth unemployment is juvenile delinquency. However, the relationship is not as simple or unidirectional as is commonly assumed. Although adult crime rates do tend to fluctuate with unemployment rates, no such clearcut relationship has been established for juvenile delinquency rates (Barton, 1976). Sociologists tend to emphasize the point that the same factors that underlie juvenile delinquency also explain a propensity for prolonged unemployment on the part of some young people. They are much the same factors that have already been mentioned in connection with school dropouts—poor school performance, low socioeconomic levels, large families, and broken homes. Truancy, dropping out, juvenile delinquency, and unemployment are interrelated, but unemployment is not necessarily the initiating factor.

Young people account for more than one-half of all persons arrested, as we pointed out in Section 1. Therefore, a rise in the youthful proportion of the population could explain a rise in the crime rate. In fact, although the population aged 14 to 24 increased by 63 percent from 1960 to 1975—more than six times the increase in all other age groups—the rise in the size of the youthful age group was not the main explanation of the increase in crime that occurred during that period. The number of serious crimes increased more than 200 percent, but the change in the age distribution of the population accounted for only 25 percent of the increase (Silberman, 1978, p. 31). The rest was explained by a rise in crime *rates*. Figure 13 portrays what was happening to rates of arrest. During the 1950s, the arrest rate went up for all the age groups shown in the chart, but around 1960 the arrest rate for adults aged 25 or more tended to level off, whereas those of the youthful age groups rose markedly and quite persistently.

Part of the increase in arrest rates is probably explained by more complete reporting, but such factors as increased urbanization and changes in the characteristics of the population in large cities clearly played an important role. And, before we dismiss altogether the influence of increased unemployment on arrests of young people, it is well to note the sharp increase in the rate of arrests of young people as well as adults between 1974 and 1975, when the unemployment rate rose to the highest level of the entire postwar period.

One reason for this increased propensity toward crime, according to Silberman (1978, pp. 31-32), is what might be termed "demographic overload." The growth in the size of the 14- to 24-age group was so large relative to the growth of the adult population that the "conventional means of social control broke down." He also points out that delinquency rates have always been high among migrant groups, while social controls have been weakened in recent decades by the "older generation's uncertainty about its own values."

One of the most illuminating studies of juvenile delinquency collected longitudinal data for a cohort of all boys born in 1945 who lived in Philadelphia at least between their tenth and eighteenth birthdays (Wolfgang, Figlio, and Sellin, 1972). The authors found that race and socioeconomic status were the most strongly related to whether or not the young person had an offender classification. Beginning at age 10, there was a steady rise in arrests, peaking at age 16, and dropping rather markedly at age 17. "We may take the years 14 to 17 as being

Figure 13. Persons arrested per 100,000 population,
selected age groups, and unemployment rate, 1950 to 1977

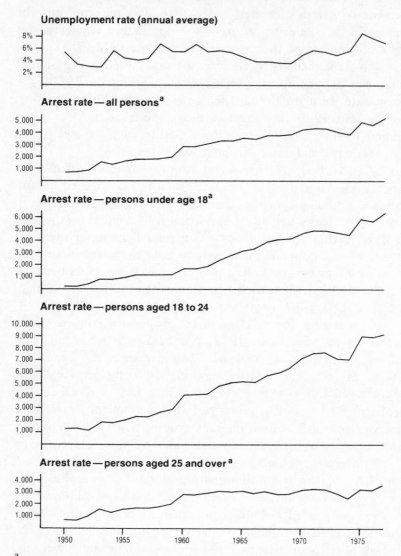

[a]The arrest rate for persons under age 18 is computed per 100,000 aged 10 to 17;
that for persons aged 25 and over is computed per 100,000 persons aged 25 to 69;
and that for all persons is computed per 100,000 persons aged 10 to 69.

Source: U.S. Bureau of the Census (1975, part 1, p. 415); *Statistical Abstract of the
United States, 1978,* p. 186; U.S. Bureau of the Census (1965, 1971, 1974); The
President (1979, p. 214).

those in which adolescent delinquency blooms" (Wolfgang, Figlio, and Sellin, 1972, p. 216). Also very significant was the fact that, the earlier the offender commits his first offense, the greater the number of offenses he will have committed by the end of his seventeenth year.

When one thinks of a juvenile delinquent one tends to think of a young male, and, on the whole, this is correct. Arrest rates for young women are far below those for young men, although there has been a tendency for them to rise in recent years. And especially pertinent to the concerns of this report is the finding of a Los Angeles study that the delinquency rate among juveniles 14 to 17 years old who were not enrolled in school was about 2.5 times higher than the rate for those who were enrolled (Simpson and Van Arsdol, 1967).

Statistics on offenses cleared would be preferable to those on arrest rates but are not available for detailed age groups. They do show, however, that the crimes most likely to have been committed by persons under age 18 are burglary, larceny-theft, and motor vehicle theft (Federal Bureau of Investigation, 1978, table 23).

Although crime and juvenile delinquency rates are high in inner-city areas, they have been rising in other kinds of areas as well. Moreover, although arrest rates are much higher for young blacks than for young whites, there is considerable evidence that young blacks are more likely to be apprehended by the police. It is also well to keep in mind the evidence that the economic impact of white-collar crime, much of which is undetected or ignored, is far greater than that of the crimes against property for which young blacks are often apprehended.

Illicit Earnings

How do young people who are neither in school nor in the labor force, or who are unemployed over long periods of time, support themselves? Clearly, crime plays a role. It is frequently alleged, also, that "the welfare state" makes it possible for young people to subsist at the expense of the overburdened taxpayer. This is true only in a qualified way. To be eligible for unemployment insurance, an individual must have had a minimum amount of earnings or a minimum number of weeks of employment in the base period (approximately the preceding year), and the rules typically call for earnings spread over several quarters or employment or work amounting to at least 20 weeks. Young people who have held only short-term jobs often cannot meet this requirement. Moreover, once a young person has passed his or her 18th birthday, no payments can be made on his or her behalf under the Aid to Families with Dependent Children (AFDC) program, unless the youth is enrolled in school or is a mother.

Nevertheless, many young people do benefit from AFDC payments. Probably the most important category consists of young mothers who are unmarried or whose husbands are absent from the home (discussed more fully in Section 3). There are undoubtedly, also, young fathers who receive some support from AFDC entirely unofficially, perhaps especially in the form of meals consumed with the mother and her children, even though they are living "around the corner."

Possibly more significant than welfare payments is the role of illicit earnings. The evidence on this comes largely from the work of researchers who have conducted intensive studies of the lives of young people in the ghetto, for official statistics shed no light on illegal earnings. For example, in a study of a small sample of young black males in Harlem, augmented by personal observation, Friedlander (1972, p. 174) concluded that "hustling was pervasive in Harlem. Nearly every respondent had some contact with an activity that could be considered hustling. Many of the respondents were aware of the risks and penalties for these assorted illegal activities, and most preferred the safer activities, such as gambling and running numbers, despite the higher incomes associated with narcotics."

Also shedding much light on the role of illicit earnings in providing income for unemployed young blacks and Chicanos in Watts and East Los Angeles is a study by Bullock (1973). The fact that illicit earnings, although irregular, can often be far higher than earnings on low-paid jobs available to these youngsters is clearly brought out.

Care should be taken, however, not to exaggerate the role of illicit earnings. Some experts think that they account for income to only a small fraction of ghetto youngsters. Even so, to the extent that they are a factor, they can be a barrier to participation in manpower programs.

Discouraged Workers and Opt-Outs

Youth unemployment statistics do not tell us the entire story about young people who are not working. As Figure 2 shows, about 5.7 percent of all youth aged 16 to 21 are not in the labor force, not in school as a major activity, and not homemakers. Figure 3 shows that the percentage is higher among blacks, especially young black men. Moreover, the percentage has been rising among young black men. Some of this group are discouraged workers, some are society "opt-outs," and some are probably engaged in illicit activities.

It can be argued, as does Trow (forthcoming), that the labor force data may well overstate the percentage of minority group youth who genuinely want work and cannot find it. On the one hand, as we have suggested earlier, some of the job-seekers among 16- to 17-year-olds who are still in school do not represent a disturbing aspect of unemployment. On the other hand, the evidence that some young people in ghetto areas are recipients of illicit earnings suggests that certain youths may report themselves as unemployed or not in the labor force simply because they do not want to reveal the source of their earnings.

Evidence that the usual labor force data based on the Current Population Survey (CPS) of the U.S. Bureau of the Census may overstate the extent of youth unemployment comes from comparison of the CPS data with data from the National Longitudinal Surveys (NLS) that have been analyzed at Ohio State University under the direction of Herbert Parnes. The NLS data, for example, showed that 46 percent of young men aged 16 to 17 were employed in 1966, compared with 36 percent on the basis of CPS data, while the black-white differences in percentages with jobs were somewhat lower in the NLS data (Freeman, 1979). Two possible reasons have been advanced for this difference: (1) The NLS data are based on responses by the young persons themselves and may reflect the true employment status of the youths more accurately than responses in the CPS, which may be given by any member of the household; and (2) to some extent, the NLS data may include a somewhat more stable group of young persons.

Despite these questions about the accuracy and interpretation of the unemployment data, there is little question that the situation of many youths, especially in the inner city, presents a social problem of major dimensions.

3

A Note on
the Special Problems
of Young Women

Thus far, we have paid little attention to sex differences, but the problems of young men and young women differ in significant respects and call for somewhat different policy emphases. Particularly important in this context is the problem of teenage pregnancies.

Unemployment

Unemployment rates of young men and young women do not differ greatly within the same race and ethnic groups, although those of young women tend to be slightly higher (Figure 14). This is not surprising in view of the fact that unemployment rates of women generally tend to be higher than those of men, chiefly because of the greater propensity of married women to move into and out of the labor force. However, in the case of young women, single or married, this may not be the main explanation of higher unemployment rates, since young people of both sexes move into and out of the labor force frequently. The higher unemployment rates of young women are probably attributable to the fact that barriers to their employment are even more serious than they are for young men.

The seriousness of unemployment rates is undoubtedly

Figure 14. Sex differences in unemployment and school dropout rates,
for selected youthful race and ethnic groups

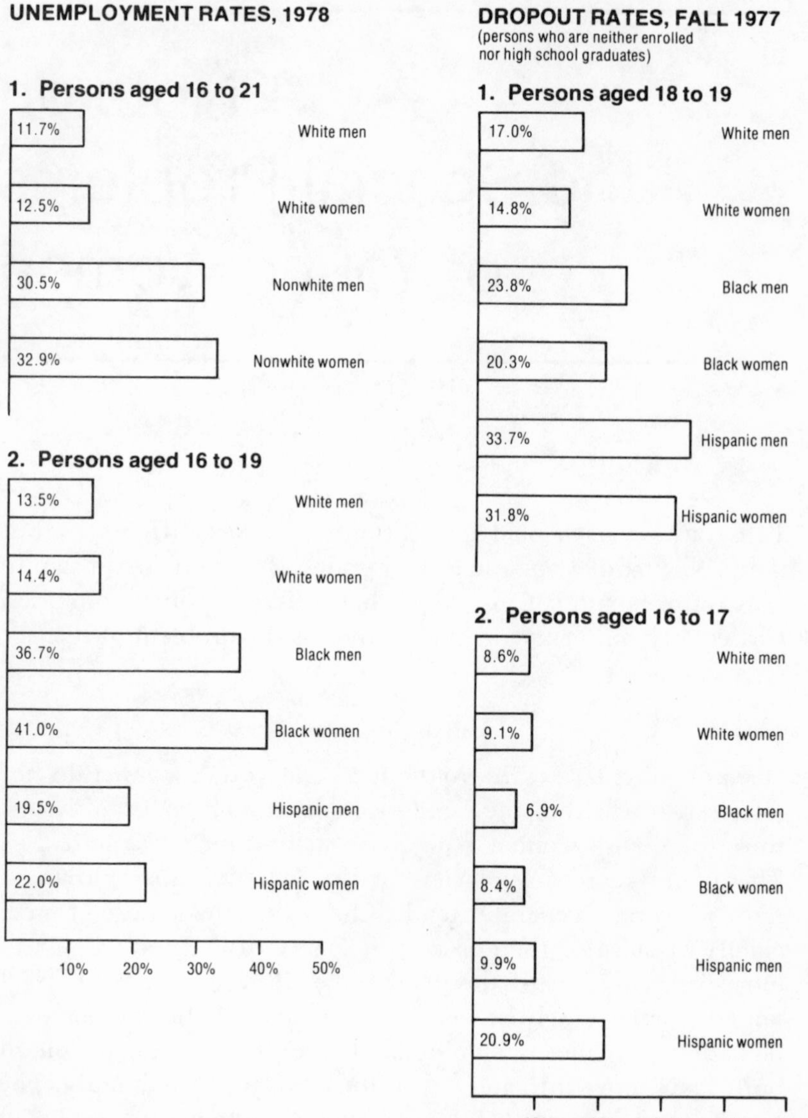

UNEMPLOYMENT RATES, 1978

1. Persons aged 16 to 21

11.7%	White men
12.5%	White women
30.5%	Nonwhite men
32.9%	Nonwhite women

2. Persons aged 16 to 19

13.5%	White men
14.4%	White women
36.7%	Black men
41.0%	Black women
19.5%	Hispanic men
22.0%	Hispanic women

10% 20% 30% 40% 50%

DROPOUT RATES, FALL 1977
(persons who are neither enrolled
nor high school graduates)

1. Persons aged 18 to 19

17.0%	White men
14.8%	White women
23.8%	Black men
20.3%	Black women
33.7%	Hispanic men
31.8%	Hispanic women

2. Persons aged 16 to 17

8.6%	White men
9.1%	White women
6.9%	Black men
8.4%	Black women
9.9%	Hispanic men
20.9%	Hispanic women

10% 20% 30% 40% 50%

Source: U.S. Bureau of Labor Statistics (1979, tables 7 and 55); U.S. Bureau of the Census (1979b, table 1).

particularly true for minority group young women. In a study of black, teenage girls in New York City, for example, Wallace (1974) found that they were among the least preferred workers and experienced major difficulties in finding jobs. They lacked information about how to get a job, were poorly served by placement and other agencies, lacked child-care facilities if they were mothers, and often had attitudes of discouragement about employment opportunities that stemmed from the adverse experiences of their parents. Furthermore, many employers in New York City rejected girls who did not have high school diplomas.

Young women, of course, are also more likely to be both out of school and out of the labor force than young men, as Figure 3 shows, and the chief reason for this is that they are more likely to be keeping house and caring for children.

Dropout Rates

Historically, the high school graduation rate of young women has tended to exceed that of young men in the United States, and this continues to be true. Moreover, among all three race and ethnic groups included in Figure 14, the percentage of young women aged 18 to 19 who were not enrolled in school and not high school graduates in 1977 was somewhat smaller than among men of the same age. The relationship was reversed, however, among 16- to 17-year-olds, and the difference is particularly pronounced in the Hispanic population. Thus, those girls who do drop out leave school somewhat earlier than boys.

It is when we consider reasons for dropping out that we encounter striking differences between the sexes (Figure 15). In a 1963 survey (Perrella and Bogan, 1964), marriage and pregnancy were mentioned as the main reasons by far the most frequently by white women and even more frequently by non-white women.[1] Among men, this reason was rarely mentioned, despite their involvement in marriage or pregnancy, although a

[1]Despite an intensive search, we have not found more recent detailed data on reasons for dropping out, for boys and girls separately, than those in Figure 15, based on a survey in the early 1960s.

Figure 15. Reasons most frequently given for dropping out of school, persons aged 16 to 21 no longer in school, by sex and race, 1963[a]

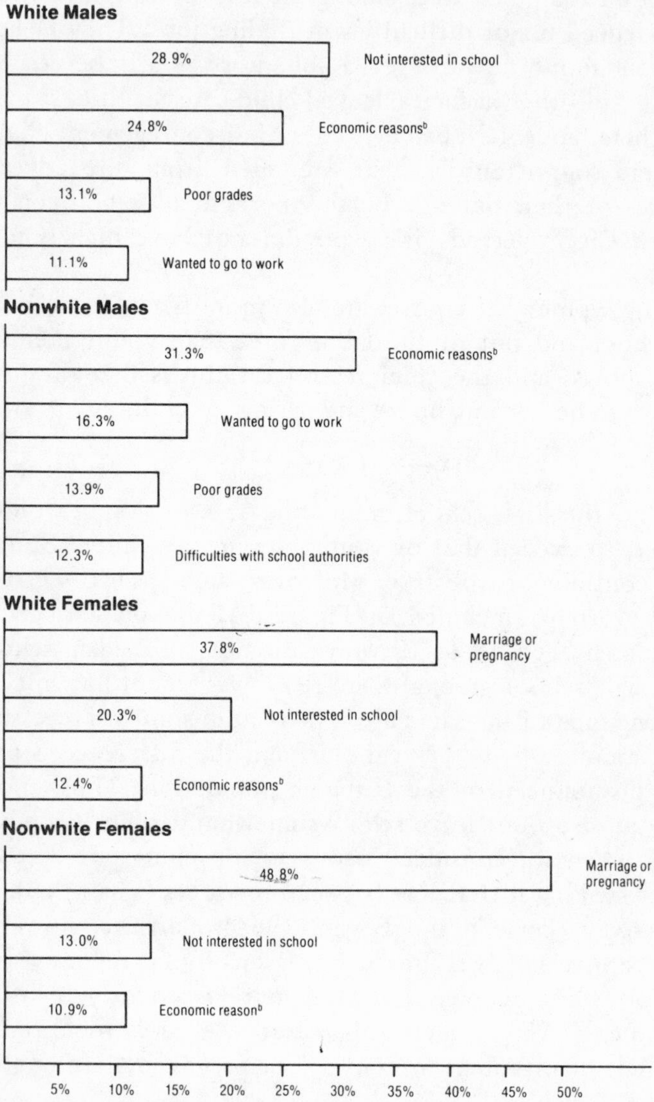

White Males

| 28.9% | Not interested in school |

| 24.8% | Economic reasons[b] |

| 13.1% | Poor grades |

| 11.1% | Wanted to go to work |

Nonwhite Males

| 31.3% | Economic reasons[b] |

| 16.3% | Wanted to go to work |

| 13.9% | Poor grades |

| 12.3% | Difficulties with school authorities |

White Females

| 37.8% | Marriage or pregnancy |

| 20.3% | Not interested in school |

| 12.4% | Economic reasons[b] |

Nonwhite Females

| 48.8% | Marriage or pregnancy |

| 13.0% | Not interested in school |

| 10.9% | Economic reason[b] |

5% 10% 15% 20% 25% 30% 35% 40% 45% 50%

[a]Data relate to the main reason given by each respondent.

[b]Economic reasons include unemployment in family, to support family, needed money, and so on.

Source: Perrella and Bogan (1964, table A-3).

very small minority (not shown in Figure 15) did give it as the main reason. "Not interested in school" was mentioned most frequently by young, white men, whereas young, nonwhite men were especially likely to mention economic reasons.

In interpreting reasons mentioned for dropping out, it is well to keep in mind the possible ambiguity of some of the responses. As we noted in Section 2, some of those who have made intensive studies of dropouts believe that young people who eventually drop out tend to have developed problems of maladjustment in school in their early adolescent years or at an even younger age. And yet, when asked the reason for dropping out, a youth may hesitate to admit that poor school performance was the reason and may prefer to mention economic reasons. Even so, it is reasonable to expect nonwhite men to mention economic reasons relatively more frequently than white men in view of the generally lower-income level of nonwhite families. When a young woman gives marriage or pregnancy as the main reason, moreover, this is likely to reflect the true situation, although, as we shall note later, there is evidence that girls who are poorly adjusted in school are particularly likely to become pregnant.

Teenage Pregnancies

In spite of the pronounced drop in the birthrate since the late 1950s, teenage pregnancies continue to be a serious problem—not only for the individuals involved but for society as a whole. School policies can do much to determine whether the teenage mother is forced to terminate education abruptly as a result of her pregnancy or whether she is encouraged to complete her high school education. The adverse effects of teenage pregnancies are not confined to young mothers. If the response is early marriage—and even sometimes if it is not—the young father may drop out of school at a stage in life when he has difficulty getting a good, steady job. A particularly informative study of the impact of early marriage and early pregnancies on poverty in later life is Schorr (1966), and there are a number of more recent studies. In a study based on longitudinal data from Project Talent, Card and Wise (1978) found that teenage mothers and teenage fathers acquired less education than their contemporaries, were more often limited to lower-level jobs or, in the case of women, to dead-end jobs, and experienced less stable marriages than their contemporaries.

Joseph A. Califano, former Secretary of the U.S. Department of Health, Education, and Welfare, was reported to have become alarmed several years ago when he learned that one million teenage girls, or one out of every ten, become pregnant every year ("Birth of Budget Item," 1978). Of these young women, nearly 600,000 carry their babies to term. About 100,000 pregnancies are terminated by miscarriages and 300,000 by abortions.

Actually, the number of live births to mothers aged 15 to 19 has been declining in recent years, reflecting both a decline in the number of young women in this age group in the population and a decline in their age-specific birthrate (Figure 16). Moreover, the increase in number of births that occurred in the 1960s was entirely explained by the rise in the size of this age group, even though the birthrate declined. However, the rate of illegitimate births to mothers in this age group has been rising quite steadily, while the percentage of births to mothers aged 15 to 19 that were illegitimate rose from about 15 percent in 1960 to about 40 percent in 1976. This reflects, in large part, a decline in the tendency of young mothers to marry in response to pregnancy. In view of the mounting evidence that early marriages occurring in response to pregnancy tend to be unstable and that there is decreased social stigma associated with keeping a baby born out of wedlock, it is not clear that the rise in the percentage of illegitimate births is regrettable per se. The young mother, whether she is married or not, is likely to be confronted with a difficult problem.

Although the number of births to girls less than 15 years of age is small, the problems they present are especially difficult. Health hazards to the mother and to the baby tend to be more serious for this age group (also for 15- and 16-year-olds) than it is for those in their late teens. The percentage of illegitimate births is also much higher among those under 15 than among 15- to 19-year-olds, partly because there are often legal obstacles to marriage at these early years and partly because both parents and society oppose such early marriages.

Although the increase in the proportion of illegitimate births has been more pronounced among whites, both the rate of illegitimate births and the percentage of all births that are illegitimate continue to be much higher among blacks. In 1976 there were 12.7 illegitimate births per 1,000 white women aged 15 to 19 compared with 83.2 per 1,000 black women in the same age group, while 24.8 percent of all births to white mothers and 79.7 percent of those to black mothers in this age group were illegitimate (U.S. National Center for Health Statistics, 1978, table 12). Part of the explanation of the higher rate of illegitimacy among blacks is conception at an earlier age and, associated with this, fewer marriages after the onset of pregnancy.

Other facts that are important to an understanding of the frequency of teenage pregnancies and of policies needed to meet the problems are the following:

• The prevalence of sexual intercourse among teenagers has been rising rapidly, probably associated with the drop in the age of puberty. A group of Johns Hopkins researchers who have been conducting surveys since 1971 have found that the percentage of young women who had had intercourse by age 19 rose from 55 percent in 1971 to 63 percent in 1976 (Zelnick, Kim, and Kantner, 1979). The increase was more pronounced for white teenagers, but the percentage continued to be higher (83 percent) among blacks than among whites (60 percent). The researchers also found that the median age of young women at the first act of sexual intercourse was 16.6 years for blacks and 18.4 years for whites. Eight in ten of the pregnancies of girls under age 19 are premarital.

• Although the use of contraceptives by teenage girls has been rising, researchers have found that only about one-third of the girls who are sexually active use contraceptives regularly (Zelnick and Kantner, 1978). Ignorance or lack of access are not always responsible for the failure to use contraceptives. Intensive studies of teenage mothers have indicated that many pregnancies occur because the girl has allowed herself to go further than she intended. Some girls, also, do not want

Giving Youth a Better Chance

**Figure 16. Number of live births to all mothers and unmarried
mothers, birthrate, and number of girls in population, 1950 to 1976**

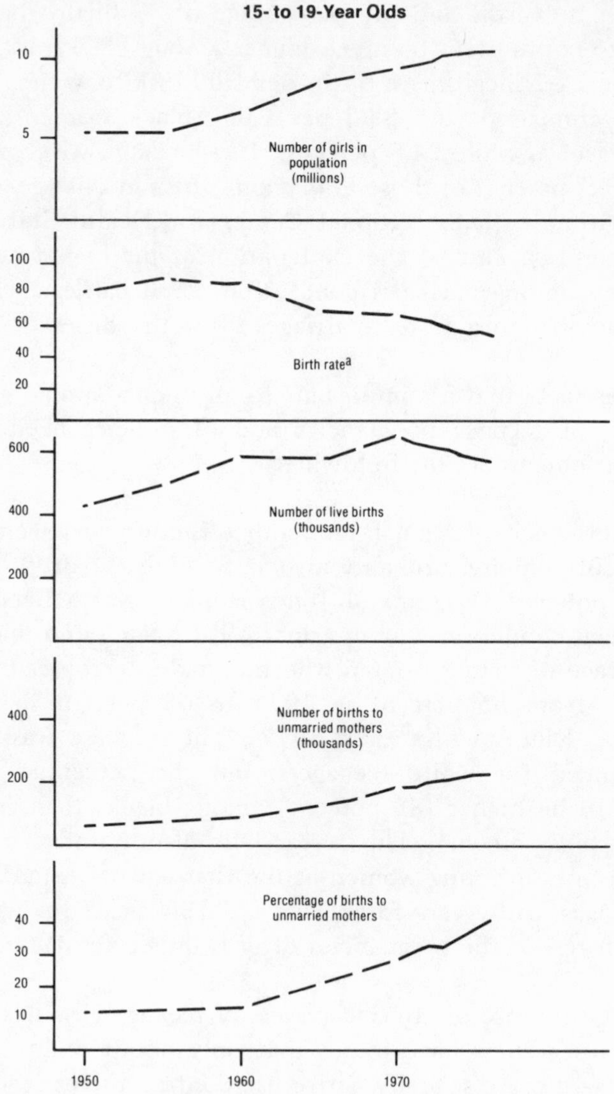

15- to 19-Year Olds

[a]Number of live births per 1,000 girls in the age group.

[b]Note that the scale used for girls aged 10 to 14 differs from that used for those aged
15 to 19.

Source: Computed from data in *Statistical Abstract of the United States, 1978* (pp.
60, 65); U.S. Bureau of the Census (1965, 1974, 1978).

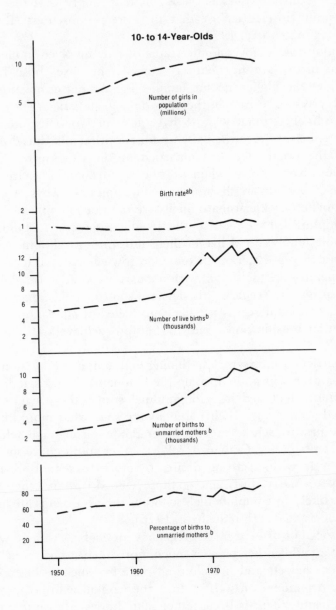

10- to 14-Year-Olds

Number of girls in
population
(millions)

Birth rate[a][b]

Number of live births[b]
(thousands)

Number of births to
unmarried mothers [b]
(thousands)

Percentage of births to
unmarried mothers [b]

to use contraceptives because this may imply that they are expecting intercourse or that they are promiscuous (Rains, 1971; Furstenberg, 1976).

* Data on the socioeconomic status of girls involved in illegitimate births are not entirely reliable, because those from middle- and higher-income families are in a better position to find ways of escaping the illegitimacy statistics. They are more likely to marry or to have an abortion. They are also more likely to give the baby up for adoption and thus do not join the population of unmarried mothers caring for their babies. Nevertheless, data on the socioeconomic status of teenage parents are illuminating in a number of ways. A large proportion of illegitimate births are to young people who are unemployed, have relatively little education, come from low-income families, and live in the South or in rural nonfarm or central-city areas. Low-income and low-educational levels of the parents are associated with nonuse or sporadic use of contraceptives by teenage girls. There is some evidence that sexually active adolescents are likely to have low educational and vocational aspirations and to be low achievers (Chilman, 1976).

* Of particular interest is the finding that, among young unmarried mothers in a low-income predominantly black sample in Baltimore included in a longitudinal study, those who continued to live with their parents were somewhat more likely to return to school and to be graduated from high school (Furstenberg and Crawford, 1978). Other studies have shown that girls with a strong desire to return to school are less likely to marry, but, among those who do marry, they are more likely to complete high school if their husbands are high school graduates (Furstenberg, 1976).

* The social costs of teenage pregnancy are high. A woman who bears a child in her teens is much more likely to be forced to support herself and her children on a low income or to become dependent on welfare than the woman who postpones childbearing. This is because her schooling is interrupted; she often has additional children soon after the first; her employment opportunities are limited as a result of her low level of

education and her child-rearing responsibilities; and, even if she does marry, her husband is likely to have low earnings and it is highly probable that the marriage will end in separation or divorce. It has been estimated that in 1975 about $4.7 billion, or one-half of total payments in the Aid to Families with Dependent Children (AFDC) program were made to women who were either teenage mothers or who had borne their first children while still teenagers. These expenditures did not include the costs of food stamps or of Medicaid. However, while nearly one-third of all mothers aged 14 to 30 who had not graduated from high school lived in households receiving AFDC payments, only 11 percent of those who were high school graduates lived in such households (Moore, 1978).

- It is sometimes alleged that the availability of AFDC encourages teenage pregnancies, or even that teenage girls deliberately become pregnant in order to become eligible for AFDC and thus to become independent of their parents. However, researchers who have made careful studies of teenage mothers have not found much evidence in support of these allegations (Moore and Caldwell, 1977; Moore, 1978; Furstenberg, 1976). These researchers have also concluded that the great majority of births to teenage mothers are unplanned and unwanted.

What about policies toward teenage pregnancies? There have been many significant changes since the early 1960s, when the problem was largely neglected. The federal government has gradually increased funds available for maternal and child health services to low-income mothers and for family planning services. However, Congress cut off funds several years ago for financing abortions for low-income mothers, except when the mother's health was endangered, and a number of states have done likewise or are experiencing controversies over their policies. The battle between pro-abortionists and right-to-life advocates has become intense.

Public opinion now supports sex education in the schools by a large majority, and such programs are quite widespread, in many cases beginning in the lower grades. There has also been a tendency to develop programs to assist teenage mothers in completing their schooling, but these are not nearly prevalent enough. Probably the most impressive growth has been in the availability of family planning services, but there are still many areas that are inadequately served, especially in suburbs and small communities (Dryfoos and Heisler, 1978).

On the whole, we continue to be far behind certain other industrial countries such as Sweden and the Netherlands in providing services for unmarried mothers (Klerman and Jekel, 1973).

From the perspectives of this report, the evidence that teenagers of both sexes who are not strongly motivated toward educational achievement are more likely to become involved in teenage pregnancies is especially important. Would the changes in school structure and school policies that we shall discuss later motivate more of these youngsters toward educational achievement and make them more wary of activities that interfere with educational progress?

The Motivation of Young Women

Before leaving the question of sex differences, we need to refer to sexist attitudes toward school programs of young women that impede their educational achievement and ultimately their career options. This problem was discussed at some length in the Carnegie Commission's report on *Opportunities for Women in Higher Education* (1973b), where the importance of overcoming the sex stereotypes that affect the interests and motivation of girls from early childhood onward was stressed. The secondary school experience is crucial in this context, because it is at this stage that girls may decide that it is not important to continue taking courses in mathematics and science, in which their performance tends, on the average, to be somewhat inferior to that of their fellow male students. Although the situation is improving, there are still too many counselors who have not abandoned older attitudes about females—to the effect that they are less likely than males to need prolonged study of mathematics or science since they will marry or, in any event, enter occupations in which advanced knowledge of such subjects is not needed. And yet deficiency in mathematical training blocks a woman in college from majoring in many of the fields that lead to promising professional occupations and tends to shunt her into courses in the humanities or the "softer" social sciences that do not lead to promising careers under the employment market conditions that have prevailed in the 1970s and will continue into the indefinite future. With advancing technology, moreover, many fields, such as business administration, that once did not call for much mathematical background now demand it.

A closely related problem is the tendency of high school counselors—probably less prevalent now than in the past—to discourage young women of low-income or working-class backgrounds from pursuing academic programs and to steer them into commercial or other vocational programs, even when they clearly have the ability to go on to college.

We believe that females should have opportunities equal to those of males to develop their highest skills.

4

The Importance of Being Sixteen: A New Age for Free Choice

The School-Leaving Age

Central to the proposals made in this report, whether they relate to schools or the labor market or service opportunities, is the issue of the school-leaving age. We believe that compulsory schooling should not extend beyond the sixteenth birthday and that from then on young people should have a wide variety of options for more advanced education in different types of schools and colleges, or for combinations of work experience and education, or for training in a choice of environments, or for cultural or community activities, or for service.

The main reason for this recommendation is that there is ample evidence that many young people are held in school too long—in this country and in other industrial countries—and that they would benefit from opportunities for experiences that would seem more challenging and closer to the "real world" than school, especially the big-city school. Most proposals for education reform in recent years have advocated lowering the school-leaving age, at least if it calls for compulsory schooling beyond age 16. The Kettering Commission goes so far as to recommend a school-leaving age of 14 (see Section 5), but this does not seem feasible to us because it would create too many problems in a society that now offers few employment opportunities for 14- and 15-year-olds, does not officially count them as part of the labor force (even when they are working or seeking work), and offers almost no prospect of improving job opportunities for them in the normal labor market.

In fact, 16 is the present school-leaving age in most states. However, in 1977 there were nine states in which the school-leaving age was either 17 or 18—Hawaii, Nevada, New Mexico, Ohio, Oregon, Pennsylvania, Texas, Utah, and Virginia (Table 1). Several states have lowered the school-leaving age in the last few years.

The trend toward raising the school-leaving age that has prevailed in the past was supported by organized labor, which had an interest in keeping youth from competing for jobs, and union interests are likely to resist efforts to lower the school-leaving age where it is still above age 16. The alarming situation in big city schools has, however, convinced many people that forcing young people to stay in school has created many of the disciplinary problems that those schools face.

Associated with provisions for compulsory schooling, of course, have been child labor laws that limit the amount of work a young person can do, require work permits for those below a certain age, prohibit the employment of young people in proximity to moving machinery, and so on. We shall return to those requirements in Section 13.

Recommendation 1: *The legal age for the end of compulsory schooling should be no later than the 16th birthday. States with a higher school-leaving age should revise their legislation, but they may need to plan for gradual implementation so that opportunities for training, community service, and other activities for those who leave formal schooling at age 16 can be expanded.*

Table 1. Age ranges for compulsory school attendance, by state, 1977

State	Age range	State	Age range
Alabama	Between 7 and 16	Nebraska	Not less than 7 nor more than 16
Alaska	Between 7 and 16	Nevada	Between 7 and 17
Arizona	Between 8 and 16	New Hampshire	Between 6 and 16
Arkansas	Between 7 and 15 (both inclusive)	New Jersey	Between 6 and 16
California	Between 6 and 16	New Mexico	Attained 6 and until attaining 17
Colorado	Aged 7 and under 16	New York	From 6 to 16
Connecticut	Over 7 and under 16	North Carolina	Between 7 and 16
Delaware	Between 6 and 16	North Dakota	Aged 7 to 16
District of Columbia	Between 7 and 16	Ohio	Between 6 and 18
Florida	Attained 7 but not 16	Oklahoma	Between 8 and 16
Georgia	Between 7th and 16th birthdays	Oregon	Between 7 and 18
Hawaii	At least 6 and not 18	Pennsylvania	Not later than 8, until 17
Idaho	Aged 7 but not 16	Rhode Island	Completed 7 years of life, not completed 16 years
Illinois	Between 7 and 16		
Indiana	Not less than 7, not more than 16	South Carolina	Aged 7 to 16
Iowa	Over 7 and under 16	South Dakota	Aged 7 and not exceeding 16
Kansas	Aged 7 and under 16	Tennessee	Between 7 and 16
Kentucky	Aged 7 and under 16	Texas	As much as 7, not more than 17
Louisiana	Between 7 and 15	Utah	Between 6 and 18
Maine	Between 7th and 15th anniversaries	Vermont	Between 7 and 16
Maryland	Between 6 and 16	Virginia	Reached 6th birthday, not passed 17th birthday
Massachusetts	Between 6 and 16		
Michigan	Between 6 and 16	Washington	Child 8 and under 15
Minnesota	Between 7 and 16	West Virginia	Begin with 7th birthday, continue to 16th birthday
Mississippi	From 7 to 13		
Missouri	Between 7 and 16	Wisconsin	Between 6 and 16
Montana	Is 7, not yet reached 16th birthday	Wyoming	Between 7 and 16 inclusive

Source: U.S. National Center for Education Statistics (1978a, table 23).

Options for the 16-Year-Old

From their sixteenth birthday, or after completion of the school term following their sixteenth birthday, a wide variety of options should be available to youths. These would include the following and perhaps others as well:

- Continuation in secondary school but with greatly increased opportunities for combinations of work experience, training, and education—see Section 6. (The issue of changes in the structure of secondary schools will be considered in Section 8.)
- Enrollment in a middle college. The middle college would combine the last few years of high school and the first few years of college. Examples are (1) proposals for a middle college that have been considered but not adopted within the City University of New York and (2) Seattle University's program, which includes the last three years of high school and the first three years of college.
- Enrollment in a community college. This is currently possible in some states for those who have graduated from high school and, in a few states (for example, California), for those who have passed special competency tests. We believe that individual community colleges or systems should experiment with admission at age 16. Some experiments might require a minimum competency test; others might not.
- Expanded and more varied apprenticeship programs—see Section 13.
- Other on-the-job training opportunities—see Section 13.
- The Job Corps and other similar programs—see Section 14.
- Jobs, including subsidized jobs—see Section 13.
- Youth service in the community, or in conservation and other similar programs, or in the armed forces—see Section 17.

These options are portrayed in Figure 17. It should be explained that *each of the options for 16- to 17-year-olds should ideally lead to any one of the options available for those 18 and older.*

Recommendation 2: *Beyond the sixteenth birthday, a young person should have the option of proceeding to (1) additional secondary schooling and work options, (2) middle college and work options, (3) community college and work options, (4) apprenticeships, (5) work or training programs, or (6) youth service.*

Each of the options available to 16- and 17-year-olds should lead to any of the options available at age 18 or older.

Whose Responsibility?

It is not our intention that a young person should be set adrift at age 16 or that the school should abdicate its responsibility. As will be discussed at greater length in Section 6, we believe that secondary schools should have much more adequate counseling and placement services than most of them now have and that it should be the responsibility of the school to make every effort to open up one of the options indicated in Figure 17 for every youngster approaching age 16. Many, of course, will opt to stay on in secondary school but usually with an opportunity to enroll in an alternative school or a magnet school, as we propose in Section 8. Many, however, will do better in an entirely new environment, such as a community college, an apprenticeship program, or a job.

In fact, we believe that secondary schools should be required to follow all of their students for at least two years after they leave school, regardless of their activity. Some students will inevitably disappear, but the school should be in a position to keep track of the great majority, and counseling and placement services should always be available for a school-leaver who has had trouble settling into a training program or finding a job, or who simply wants to shift to another option. This would be somewhat similar to the responsibility of the Careers Service in Great Britain (see Section 6).

Under certain circumstances, the school could transfer its responsibility to another agency, for example, a community college in which a student is enrolled. In some communities, moreover, it might be preferable for a community college to take on

Figure 17. Paths from childhood to adulthood

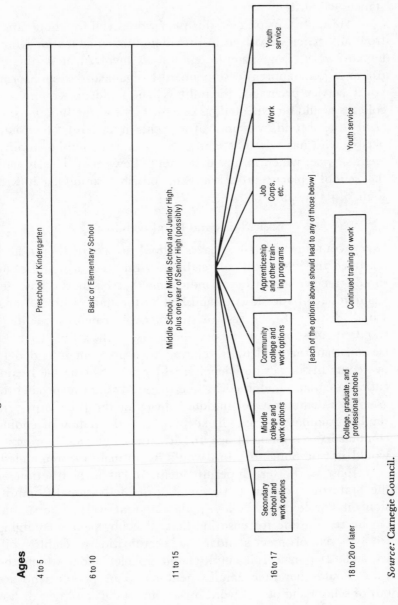

Ages

4 to 5 — Preschool or Kindergarten

6 to 10 — Basic or Elementary School

11 to 15 — Middle School, or Middle School and Junior High, plus one year of Senior High (possibly)

16 to 17 — Secondary school and work options | Middle college and work options | Community college and work options | Apprenticeship and other training programs | Job Corps, etc. | Work | Youth service

[each of the options above should lead to any of those below]

18 to 20 or later — College, graduate, and professional schools | Continued training or work | Youth service

Source: Carnegie Council.

the responsibility for the future of all school-leavers—circumstances will differ.

An important part of this plan would call for cooperation from all agencies involved in providing further education, training, or work. For example, employers involved in on-the-job training, joint apprenticeship boards, organizations sponsoring youth service programs, the military, and middle or community colleges would be expected, as one of their routine functions, to notify the secondary school of any change in status of a young person who has left that school. So would the public employment service, which in any case should be working closely with the school's placement service and possibly supplying it with some of its personnel.

Basic Skills and Employability

Every young person who leaves school at age 16 should have mastered the basic skills of reading, writing, and arithmetic and should receive a certificate indicating that he or she has met standards for basic skills established by the state or by the local school district. In the case of students who cannot meet these standards, it should be the responsibility of the school to make certain that the student is referred to a program intended to overcome his or her deficiencies, which might be an adult education program conducted by the school district, a special program at a community or middle college, or the Job Corps or a similar training program. In keeping with the policy of ending compulsory schooling at age 16, attendance at such a program would not be obligatory but would be strongly recommended.

John W. Porter, Superintendent of Public Instruction of the State of Michigan and a member of the National Commission on Employment Policy, maintains that every state should (1) be responsible for ensuring that all young people emerging from its schools meet standards of certification of employability and (2) pursue full employment policies under which the state would guarantee employment to young people who are out of school and out of work by serving as the employer of last resort. The high costs associated with serving as employer of last resort, he argues, would force the state to take vigorous steps to ensure that jobs were made available in private industry and nonprofit agencies.

Recent legislation enacted by the state of Michigan does not go as far as this, but it takes steps toward these twin goals through three measures:

1. The Youth Employment Clearinghouse Act of September 28, 1979, creating a youth employment clearinghouse within the state department of labor, which will be responsible for assembling comprehensive data on all unemployed youth in the state, evaluating youth employment programs, and submitting an annual program to the legislature and governor making recommendations concerning the funding of youth employment programs.
2. An amendment to the state's education legislation, requiring that counseling and guidance staffs in each school district devote an appropriate portion of working time and effort to employment counseling and placement services for pupils 16 to 19 years of age who do not intend to enroll in college or who desire part-time employment while continuing their education. The legislation also provides that school districts may enter into agreements with other school districts or units of local government in establishing counseling and placement services and that the state public employment service and other appropriate state agencies must provide assistance to school districts establishing such services.
3. The Full Employment Planning Act of 1978 (a state version of the Humphrey-Hawkins Act), which provides that the state department of labor must submit an annual projection of labor demand and supply in the state and prepare an annual employment plan that will increase both subsidized and unsubsidized employment opportunities, increase the employability of disadvantaged members of the labor force, and increase the effectiveness of the public education system in equipping youth with skills, attitudes, and experiences necessary for a successful transition to the labor force.

These policies are of special interest, because they move

toward explicit recognition of the joint responsibility of the school system and of labor market agencies for both the employability and employment of youth at the state level. The Council of Chief State School Officers endorses similar policies.

Recommendation 3: *The responsibilities of secondary schools for school-leavers should not end at age 16. School districts should be required to ensure that those leaving school have acquired basic skills or are provided with opportunities for making up their deficiencies. School districts should also ensure that school-leavers are referred to appropriate education, training, work, or service programs and should follow the progress of school-leavers for at least two years after their departure from school.*

Part II

Schooling

5

Current
Reform Proposals

Recent Proposals

In the 1970s, three distinguished groups issued reports on the education of adolescents in the United States. Their diagnoses of what was wrong were remarkably similar, and their recommendations were also quite similar. The reports were:

- *Youth: Transition to Adulthood.* Report of the Panel on Youth of The President's Science Advisory Committee. (James S. Coleman, Chairman, and hereafter referred to as the Coleman Panel.) Washington, D.C.: Office of Science and Technology, Executive Office of The President, 1973.
- *The Reform of Secondary Education: A Report of the National Commission on the Reform of Secondary Education.* (B. Frank Brown, Chairman; Commission established by the Charles F. Kettering Foundation.) New York: McGraw-Hill, 1973.
- *The Education of Adolescents: The Final Report and Recommendations of the National Panel on High School and Adolescent Education.* (John H. Martin, Chairman and Director.) Washington, D.C.: U.S. Office of Education, 1976.

As these groups saw it, the problems were as follows:

1. Young people received too heavy a dose of schooling for too long a period, unmixed with knowledge of the world of work or experience in work or community service.
2. Young people were segregated in their own age group and had little experience of association with other age groups or of appreciation of the problems of other age groups. (This was emphasized especially in the Coleman Panel report.)
3. Large city schools had become too big and too impersonal and had the most severe problems of discipline, violence, absenteeism, and dropouts.
4. Opportunities for work were impaired both by protective legislation and by inflexible school hours.
5. The quality of education was damaged by the necessity of keeping many young people in school long after they derived any real benefit from it and the accompanying need to develop watered-down programs to keep these youngsters busy.
6. The capacity of modern schools to exercise authority and influence over the development of young people was greatly weakened by the influence of mass media (especially television) and by the influence of peer groups. The drift of families away from religion and the permissiveness of modern parents made the schools seem excessively authoritarian to children.

Among the important recommendations made by one or more of these groups were the following:

1. Young people should not be compelled to be in school beyond their sixteenth birthday (the Kettering Commission recommended a school-leaving age of 14).
2. Alternatives to the comprehensive high school should be created. Smaller schools and smaller classes should be stressed. Schools should become more specialized, so that students could pursue their interests under the guidance of especially skilled teachers (the Coleman Panel emphasized specialization more than did the other two groups).
3. Children should be exposed to career education at an early age, but this should take the form of teaching them about the

world of work in the early years and gradually be expanded
to include visits to work places, followed by actual work
experience in the last two years of high school.

4. School hours should be made more flexible to accommodate
opportunities for work, and students should be given academic credit for work experience.

5. Work that takes the form of community service is particularly desirable, giving young people a feeling of involvement
in community problems and of contributing to their solution.

6. Schools should maintain a placement service as an integral
part of career education.

7. Instead of subsidizing schools, educational support from age
16 on should be provided through vouchers, which the recipient could use at his or her discretion for schooling and other
skill acquisition at any subsequent time of life (Coleman
Panel).

8. Youth service activities should be expanded and should be
available to those aged 16 to 24, with a commitment required
for only one year but with the option of staying on for two
years (Coleman Panel).

9. Development of educational programs within industry (Coleman Panel).

The three reports were reviewed by the Rand Corporation
for the Assistant Secretary for Planning and Evaluation of the
U.S. Department of Health, Education, and Welfare (Timpane
and others, 1976). The review was critical of the Coleman
Panel's contention that young people were segregated from
adults, largely on the ground that many young people enter the
labor force at ages 16 or 17. It also tended to throw cold water
on some of the recommendations, suggesting, for example, that
individualized and flexible secondary education programs are
desirable but may be difficult to attain and that smaller high
schools may create a more human scale but may be more costly
and less integrated. It warned that collective bargaining
processes are likely to limit the high schools' capacity for innovation. However, it pointed out that, in an era of declining
enrollments, large high schools would gradually get smaller and

school districts should not worry about that. "Sub-schools" might enhance these gains without adverse results, but drastically smaller schools might impose limitations on the number of courses available to students. In addition, serious consideration should be given to voucher plans, and great emphasis should be placed on staff development plans that would enable teachers to cope more successfully with new problems and new situations.

In a later paper, Timpane (1978) placed particular emphasis on one of the phenomena that is likely to make school reform at the secondary level especially difficult. This is the development of complex bureaucracies within school systems. The bureaucracy, he notes, is "characterized by multiple levels of authority (especially in the largest urban school districts) and by the growth of rule making, centralized personnel systems, etc." (p. 9). We have also "seen an explosion of specialization in administration. Assistant principals, assistant superintendents, curriculum supervisors, and district planning officers have appeared in every school system" (p. 10).

Early in 1979, the then U.S. Commissioner of Education, Ernest L. Boyer, proposed a restructuring of the American school system that was consistent with some of the earlier proposals and in some respects went beyond them (Boyer, 1979, p. 14). The system was outlined as follows:

Basic or elementary school—4 to 5 years. Here children would become well grounded in the basic skills.

Middle school—5 years. During this period students would "continue a rigorous exposure to the basics of language and mathematics. But they would also study their contemporary world—examining the organizational, economic and social structures of which they are a part."

Transition schools—2 or 3 years. These would be places "where students would specialize somewhat and develop their unique talents." They would extend the opportunities now opening up in many school districts for students "to work and learn beyond the campus." Examples of what Boyer had in mind are:

• A school for the arts that would be linked to community theater groups, galleries, museums, and orchestras.

- A school for business that would offer on-the-job training a day or two each week.
- A health-professions school that would be linked to hospitals and clinics in the community.
- A social-service school that would include apprenticeships at retirement homes, community agencies, and city parks.
- A "university in the school" program that would offer collegiate study in science, mathematics, or the humanities for academically advanced students.
- Finally, language and general education would be stressed throughout all of formal education.

Boyer's recommendations, along with those of the three groups outlined earlier, appear to repudiate James B. Conant's well-known support of the comprehensive high school in his first report (1959) prepared for the Carnegie Corporation. It should be kept in mind, however, that Conant's first study was concerned with schools in moderate-sized communities. He advocated a comprehensive high school that would serve all the students in the community, offering a choice of academic, general, and vocational curricula. Equally important was the following recommendation (p. 46):

It should be the policy of the school that every student has an individualized program; there would be no classification of students according to clearly defined and labeled programs or tracks such as "college-preparatory," "vocational," "commercial." . . . It will turn out that many students of similar ability and vocational interests will have almost identical programs, but a student who has elected an academic sequence may shift to a vocational sequence and vice versa. Furthermore, with individualized programs, the students themselves do not feel that they are labeled according to the program they have chosen in the ninth or tenth grade.

This first report did not discuss, except in passing, the

problems of big-city schools. One of its major concerns was that many high schools were too small to offer a desirable combination of programs, and it advocated district reorganization to reduce the number of such schools.

In his second report, Conant (1961) turned to the contrast between schools in the slums and schools in the suburbs. The book includes striking descriptions of the miserable living conditions of children in the slums—conditions that make it virtually impossible to do homework or even in some cases to get a good night's sleep or to have a good breakfast before starting off to school in the morning. Further, Conant pointed out, "the contrast in money available to the schools in a wealthy suburb and to the schools in a large city jolts one's notions of the meaning of equality of opportunity" (p. 3).

> ... I am convinced we are allowing social dynamite to accumulate in our large cities. I am not nearly so concerned about the plight of suburban parents whose offspring are having difficulty finding places in prestige colleges as I am about the plight of parents in the slums whose children either drop out or graduate from school without prospects of either further education or employment. In some slum neighborhoods I have no doubt that over a half of the boys between sixteen and twenty-one are out of school and out of work. Leaving aside human tragedies, I submit that a continuation of this situation is a menace to the social and political health of the large cities [p. 2].

Conant could have been writing these words as well in 1979 as in 1961.

In more recent years, Conant has been followed by other writers on schools whose works are worthy of attention. Particular mention should be made of Silberman (1970), whose book is valuable not only for its incisive criticisms but also for its descriptions of certain highly innovative schools at the secondary level. Another provocative work is that of Sizer (1973), which suggests changes somewhat similar to those emphasized by the three panels discussed earlier but in a more flexible and possibly more feasible way. Sizer's emphasis is on combining the academic experience of the student, not necessarily with opportunities for work, but with opportunities for a wide variety of experiences within the community. A pupil might, for example, be given a chance to accompany a policeman for a week, or to participate in an orchestra, or to join in a discussion group under community auspices, or to travel. Bailey (1976) is similar in his critique of existing education and in his suggestions but gives special emphasis to the challenge of training young people for public service.

Mention should also be made of a report issued by the National Association of Secondary School Principals (1975), which was important because it showed that those who would have to implement changes in the secondary schools agreed with many of the criticisms and proposals for change that were being made by the groups we have been discussing. Among the recommendations in this report (pp. 17-18 and 58-59) were:

- The secondary school curriculum should be redesigned and placed in a more comprehensive setting. Opportunities for service and work, serious contact with adult institutions, and experiences that span age and ethnicity need to be a part of secondary education.
- The identification and design of learning opportunities in the community must become a new curricular priority for the school.
- The opportunities to learn through action and participation will vary. Some students may find value in job situations. Others may prefer volunteer work in social service agencies or special interest organizations. Still others may organize and contract with public or private agencies, through the school, to provide a specific service. For still others, the school itself may provide the opportunity for a responsible role as tutor or recreation leader or aide.
- A number of imaginative programs should be developed by secondary and postsecondary education to assure a smooth

flow of students from secondary school to postsecondary status. Distinctions should be eased so that youth may have the option of being secondary school students or postsecondary students, or both, or part-time students of one or the other institutions. To plan and implement this flow, strong school-college liaison councils should be formed to meet on a regular basis. Secondary schools should initiate the formation of these councils.

The association also issued a useful pamphlet in 1974 summarizing 25 exemplary action-learning programs selected from descriptions of programs submitted by 2,000 secondary school principals. The 25 programs included varying combinations of cooperative education, work experience, career education, and community service and were found in varied types of communities, large and small, and in a few cases in Catholic schools (National Association of Secondary School Principals, 1974).

An International Perspective

The United States is by no means alone in debating far-reaching changes in its secondary schools. Many of the ideas discussed here, and especially the desirability of earlier exposure to work experience on the part of students, are being considered and in some cases have been adopted in other industrial democracies. The prolongation of compulsory schooling in western Europe (which has typically involved raising the legal school-leaving age from 14 to 16 over the last several decades), plus the tendency of growing proportions of young people to continue on to postcompulsory education, often under societal or parental pressure, has by no means been an unmixed blessing. On the one hand, as Torsten Husèn (1977, p. 23) puts it, "equalization of formal access to education is expected to result in equalization of life chances." On the other hand, for many young people, it fails to accomplish that. As Husèn (p. 23) goes on to point out:

Another serious problem is the "new underclass" that is recruited among those who (often right from the beginning) are academic failures in the race: backward readers, dropouts and others, many of whom are from underprivileged homes. . . . In several big city secondary schools in Europe and North America about 30-35 per cent of all the 13-16 year-olds are simply not present in their classrooms at a given day. They have "voted with their feet." The early leavers with low and even without qualifications quit school with extremely negative attitudes and with low job expectations. The International Evaluation Study conducted by the International Education Association in some 20 countries . . . most of them industrial, showed that among the academically weak students negative feelings toward school increased during the last few years of mandatory schooling. To many of them school was perceived as just a jail.

Husèn recently participated in a four-member committee appointed by the Organization for Economic Cooperation and Development (OECD) to conduct a review of educational policy in the United States, with particular reference to federal policies and programs for the disadvantaged, under the chairmanship of Peter Karmel, chairman of the Tertiary Education Commission of Australia. A draft of the committee's report was submitted to OECD in May 1979, but is not yet available to the public.

The changes that are going on in school systems in a number of countries are discussed in the Carnegie Council's series of volumes on *Education and Youth Employment,* which is listed in Appendix B. Perhaps the most far-reaching and detailed set of proposals, reflecting many of the ideas that are being discussed on an international scale, is presented by the author of the volume on Belgium, sociologist Henri Janne (1979, pp. 109-110), who recommends that youth needs "deschooling," which means among other things:

· Individualization of training.
· Continuous, positive orientation and guidance through an optimal and flexible credit system.
· Alternatives to the classroom system with provision for diversity of age and size of groups.
· Less instruction in learning rooms and more through activities

carried out where things happen and where knowledge and skills are produced.

- Alternation of work and studies for the 14- to 15-age and 18- to 19-age groups, based on national standards of equitable earnings.[1]
- Recurrent education provided on the basis of paid educational leaves, by law or collective bargaining, for all types of studies (professional, vocational, general) for self-improvement or for community life, and at all levels.

The country studies also provide a number of other interesting examples of reforms or controversies affecting secondary education:

Great Britain

A sudden shift in the focus of debate, now that comprehensive secondary schools have largely replaced the former elitist grammar schools and unselective modern schools, toward a new concern with educational standards and with the links between education and the world of work (Maclure, 1979).

Federal Republic of Germany

Continuing heated controversy over proposals to replace the existing, social-class-oriented, three-level school system by a comprehensive secondary school—a reform long since accomplished in Great Britain, Sweden, and other countries (von Dohnanyi, 1978).

Sweden

Mandatory work-education councils (much like those proposed to operate on a voluntary basis by Willard Wirtz and the National Manpower Institute in the United States—see Section 6),

---

[1]Apparently, in recommending alternations of work and study for the 14- to 15-year-olds, Janne had in mind the fact that many of these young people would be leaving school at age 15. He evidently felt that the 16- and 17-year-olds, who were beginning their upper secondary education, needed concentrated schooling, while the 18- and 19-year-olds, who would be completing upper secondary schooling and going to work or into the university, would benefit from exposure to work experience.

bringing together school and labor market representatives in communities throughout the country, to plan work-study programs and ease the transition from school to work (Rehn and Petersen, forthcoming).

Denmark

Work-education centers, located on campuses outside the cities, in which disadvantaged young people not only pursue a program combining education, occupational training, and work experience, but also provide for the physical needs and management of the center by farming, fishing, repairing motor cars, operating the kitchen, and the like (Rehn and Petersen, forthcoming).

Poland

Broadened opportunities for graduates of both academic and vocational programs in secondary schools to be admitted to institutions of higher education (Liberska, 1979).

Japan

The development of more than 350 educational institutions, operated by industrial firms, that provide the equivalent of a high school education, combined with intensive technical training, on a highly selective basis, to students whose educational costs are met by the company and who are guaranteed full-time jobs with the company on satisfactory completion of the program (Kato, 1978).

Mexico

Caustic criticism by the authors of policies that provide a much larger percentage of the Gross National Product for education of children of the highly privileged than for children of the poor, in a country with strong democratic and egalitarian aims (Medina and Izquierdo, 1978).

South Asia

The author recommends that primary education be made more accessible to poor children by developing opportunities for part-time school attendance, involving flexibility of school hours and course duration to conform with the agricultural cycle and the pattern of children's labor in family subsistence activities (Ahmed, 1978).

The last point is of special interest, because it suggests that in less-developed countries full-time schooling at the primary level may have disadvantages that are somewhat similar to those of full-time schooling at the secondary level in developed countries.

The Organization for Economic Cooperation and Development (OECD) has sponsored a continuing series of studies and reports on the transition from school to work in recent years, often involving policy proposals similar to those discussed in this report. Reports concerned primarily with employment policy will be discussed in Part III, but at this point mention should be made of a 1976 OECD report, *Beyond Compulsory Schooling: Options and Changes in Upper Secondary Education.* While refraining from formal recommendations, that report concludes by identifying trends that are common to a number of countries:

• A movement away from the sharp separation of general and vocational education that was characteristic of traditional secondary schooling in many European countries, and usually, but not invariably, toward the comprehensive school.
• Emphasis on diversification of the structure of studies to increase a student's options.
• Reorganization of vocational education, in a variety of ways in different countries, but with a general trend toward greater public responsibility for the quality and financial support of vocational education and for ensuring that the general education of those choosing a vocational stream is not neglected.
• Alternation of education and employment, through part-time study for pupils involved in on-the-job training, cooperative education, and greater involvement of community agencies in providing opportunities for service to young people.

China

Education in China has some lessons for the West—not always the expected ones.[2] With the onset of the post-Cultural Revolution in 1970 and the arrest of the Gang of Four after Mao's death in September 1976, it became clear to the Chinese leadership that the quality of education, especially at the higher education level, had suffered severely during the Cultural Revolution and that the renewed aspirations for industrial and technological development would require a revitalization of high standards in the secondary schools and the universities.

In China, a child proceeds through five years of primary school, three years of junior middle school, and two years of senior middle school. The aims set forth by Boyer (1979) for middle schools in the United States are similar to those of the middle schools in China, which Boyer visited in 1975. A graduate of a senior middle school may apply for entrance to a university, but only a small proportion of applicants can be admitted. The former policies of forcing urban youth to move out to distant rural areas, participate in the work life of the communes, and become eligible for university admission only if selected by their communes are being abandoned. Although primary school enrollment is close to universal, the percentage of the age group in middle schools (40 percent) is much lower than in the United States (90 percent), and in higher education 0.7 percent compared with 35 to 40 percent in this country.

Chinese educational policies emphasize inculcating an appreciation of the dignity of work and blending education and work. Students visit factories and communes to see people at work, including their parents, and, wherever possible, shops and gardens are included in the schools. Students are expected to work 15 percent of the time in the school or in an outside fac-

---

[2]Four members of the Carnegie Council participated in a visit to China under the chairmanship of Clark Kerr in spring 1978. The major focus of the group, 21 members in all, was on the relations between education and work in the People's Republic. Our discussion is largely based on the report of the group by Kerr (1978), with contributions by other members.

tory or agricultural commune. Such work now includes mental as well as manual labor, whereas the former policy was to elevate the status of manual labor and to denigrate mental labor. Students are also encouraged to spend two years or more at work between secondary and higher education. Although work projects in schools seem to some American observers to be of questionable value, the efforts to orient students toward work and to give them some working experience outside the school are impressive.

Also impressive are the children's palaces, which are maintained in cities and in some suburban areas as well, to provide cultural and recreational activities after school for children aged 7 to 16 who attend local primary and junior middle schools. Students must apply for admission, which is based on intellectual ability, special talents, behavior, and good health. By no means are all children admitted. Training classes include such activities as music and art work, building radios or model ships and airplanes, theatrical presentations, and sports. A corps of paid full-time teachers is assisted by unpaid volunteers. Although classes are conducted in an orderly fashion, the atmosphere is less formal than that of the schools.

The children's palaces exemplify the Chinese emphasis on development of the individual, even within the framework of a totalitarian society and of indoctrination in the schools. While they would be even more impressive if they accommodated all children, they meet a need that is being neglected in some of our school systems, as we shall point out later.

6

Education for Work
and Work as Education

Work-Experience Programs

It is clear that many high school students—and junior high
school students as well—are getting little out of school, because
they simply do not see the relevance to their future lives of
what the school is attempting to teach them. We believe that
school might become more meaningful to them if there were
more options available for combinations of school and work
experience. Even for those students who are doing well in
school, opportunities for work or community service are likely
to make valuable contributions to a better understanding of
how society works and to a better appreciation of the relationship between their academic studies and the responsibilities
they will be assuming in adulthood. Such opportunities will aid
youth in gaining a sense of maturity and independence, and in
many cases earnings from work will be urgently needed for immediate purposes or may be set aside for college costs.

We do not mean to suggest that every secondary school
student should spend part of his or her time at work. The option should be there, but it should be entirely voluntary. There
will be some able students pursuing a science program, for
example, who will want to devote full time to study and should
have that option, although a one-semester internship in a labora-
tory, for example, might have great value. Nor do we propose

that all work available to high school students should be paid work. An opportunity to serve the community in a voluntary, unpaid capacity will attract many high school students and in some cases contribute far more to their personal development than a routine, paid job.

During the 1970s, the career education movement, associated especially with the name of Sidney P. Marland, Jr., former U.S. Commissioner of Education (see Marland, 1974), has grown and is supported by a special federal program. Advocates of career education believe that children should begin to learn about the world of work early in their school careers, at first in a classroom environment, and later through visits to factories and other workplaces. By the time they are in senior high school, career education, in the view of some of its advocates, should take the form of actual work experience in many instances. If the work is closely related to the student's educational program or, alternatively, if it takes the form of community service, so much the better. In addition, many advocates of career education believe that there should be no "tracking" of students in academic, general, and vocational programs. All students should have some exposure to both academic and vocational training, but with differing emphases.

Many students, of course, are in the labor force, with or without any special program in their schools, as we noted in Section 2. But unemployment rates of students are high in some areas, particularly in inner cities. Involvement of the school in developing jobs for students could make a great deal of difference both in preventing unemployment and in enhancing attachment to the school.

There will be critics who will argue that our emphasis on providing options for work experience for all high school students is simply a manifestation of a narrow adherence to the "work ethic." We do not see it as such. Rather we agree with Willard Wirtz and the National Manpower Institute (1975, p. 3) when they said: "An education-work policy is not one that misconceives of education as having for its purpose the preparation of people for work. Rather, it *includes* this purpose as part of education's function of preparing people for life, of which work is one part; it takes full account of learning as a human value in itself."

There will also be those who will suggest that opportunities for work experience will not do much to prevent absenteeism and dropping out, because the seeds of a propensity to drop out or to become a chronic truant tend to develop long before senior high school. It surely must be conceded that work-experience programs will not eradicate dropping out and chronic truancy, but we believe that they *will* increase the holding power of the school for many. In order to accomplish this, however, the school must be very much involved in the whole process of seeking out job opportunities for students—as we shall emphasize later—so that the school's image becomes one of opening doors to the world of work rather than of keeping youngsters confined in what seems to many of them a prison-like atmosphere. This image of the school can influence those who have not yet reached the senior high school stage—through the experiences of their older siblings or friends—as well as those who are already there.

Several experts who read and commented on an earlier draft of this report pointed out that success in finding work for all or most students would make employment opportunities for out-of-school youth even worse. We concede that this might be a short-run effect, but the long-run objective would be to diminish the number of young people who drop out or graduate without basic skills. Increasing the proportion of young people who graduate from high school and improving their preparation, of course, will not increase the number of jobs available for them in the absence of other developments, but there are several reasons for believing that this consideration need not be a major concern: (1) the anticipated decline in the youth population; (2) the probability that relatively more youths leaving secondary school will be involved in a variety of on-the-job, apprenticeship, or other training programs, or in youth-service programs, if our recommendations are adopted; and (3) the probability that at least some jobs will open up for qualified youths in firms now refusing to hire young people without previous work experience and basic skills.

We recognize that the job market for high school graduates cannot be expected to improve markedly in the absence of vigorous full-employment policies. As many critics have pointed out, the antipoverty legislation of the 1960s was an expression, in large part, of an exaggerated faith in the possibility of eradicating poverty by raising educational attainment levels, especially among the young (Levin, 1977; Jencks and others, 1972; Gordon, 1972; among others). During the 1970s, we have seen greater relative emphasis on such measures as direct job creation in the public sector to reduce unemployment.

Yet we believe that there is more at stake than success in reducing the number of young people whose destiny otherwise is poverty. The chronic truants and dropouts, especially in inner-city areas, are truly a "lost generation" whose destiny is not only poverty, but a complete lack of appreciation of the value of education, along with a high propensity for a life of crime. One purpose of our strong endorsement of greater emphasis on work-experience programs—along with many other changes in the schools to be discussed in later sections—is to make the school experience more meaningful for young people who are deriving little or no benefit from it today.

At this point, it may appear that we are mainly concerned about the disadvantaged, and, therefore, the reasons for our support of work experience for all students will be questioned. The answer is that we believe that a large proportion of students in all types of schools would benefit from work experience or community service. Although the most serious problems are found in inner-city schools, it is clear that schools in suburban and smaller communities also have problems of boredom, absenteeism, and alcohol and drug abuse. More constructive use of the students' time, especially in the afternoon, would almost certainly alleviate some of these problems.

In addition, a major theme of this report is that most programs for youth should be available to all youth and should bring young people from the various socioeconomic and racial groups together. There has been too much emphasis, in our judgment, on targeting programs to the disadvantaged.

The Neighborhood Youth Corps

We have had one nationwide work-experience program for high school students in the United States—the Neighborhood Youth Corps (NYC), succeeded by the Summer Program for Economically Disadvantaged Youth (SPEDY) and other limited work-experience programs for in-school and out-of-school youth under the Comprehensive Employment and Training Act of 1973 (CETA). In 1977, manpower programs for youth were substantially expanded under the Youth Employment and Demonstration Projects Act (YEDPA), which included some features of special interest in the context of work experience programs for high school students.

The NYC program was created under the Economic Opportunity Act of 1964 and was designed to keep low-income young people in school, get them back to school, or increase their chances of becoming employable if they were school dropouts. The in-school program emphasized job market orientation and work experience. Skill training was emphasized for out-of-school youth. Apart from the summer program, however, in which 567,000 young people were involved in 1971, NYC was quite small. First-time enrollments in that same year included 120,000 in the in-school program and 53,000 in the out-of-school program, many of them from families on welfare.

NYC has been evaluated by a number of investigators, with generally negative results in relation to prevention of dropping out or improvement in the employability of the young people involved. And yet, as Mangum and Walsh (1978, p. 56) put it, "the picture is not totally bleak." They cite one study that classified as "mildly encouraging" the evidence concerning the impact of work experience on crime and delinquency, as well as another study that emphasized the usefulness of the program in providing income maintenance even though it had only modest impact on employability. Their main conclusion, however, was that "the evidence of seventeen years of research and evaluation indicates that whenever the hard-core disadvantaged were segregated in any program, failure was almost inevitable" (p. 58). Work-experience programs, in addition, had to be supplemented

with skills training and effective job development and placement efforts to have an impact on eventual employability.

Youth Incentive Entitlement Projects

Despite the negative experience under NYC, an important feature of YEDPA, which is being intensively watched by manpower experts, provides for Youth Incentive Entitlement Pilot
Projects. Pilot projects lasting for 18 months, under which economically disadvantaged 16- to 19-year-olds are guaranteed
work if they agree to finish high school, are being tested in 17
large and modest-sized communities that were selected at the
end of 1977 on the basis of proposals that were judged the most
promising in a competitive process that began with preapplica-
tions from 153 CETA "prime sponsors."[1] A unique feature of
the program, at least in the larger cities included, is its design as
a "saturation project," embracing all young people in the demonstration area that meet the eligibility conditions—(1) reside in
the project area, (2) be in the 16- to 19-age group, (3) be a
member of a family receiving cash welfare or a family with income at or below the poverty level (now $6,700 for a family of
four), and (4) maintain satisfactory school and work attendance
performance standards. The program is also unique in its requirement for school performance standards.

Employment during the school year under the program
may not exceed 20 hours a week and must last not less than six
months or more than nine. In the summer, employment is to be
full-time or a combination of part-time work and training. All
prime sponsors selected for the project receive the funds needed
to pay wages plus costs of administration. Under general provisions of the legislation, wages must amount to the higher of the
federal minimum wage, the state or local minimum wage, or the
prevailing rates of pay for the occupation concerned (with certain exceptions involving special arrangements approved by the
relevant labor union or arrived at through collective bargaining).

---

[1]A prime sponsor, as defined in the 1973 CETA legislation, may be a state, a unit of
general local government with a population of 100,000 or more, or a combination of
units of local government.

Earnings received by any youth under the act are to be disregarded in determining the eligibility of the youth's family for such income-tested benefits as AFDC, Medicaid, food stamps, and housing subsidies.

The U.S. Secretary of Labor is also authorized to approve projects involving subsidies to private, for-profit employers, arrangements with unions to permit youths to enter apprenticeship training, and inclusion of youth under the jurisdiction of the juvenile or criminal justice system with the approval of appropriate authorities.

All the demonstration projects are scheduled to terminate on June 30, 1980, and final evaluation will, of course, not be available until some time thereafter.[2] Two reports by the Manpower Demonstration Research Corporation (MDRC) are, however, available on the early stages of the project (1979a and 1979b). By September 1978, 37,000 youngsters, averaging 16.8 years in age and 9.7 grades in school completion, had been enrolled in the program. In the school semester prior to their enrollment, 93 percent were in high school or in a high school equivalency certificate program, while 7 percent were out of school. However, 14 percent had dropped out of school at some time for at least a semester.

The enrollees came heavily from minority groups, with blacks accounting for 74 percent and Hispanics for 8 percent (chiefly in Monterey County, California; Albuquerque; and Denver).

Patterns of employment differed somewhat between the Tier I communities—chiefly the larger cities plus the 19 rural counties in Mississippi that were involved—and the Tier II communities, which were predominantly smaller, but also included

[2]The sites selected for the demonstrations were Baltimore (four complete high school zones and part of a fifth); Boston (four school districts); Cincinnati; Denver; Detroit (five high school zones); King and Snohomish counties (including the city of Seattle), Washington; 19 rural counties of Mississippi; Alachua County, Florida; Berkeley, California; Dayton, Ohio (one census tract); Hillsborough County (including the entire city of Nashua), New Hampshire; Monterey County, California (the rural Gonzales Union High School District); New York (part of one school district in Brooklyn); Philadelphia (one census tract in North Philadelphia); seven school districts in rural Steuben County, New York; and Syracuse.

portions of New York and Philadelphia. By September 1978, about 61 percent of the employment (measured in terms of job hours) in the Tier I areas and 51 percent in the Tier II areas were in public agencies (including public schools). Nonprofit agencies accounted for about 26 percent in both groups of areas, while private, for-profit employers accounted for 22 percent in Tier II areas and 12 percent in Tier I areas. However, some areas stood out with much more involvement of private, for-profit employment than the average—Detroit with 32 percent, Hillsborough County (New Hampshire) with 64 percent, Monterey County (California) with 67 percent, and Philadelphia with 65 percent.

One feature of the program worth noting is that, although it is clearly designed to prevent dropping out and to encourage dropouts to return to school, the enrollees are not all potential dropouts. This is because family poverty, which is presumably more easily determined, is the key eligibility criterion, rather than identification as a potential or actual dropout. We learned that in the Berkeley, California, program, for example, some of the students (though a small proportion) had A or B averages. However, about one-half were two grade levels behind.

Other particularly interesting features of the Berkeley program are (1) an individualized performance agreement with each student, designed to improve the level of school performance compared with the past, (2) frequent conferences between each student and the school staff member assigned to monitor his or her school performance, (3) a weekly attendance report, and (4) sessions in which students participate in demonstrations of what to do and not to do in a job interview. The students seemed very appreciative of the frequent conferences with staff members—something they had not experienced before.

Among those in the Berkeley program are a number of handicapped young people who could not be served in any other type of manpower program. This results from the saturation principle, and some of the handicapped are attending special schools. In addition, there are a few who were referred by criminal justice agencies. Also, there are about 75 dropouts in the 18- to 19-age group who are working toward a General Edu-

cation Development (GED) certificate at the Berkeley Adult
School or Vista College.

Tutors are offered to students whose reading ability is two
or more years below grade level, while some students who are
doing well in school are working through the project as "peer"
tutors. All those whose grade point averages fall below C are
given additional counseling and tutoring.[3]

The second of the two MDRC reports (1979b, pp. xix-
xxiii) reached certain tentative conclusions that are of interest:

1. The 17 programs made strong efforts to reach out and serve
   the target population but were more successful in reaching
   in-school than out-of-school youth. The particular program
   configuration of entitlement "may not be the most effica-
   cious vehicle for reaching a large percentage of dropouts."
2. It does not appear that large numbers of youths declined to
   apply because of the information and paperwork burden.
3. There was an adequate supply of work experience opportunities and sponsors were able to generate a pool of potential
   work sponsors with minimal trouble.
4. The types of worksites developed were by and large fairly
   typical of work-experience programs, with a heavy emphasis
   on government and nonprofit-related service and clerical jobs.
   Private-sector worksites did not generally deviate from this
   pattern and were primarily service and clerical jobs. More am-
   bitious efforts to match youths with jobs based on skills,
   special interests, and other similar criteria were largely unsuccessful, except at a few of the smaller Tier II programs that
   attempted such matching.
5. Efforts to enforce attendance and work performance standards for youths at worksites proceeded minimally at most
   Tier I programs, although youths with extremely poor work
   attendance or behavior accounted for nearly 10 percent of all
   terminations. Enforcement of work standards was generally
   pursued more diligently at the smaller programs in the Tier II
   sites.

[3]Interview with Barbara Yoder, director, Office of Community and Employment
Programs, City of Berkeley, Calif., March 1979.

6. At the minimum, educational institutions were cooperating with prime sponsors in reporting on participants' attendance and performance, although the process was slow to get underway. Again, the smaller programs had a generally easier time in monitoring these matters.

7. School systems and prime sponsors tended to agree that dropouts were unlikely to find a return to regular school settings worth the benefit of the entitlement job. This was believed to be particularly true for 18- and 19-year-old, out-of-school youths. The slow development of alternative programs, where they did not already exist, imposed some delays on the enrollment of dropouts.

8. The rapid startup, the short duration of the program as originally conceived, and other factors made it difficult to institute changes within the educational system.

9. The average cost to maintain a year-round participant slot was initially projected at $4,600, but costs varied widely within the individual sites, depending on the average number of hours worked per week by participants and program management costs.

Also of interest are the data on terminations of enrollees, although obviously related to experience in the early stages of the program. From March through September 1978, total terminations were 6,648, but 2,583 graduated, leaving just over 4,000, or about 11 percent, who left the program without graduating. Of these, more than one-half were in school, and the most common reason for terminating were "wanted other job" or "time needed for school." Nearly 600, or about 1.5 percent of the enrollees, dropped out of school, while an additional 1,100 were classified as "status unknown."

Two results are of special interest: (1) the greater ease with which the smaller programs were able to accomplish certain objectives, and (2) the reluctance of dropouts to return to high school. This latter result tends to underscore our emphasis on the desirability of other settings, such as community colleges, middle colleges, apprenticeship programs, and so on for youths who have left school.

The results of the experiment, as suggested earlier, will arouse much interest and may have a considerable influence on future legislative developments in the youth manpower field, although replication on a national scale would be extremely expensive. Clearly, some of its features, such as the frequent conferences between students and school staff members, markedly distinguish it from NYC and suggest the prospect of more impressive results.

Other In-School YEDPA Programs

The largest share of the funds in YEDPA—about $440 million in the original allocation—was for Youth Employment and Training Programs, to be conducted by CETA prime sponsors largely for unemployed and underemployed low-income youths aged 16 to 21, in or out of school. The act earmarked 22 percent of the employment and training money for in-school projects to be run jointly by prime sponsors and schools. An early report on experience under the act indicated that, where schools and prime sponsors were working together in communities, there was increased emphasis on serving in-school youths in employment and training programs, paying special attention to the problems of economically disadvantaged youths in school-based, career-oriented programs, and in tying the vocational education curriculum to jobs (U.S. Employment and Training Administration, 1978, pp. A-35 to A-41).

The Portland Program

Very different from the federal programs we have been discussing is the work-experience program of the Portland, Oregon, public high schools.[4] It operates within the framework of a state program that emphasizes career education beginning in the elementary schools and continuing in the secondary schools throughout the state (Marland, 1974, chap. 10). There is a career awareness program in the early grades that encourages

[4]Our discussion of the Portland program is based on Schneider (1978), and a telephone conversation and correspondence with the author of that article, Dr. Edwin Schneider, assistant superintendent, Portland Public Schools, March 29, 1979.

young people to explore the characteristics of the world of work. This is largely accomplished through reading and using other materials in the classroom. In the middle grades students visit workplaces to become familiar with the actual milieu of various careers. In high school, the program begins to emphasize actual work experience.

An important element in the program in Portland was a decision of the board of education to grant academic credit for work experience where feasible. It also formally adopted a policy directing the administration to develop extensive off-campus learning programs to encourage student participation and to design procedures for determining whether and in what situations academic credit should be granted for such participation. The high schools soon found that their staff was too small to accomplish the purposes of the program. As a result, a decision was made to form an organization of business and other community leaders and educators to develop a working relationship designed to "increase the involvement of the students in the community and the community in the schools" (Schneider, 1978, p. 170). This organization, called the Institute for Public Affairs Research, is funded by about $100,000 annually, most of it contributed by local business firms. The organization's first step was to conduct an inventory of enterprises and agencies in which students might become significantly involved in a learning process. The inventory is continually kept up to date through a program in which teachers receive university credit and compensation for a special course in which the major assignment is conducting personal interviews with local firms and agencies in an attempt to identify resources available for the work-experience program.

Another important feature of the program is that students themselves, with the aid of teachers, identify those institutions and organizations in which they would like to have learning experiences and then develop proposals for an off-campus experience. The student next approaches the organization to determine its interest and to seek its suggestions for modifying his or her proposal. A requirement of the program is that there must be a person in the organization who is willing to accept primary responsibility for supervision of the student's work. This "internship supervisor" is the key person involved in making an assessment of the degree to which a student has carried out the contract. Counseling by a member of the high school staff in the department most closely associated with the student's area of special interest is also involved.

Students work on assignments in government agencies, public utilities, volunteer organizations, and other types of agencies. About 2,000 juniors and seniors, or about 20 percent of enrollment in those classes, are involved in the program. A large number hold paid jobs. However, academic credit is granted only for students working on a voluntary basis. Many of these students are in internships in public or nonprofit agencies, where some of the most challenging opportunities are to be found. In addition, transportation costs are provided for needy students. Of special interest, also, is the fact that some of those participating in the program are gifted students.

The Impact of the Career Education Legislation

Work-experience programs are being developed in a number of other communities and on a statewide basis in a number of states. Undoubtedly, the Career Education Demonstration Act of 1974, which provided $10 million annually to support demonstration career education projects, has been influential in accounting for this movement. The much more comprehensive Elementary and Secondary Career Education Act, which was adopted by Congress in 1977, authorized federal expenditures of $325 million over a five-year period to support career education projects. Although it has not been fully funded, $30 million was initially appropriated for fiscal year 1979 and later reduced by $12.5 million through congressional approval of a rescission measure. No funds were recommended for the program in the Carter administration budget for fiscal year 1980, but action by Congress to provide funds appears likely. Among other things, the act provides that 85 percent of the funds are to be allocated to states and to be used by them for grants to finance career education projects sponsored by local education agencies. A local school district may use the funds for career education guidance, counseling, placement, and followup activities. It may also institute work-experience programs for students who want to explore specific careers, provided jobs can be located and the students do not displace other workers.

Wisconsin

One of the most interesting work-experience programs, particularly because it shows how funds to support such a program can be pooled from a number of different sources, is in the state of Wisconsin. Known as the In-School Placement Project, it is a cooperative venture of the Vocational Studies Center of the University of Wisconsin at Madison, the Wisconsin Department of Public Instruction, and the public employment service. The program, which was initiated in 1976, had served 25,000 students in 140 schools by the fall of 1977. Financing is almost entirely from federal funds, combining vocational education, public employment service, and CETA allocations. The program is designed primarily to serve potential dropouts and students who do not expect to go on to college or vocational school after high school graduation. The first phase of the program concentrates on job search preparation and helps students to prepare resumes, fill out job application forms, and do well in a job interview. The second phase aims at teaching students how to be successful on a job and provides opportunities for part-time work experience. The final phase is an effort to place graduating seniors in full-time jobs ("Wisconsin Schools," 1977, p. 9).

Thus far, there have been few evaluations of work-experience programs, but one such study, by the Work in America Institute, concludes that work-experience programs for high school students were most successful when the objectives of student participants, employers, and school administrators coincided. The study also provides evidence that work experience outside the classroom improved the students' ability to function as employees and to make more informed career choices (Work in America Institute, 1978).

Cooperative Education

The advantages of cooperative education, as a particular form of work-experience program, have been well known at the college level for more than half a century, largely because of the pioneering and successful programs at Antioch College, Northeastern University, and the University of Cincinnati. In recent years, supported in part by federal funds from Title IV of the Higher Education Act, the cooperative education movement has spread among postsecondary institutions. Cooperative education differs from other work-experience programs in that students typically alternate between periods in school and on a full-time job, rather than holding a part-time job while in school, and that the job must be related to the student's major field of study. A typical program of the baccalaureate type is purely academic in the freshman year, followed by alternating quarters of work and study. Under many of the programs, an effort is made to obtain jobs for the students that are related to their major field of study, for example, engineering. Dr. Asa Knowles, former president and now chancellor of Northeastern, has pointed out in various publications (for example, Knowles and Associates, 1971) that cooperative education not only provides the student with an opportunity to coordinate his academic progress with learning on the job but also provides him with an important means of financing his college education through earnings.

Cooperative education at the secondary level is less well known, but it does exist, and modest financial support is provided for cooperative work-study vocational education programs under the federal Vocational Education Act. A Massachusetts study (Winer and Hochman, 1976) indicated that nearly 90,000 high school students in the state—mostly in grades 11 and 12—were being served by work-experience programs, and that, of these, about 23,000 were in cooperative education programs. The students in cooperative programs tended to be vocational education students, and the administrative expenses of the program were met largely by federal and state vocational education funds. The majority of students in cooperative education programs were working on a half-day schedule, while most of the others were working on an alternating weeks schedule. These patterns are probably more suitable for secondary school students, most of whom live at home, than the longer periods at work that are typical of cooperative education in colleges.

Interestingly, a cooperative education and work-experience program began operation in Canada in 1977-78 as a joint federal-provincial initiative, with the federal government contributing toward the costs of approved projects. Arrangements are made by institutions and prospective employers under which full-time secondary and postsecondary students divide their time between academic and related employment settings. Federal funding rose from $0.5 million in 1977-78 to $2.0 million in 1979-80. The federal contribution to any one project is limited to 50 percent of the total project cost up to a maximum of $100,000 and for a duration of no more than two years. Wages are paid entirely by the employer. Early in 1979, all but three provinces were reported to be participating.[5]

A Federal-State Work-Study Program

Clearly, the number of provisions of federal legislation that are available to provide financial support for work-experience programs at the high school level is substantial—and we have not yet mentioned all of them. In later sections we shall consider the desirability of consolidating some of these provisions.

Existing programs, however, tend to be targeted on the disadvantaged or to be funded under the Vocational Education Act and thus destined for vocational education students. We believe that there is a strong case for a more broadly based, work-study program for high school students, modeled after the successful College Work-Study program (CWS).

In a report published in 1977, the Congressional Budget Office (CBO) considered a variety of options for combatting youth unemployment and had some interesting things to say about a possible high school work-study program (though not arriving at any policy position, in keeping with the CBO's practice). It discussed a program that would provide students with part-time jobs of not more than 20 hours a week and would offer them an introduction to work in various vocations, en-

[5]We are indebted to Donald G. Pyle of the Canadian Public Service Staff Relations Board and to W. J. H. Poole, director of the Policy and Programs Division, Youth and Employment Branch, Employment and Immigration Canada, for this information.

abling them to get a better idea of what careers they wished to pursue. A program funded at the $1 billion level and serving students only during the school. year would serve about 572,000 students, the report estimated. Full wage costs under this proposal, plus administrative costs, would be paid by the federal government.

> A program such as this could be targeted on high unemployment areas, or it could be made more generally available. It would, of course, not be of much service to those who have already dropped out of school or to those who have graduated from high school but still lack job skills and experience. It might, however, be a powerful mechanism in encouraging youth to stay in school, in eliminating some of the severe structural problems of certain youth, and in easing the transition from school to work for others [Congressional Budget Office, 1977, p. 34].

The program we propose should be developed and funded gradually, since many high schools will lack experience in administering such a program. We believe that the federal role should involve matching grants to the states, on a three to one basis (75 percent of the funds would be federal) and that allocation to individual school districts should be a function of state governments. This departure from the CWS model is suggested because of the traditional responsibility of the states for education; because the large number of high schools in the United States (nearly 24,000) would call for a sizable bureaucracy to administer such a program at the federal level; and because we believe the states should be stimulated to take the leadership in encouraging local school districts to develop a comprehensive work-experience program at the high school level, of which the work-study program would be a part. As under the CWS program, the agency employing the student would be expected to pay 20 percent of the wages, and the program would be confined to employment in public and nonprofit agencies. As we point out in Section 13, we believe that wage subsidies for private, for-profit employers should be used sparingly. Making them available under a work-study program would tend to reduce the number of jobs offered by employers to students without a subsidy.

In order to hold down the cost and also in recognition of the fact that high school students from middle- and upper-income families often have contacts that make it easier for them to find jobs than students from low-income families, we believe that the program should be income-tested initially. Income eligibility standards might later be relaxed if experience seemed to warrant it. Yet we do not believe the family income limits should be as restrictive as under either NYC or the Youth Incentive Entitlement program—we suggest an initial standard of eligibility for students from families with incomes below the median. Allocation from the federal government to the states would be based on high school enrollment and estimates of proportions of parents of high school students with below-median incomes, but funds in the first few years should be targeted to areas with high teenage unemployment rates.

The work-study program would not be designed to replace existing programs, at least in the beginning. As suggested earlier, we offer no judgment on the future of a program modeled on the present Youth Incentive Entitlement program until evaluation is completed. However, because we believe that existing classroom vocational education in high schools should be de-emphasized as work-experience programs are introduced, we contemplate some reallocation of federal vocational education appropriations to stimulate greater emphasis on work-experience programs and placement services (see Section 7).

We view the proposed work-study program as a part of a much broader work-experience program, in which high schools would be much more involved than they currently are in job development and placement activities for their students. The program might be modeled in part on the Portland program.

School placement officers and students, working together, could aim at locating jobs in public and community agencies and in private employment that would be related to the student's career aspirations and/or involve community service.

Other Essential Components
of an Education and Work Program

A successful work-experience program must be associated with related services, in the absence of which it is not likely to be successful. We have in mind (1) community work-education councils, (2) school placement services, (3) more effective counseling services, and (4) far greater emphasis on parent involvement than now seems to be the case in many high schools, especially the big-city schools.

Community Work-Education Councils

In 1975, Willard Wirtz and the National Manpower Institute issued a volume entitled *The Boundless Resource* that is based on several years of intensive investigation of the employment problems of youth, and also, to some extent, of adults. The most influential recommendation that emerges is an idea that is not entirely new but that received major impetus from their work. It is a proposal for the establishment, in at least 25 cities, of community education-work councils "through which school officials, employers, members of labor unions, and members of the public engage collaboratively in developing and administering education-work programs; and that these pilot projects be carefully evaluated over a five-year period and on a comparative basis, to determine their practicability and effectiveness" (Wirtz and the National Manpower Institute, 1975, p. 170). A few passages from the introduction to the book are worth quoting because they express a philosophy about education-work relationships with which we agree:

> A good deal of the American achievement traces in one way or another to the development of Education and Work as coordinate forces. They have, however, been distinctively separate developments controlled by independent institutional sovereignties—with the consequence that in most people's lives learning and earning pass as totally isolated chapters.
>
> This traditional separatism has come under increasing challenge. . . . The vague public awareness of

a decade ago of the human costs in compartmentaliz-
ing education and work is today developing into a
consensus that the two systems be brought together
[p. 1].

There followed a contract between the National Manpower
Institute and the U.S. Department of Labor, under which the
institute was to carry out a program of stimulating the organization of community work-education councils in selected communities. A report issued by the institute in October 1977 traces
the development and accomplishment of councils in 20 communities and the state of California, in which there is a statewide work-education council (National Manpower Institute,
1977). The progress in organizing the councils was impressive,
and officials of the institute express pleasure with the enthusiasm developed for this effort in many of the communities.[6] It
should be noted, in connection with our discussion of the work-
experience program in the Portland, Oregon, high schools, that
Portland is one of the communities involved and that the executive director of the Institute for Public Affairs Research is a
member of the planning committee of the Portland Work-
Education Council. Most of the communities involved do not
appear to be as far along as Portland in developing work-experience programs, although many of them appear to be moving
toward such programs in the future. Much of the emphasis up
to 1977 was in organizing efforts, community inventories, and
formation of initial plans for action programs.

We believe that the formation of community work-education councils is important, not only for the building of bridges
between the schools and the labor market, but also for the development of more effective manpower and education programs
for out-of-school youth and adults within communities.

School Placement Services

Placement services for youth are not very effective in the
United States. Only a small proportion of young people get jobs

---

[6]Interview of Clark Kerr and Margaret Gordon with Willard Wirtz and Jack Gentry,
February 1978, as well as other contacts with staff members of the institute.

through the federal-state public employment service. Most youths, as well as adults, get jobs through tips from "friends and relatives," or through direct application to employers. This appears to be true in western Europe also, but in Great Britain and Sweden school-leavers are far more likely to visit official employment offices than in the United States (Reubens, 1977, p. 56). The basic problem is that the public employment service in the United States has never been viewed with much favor by employers, who tend to use its services relatively little, and to some degree this situation has been made worse by the increased involvement of the public employment service in programs serving the disadvantaged, which has led employers even more to shun the service. To be sure, there are some communities in which the public employment service does an effective job, but the broad picture has always been subject to much criticism by manpower experts.

During the 1970s, there has been a movement for high schools to develop placement services, and it has recently been reported that nearly one-half of all high schools have them, but they tend to be small and not very effective. They are much more likely to be found in large than in small school districts, and in high-income than in low-income districts. In addition to the federal programs that we have already discussed providing funds that may be used for placement services, several of the states have adopted programs to provide support for school-based placement services. A report prepared by the National Manpower Institute (1978, pp. 10-11) discusses the experience under such programs.

We believe that there should be far more effective provision for placement services in high schools, close liaison between community work-education councils, the regular public employment service, and the high school placement office, and continued contact between the placement service and students over a period of several years. The placement service should be involved in developing jobs for students within the framework of the school's work-experience program, providing services for those about to graduate, and also providing services for those who are about to drop out or who have dropped out.

In large metropolitan areas, collaboration among the place-

ment services of high schools would be essential, in order to
avoid excessive competition in establishing contacts with employers. A better solution in some communities might be reliance on the community college system to provide placement
services for high school students as well as for its own students.
As we suggested in Section 4, however, we believe the high
school should be responsible for following the student's progress for at least two years following his or her departure from
the school.

    In Great Britain (Feldstein, 1973; Maclure, 1979; Reubens,
1977), there is a special youth employment service, now called
the Careers Service, that every local education authority is required to operate under national legislation. The service maintains contacts with the schools and conducts guidance interviews with a large proportion of school-leavers. Moreover, it has
statutory responsibility for following the labor market status of
school-leavers for two years following their departure from
school, but according to Reubens (1977), this responsibility is
carried out in a perfunctory manner.

    Reubens considers Japan's labor market agency to be out-
standing in its supervision of the youth labor market and its
cooperative arrangements with the educational system and with
individual schools. In the lower secondary schools, the public
employment service takes the chief responsibility for providing
vocational guidance and placement services to students. However, in 60 percent of the upper secondary schools, the principal, in cooperation with the public employment service, is in
charge, while in one-third of the upper secondary schools, and
in almost all of the junior colleges, technical institutes, and universities, the heads of the schools are in complete charge of the
services, after notification of their programs to the public employment service.

Counseling Services

It has become almost a ritual—and perhaps a futile ritual—to
recommend more adequate counseling services in the high
schools. It was a major recommendation of the first Conant report (1959), which called for one full-time counselor for every

250 to 300 pupils in the high school. In his second report on the comprehensive high school (1967), Conant reported that only 3.4 percent of the 2,000 schools that were surveyed in preparing the report had a ratio of 1 counselor to 249 or fewer students, and that the majority had a ratio of 1 to 400 or more. According to the Carnegie Commission report, *Continuity and Discontinuity* (1973a, pp. 46-47), which was concerned with relationships between high education and the schools, the situation was very unsatisfactory in 1973, with a current ratio nationwide of 1 counselor to 621 students at the senior high school level and 1 to 654 at the junior high school level. Only 14 percent of the high schools met the Conant standard.

There are many reasons for urging more adequate counseling staffs in high schools, but the growth of absenteeism makes the need more critical than it ever has been before. Not that we believe counselors should be turned into truant officers, but surely if counselors were able to see students more regularly (*and* were kept informed about the attendance records of students on their panels *and* succeeded in establishing good relationships with them), they could discuss the reasons for absenteeism with students and make efforts to have discussions with the parents.

Parents and Schools

There is a strong tradition of parental involvement with the schools in the United States. One important channel of parental influence is on local elected boards of education. A second is the National Congress of Parents and Teachers, which is organized at the federal, state, and local levels. Probably more important than either of these formal channels, however, is informal communication between individual parents and teachers or counselors. It seems clear, however, that, in relation to many pupils, this type of informal communication does not exist. The problem of absenteeism could hardly have assumed its current dimensions if there were contact between schools and parents in relation to the chronic truancy of individual students. In fact, informed observers indicate that many of the schools, especially big-city schools, have no policy of systematic communication with parents about the truancy of their children. Truant officers, they maintain, are too involved with security problems in the schools to carry out their traditional function of determining the whereabouts of absent pupils.

Even if the schools had a more effective policy of contacting parents whose children are absent, the difficulties would be great, because the parent may be at work or not available for other reasons. Although sociological studies have not found that children of working mothers are more likely to become delinquent than children of nonworking mothers, there is evidence that working mothers are somewhat less likely to provide adequate supervision for their teenage children, and teenagers who are left uncared for are more likely to become delinquents (Hoffman and Nye, 1974).

Thus, the problems of the schools are associated with broad social changes that have affected family life and family structure. The most severe examples of this are in the big-city ghettoes, where many mothers are on welfare and the father is absent from the home, but the manifestations of the impact of changes in family relationships are found in the suburbs as well in the form of high divorce rates, strained marital relationships, and at least some working mothers who do not make adequate provision for supervision of their children during after-school hours and may not even know that their children are chronic truants.

The United States is by no means alone in facing these problems. Changes in family structure are having their impact on schools throughout the industrialized world. A particularly interesting example is in West Germany, where there has been a long-standing policy of school sessions in the morning only. Education did not traditionally suffer, because children were expected to do homework under the supervision of their mothers in the afternoon. But this policy is no longer working nearly as well, with many mothers at work and with children, especially of foreign workers, on the streets in the afternoon.

Clearly, the schools cannot solve all of these problems, but many of the policies we are suggesting would help—more intimate schools, smaller classes so that teachers could maintain more continuous contact with their students (discussed further in later sections), and, above all, much larger numbers of counselors who would be able to meet their students more often and establish better contact with parents.

The Roadblocks

A serious obstacle to the development of the kinds of work-experience programs emphasized in this section is the difficulty of overcoming the aversion of employers to hiring young people. This is an important reason for recommending work-education councils. Closer links between higher schools and community colleges in providing opportunities for both work-experience and occupational training programs, to be recommended in the next section, would also help, because community colleges are often in a better position to gain employer cooperation. National leadership by employer organizations, as we suggest in Section 13, can also stimulate local employer groups to become more concerned with the problems of youth in their communities. The cooperation of unions is also vital, and here the teachers unions could play an important role if they could be persuaded to give vigorous support to the effort.

The third main problem is financial. The chief costs of more extensive work-experience programs in secondary schools will be for the more effective counseling and placement services that are required to make such programs work. Yet we have noted that in Wisconsin a way has been found to pool funds from three public sources to finance these costs. We shall consider financing issues in more detail in later sections.

Recommendation 4: *School districts should develop plans to provide voluntary opportunities for combinations of work experience, community service, and education for all of their students, especially in the last two years of high school.*

Recommendation 5: *To meet the needs of students from lower-income and lower-middle-income families, who may have difficulty finding employment through normal labor market channels, a federal-state work-study program for secondary school* *students aged 16 to 19 should be established, modeled on the College Work-Study program. We recommend an initial federal appropriation of $300 million.*[7]

Recommendation 6: *To carry out a broad-gauged work-experience program and to help meet employment needs of school dropouts and graduates, every school district should take the initiative in stimulating the development of a community work-education council if none exists. In addition, much more adequate placement and counseling services are a need that should be given high priority in all school districts.*

Year-Round Operation of Schools

In many ways, a work-experience program could be more effectively developed in a school that operated year-round. Student vacation periods would be staggered, and thus there would not be a flood of students seeking work in the summer.

Year-round operation is now a growing movement in school systems around the country, having become noticeably more popular since the 45-15 plan was developed in Valley View, Illinois, in 1968. Under this plan students alternate between 45 days in school and 15 days on vacation. A concept that is considered better adapted to secondary school is that of six terms of 45 days each, under which three equal groups of students attend four of the six terms on a staggered basis. This plan can save one-third of costs for buildings and facilities, since only two-thirds of the students are present at any one time, but it does not necessarily save on operating costs. Under such a plan all students can have two seasonal vacations, one in summer and the other in colder weather, but the student might work during at least one of these vacations.

Year-round school schedules are more prevalent in Califor-

---

[7]We favor gradual increases in this appropriation in subsequent years, but the ultimate cost of an adequate program is difficult to estimate, except on the basis of experience. Much would depend on the success of school districts in developing unsubsidized jobs for their students in private employment. Moreover, in Section 13, we recommend an expansion of apprenticeship programs for high school students, which would reduce the need for work-study jobs.

nia than elsewhere, because the state actively promotes year-round operation. Such schedules have been especially popular in rapidly growing suburbs, where the saving on the cost of additional buildings can be large, but they are also found in urban and rural districts.

One of the advantages of year-round operation is less loss of progress in learning than occurs with a lengthy summer vacation. However, it is not always easy to convince parents and students that year-round operation is advantageous. Yet positive attitudes appear to predominate in communities with year-round programs, such as Hayward, California. An interesting result of the Hayward plan is that, although learning progress does not appear to be positively affected in the early grades, the longer a child attends a year-round program, the more improvement occurs in learning compared with that in traditional programs (see Shepard and others, 1975; Rice and others, 1975).

One result of more widespread adoption of year-round schedules could well be the release of a portion of federal funds spent on the costly summer employment programs for disadvantaged youth for more effective use in promoting work-experience programs on a year-round basis. In 1979, U.S. Department of Labor plans called for spending $1.2 billion on summer youth programs that would provide 1.7 million jobs, including $740 million for SPEDY and the remainder for seven smaller programs, such as the Youth Conservation Corps ("Feds Plan 1.7 Million Jobs," 1979). Economies could also be achieved in the costs of restructuring school systems advocated in Section 8 if schools were to operate on a year-round basis.

Recommendation 7: *School systems should seriously consider shifting to year-round operation where they are not now on such a schedule.*

Other Extracurricular Activities

Some communities are almost certain to have greater difficulties than others in developing effective work-experience programs. Where there is a particularly heavy concentration of minority group youth, as in New York City's Harlem, the difficulties are likely to be especially great. Job development may also be difficult for most communities in a recession and all but impossible in a modest-sized community in which the one large factory in town has just closed down.

In such situations particularly, but to some degree in all secondary schools, other nonacademic-activity programs can be extremely important in accounting for favorable attitudes toward school and in keeping adolescents off the streets and out of trouble. Sports programs do play this role for many young people, but there is evidence that other types of nonacademic-activity programs are less emphasized than they used to be, especially in large cities, and apparently at least to some degree as a result of union policies restricting teachers' hours of work.

A recent study of activity programs in southern schools conducted at the Rand Corporation and based on a survey carried out by the National Opinion Research Center in 1973 yielded some very interesting findings. Among other things, nonacademic-activity programs were more prevalent in smaller school systems than in large-city systems, and, where they were emphasized, had positive effects on the students' academic performance and on attitudes toward school. The Rand study also analyzed data from the National Longitudinal Survey of 1972 high school seniors, which indicated positive effects of participation in extracurricular activities on school performance and also showed that participation by students was more a function of opportunity than of individual desire—in other words, the strongest predictor of the student's individual level of participation was the participation level of the other students in the same school who were also surveyed (Crain, Mahard, and Narot, forthcoming).

We also believe that extracurricular programs should emphasize participation in community activities as much as possible, along the lines of Sizer's suggestions discussed in the previous section.

Recommendation 8: *Emphasis on nonacademic activities is essential in all secondary schools, especially in situations in which work-experience programs encounter difficulties.*

7

Vocational Education: Change Everything, Including the Name

The antithesis between a technical and liberal education is fallacious. There can be no adequate technical education which is not liberal, and no liberal education which is not technical: that is, no education which does not impart both technique and intellectual vision. In simpler language, education should turn out the pupil with something he knows well and something he can do well. This intimate union of practice and theory aids both. The intellect does not work best in a vacuum [Whitehead, 1929, p. 49].

Federal, state, and local expenditures on vocational education amounted to more than $5 billion in 1975-76 and are probably higher today. Of this total, roughly 10 percent came from federal funds and the other 90 percent from state and local funds. If we measure growth from enactment of the Vocational Education Act of 1963—the most important piece of federal legislation in this area since the original Smith-Hughes Act of 1917—federal allocations rose from about $50 million in 1962-63 to $543 million in 1975-76, or more than tenfold, while state and local allocations increased from about $232 million to $4,607 million, or nearly twentyfold (U.S. National Center for Education Statistics, 1978a, p. 145). More recent figures on state and local expenditures are not available, but federal expenditures for vocational education reached approximately $800 million in 1978-79. The increases were, of course, much smaller after adjusting for inflation. In terms of constant dollars the federal appropriation for vocational education rose from $50 million in 1962-63 to about $350 million in 1978-79.

The growth in enrollment in federally aided vocational education classes has also been spectacular—from slightly more than 4 million in 1962-63 to nearly 15 million in 1975-76. By far the largest enrollment (nearly 9 million) was at the secondary level in 1975-76, while slightly more than 2 million was at the postsecondary level, and the remaining enrollments were accounted for by adults (U.S. National Center for Education Statistics, 1978a, p. 144).

Yet there are substantial doubts that vocational education is generally effective, especially at the secondary level. The uneasiness of Congress about the situation is indicated by the fact that, in enacting the Education Amendments of 1976, Congress mandated a four-year study by the U.S. National Institute of Education (1977a), with funding of $1 million a year, to evaluate vocational education. The study is scheduled to be completed in September 1981.

The Council has had a study of vocational education under way for several years, and part of what we have to say about the subject is based on the results of that study (Grasso and Shea, 1979).

Before commenting on the outcomes of vocational education, however, we need to recognize that the term *vocational education,* as used in the United States, encompasses a wide variety of programs under numerous auspices, not all of which benefit from federal and state vocational education funds. Occupational and skill-training programs are found in high schools; collegiate institutions (especially community colleges); noncollegiate postsecondary institutions, including area vocational schools, technical institutes, and proprietary schools;

manpower programs under the U.S. Department of Labor; private firms, including on-the-job training and apprenticeship programs; the armed forces; and various organizations.

Generalizations about the outcomes of this enormous array of programs would be inappropriate, and most evaluative studies are limited to particular types of training, such as high school vocational education, postsecondary vocational education, or manpower programs. We are concerned primarily with vocational education that is financed by federal and state vocational education funds, especially at the high school level. Even within this narrower framework, there are some training programs that are excellent and some that accomplish little or nothing. However, the following generalizations seem to be supported by various studies:

- Among male youth with identical years of schooling (for example, 12), those who have had school-based occupational training are, on the average, no better off and no worse off in terms of unemployment experience, rate of pay, or job satisfaction than those who have pursued general or academic studies. Vocational education for girls and young women probably does reduce slightly their subsequent unemployment and increases their earnings. Among boys, vocational education in school makes little or no difference for subsequent unemployment. (This difference may be explained by the fact that girls train mostly for office work, whereas boys train for blue-collar occupations, in which employment is less stable.)
- Some studies have indicated that graduates of high school vocational programs earn more initially than other high school graduates but that this advantage tends to diminish as the years go on. It is attributed by some analysts to better placement services for vocational students.
- Vocational and office subjects are frequently cited when young people are asked to name the subject they enjoyed the most in high school. Very few name such a course when asked what subject they "disliked the most."

- At both the secondary and postsecondary level, cooperative education programs, though small in terms of total numbers served, typically work well for both students and employers.
- Many experts believe that occupational education at the postsecondary level is likely to be of higher quality than at the secondary level (for example, McGurn and Davis, 1976). Even at the postsecondary level, however, there is a need for closer relationships between community colleges, for example, and employers in the industry concerned, as we note in Section 13 in our discussion of the desirability of apprenticeships in the electronics industry. In recent years, there has been a significant trend toward the development of cooperative education in community colleges, in which students receive part of their training in industry settings.
- There are indications that, among large-city schools, some of those that specialize in technical education have records that are superior to those of the general run of inner-city high schools. This may well reflect the fact that students who attend technical schools have made a deliberate choice to attend, have formed career objectives, and are likely to be highly motivated. Teachers in such schools, also, are frequently especially motivated. However, a New York City study (Taussig, 1968) found that, in general, rates of unemployment of vocational graduates from the city's high schools tended to be extremely high and did not seem to be better than those of graduates of other curricula over the long run.
- Several studies suggest that high school vocational education followed by apprenticeship is more effective than either experience by itself as a channel to skilled jobs in the metal and construction trades.
- There would be a strong case for increasing emphasis on vocational education in high schools if it increased the holding power of the schools, but, on the whole, the evidence seems to indicate that, at least among males, dropout rates are higher for vocational students than for students in other programs, even when students are controlled for ability and socioeconomic status (Reubens, 1974, p. 314).
- Unfortunately, studies of the outcomes of vocational educa-

tion have rarely, if ever, been designed to permit special analyses of their impact on disadvantaged students. Yet the evidence on the incidence of violence and absenteeism in big-city schools leads one to suspect that vocational education can hardly be more effective than other types of programs in schools with large concentrations of disadvantaged students.

• One of the major obstacles to evaluation of vocational programs is that the statistics are notoriously deficient. Those we have cited previously on enrollments are actually counts of course enrollments and involve much double-counting of individuals. Moreover, the data make no distinction between students who are in a vocational "track" and those who simply take a course or two in home economics or manual arts. Estimates based on the National Longitudinal Survey of 1972 High School Seniors indicate that there are about 2.5 million participants in occupational programs in high schools, in contrast with the 9 million previously cited from the course enrollment data.

• Despite recognition—especially in connection with enactment of the Vocational Education Act of 1963—that a disproportionate percentage of total enrollments were in agriculture and home economics, the number of enrollments in such programs has, on the whole, continued to grow.

• The battle among various interests for a share of the total pie of vocational education funds is serious in many states. In a number of states, the dominant force is the State Board of Education, in which the interests of elementary and secondary education are predominant and tend to control the allocation of vocational education funds. Community colleges are more likely to be represented on boards of higher or postsecondary education and often have difficulty in struggling for their share of vocational education funds. In some of the states, moreover, there are conflicts over what share of postsecondary vocational education funds should go to community colleges and what share to postsecondary area vocational schools.

• It is very difficult for high schools to keep their equipment in many vocational courses up to date. This consideration reinforces many others that suggest shifting vocational education out of the classroom as much as possible. In industries with rapidly advancing technology, the costs of maintaining up-to-date equipment in classrooms are prohibitive. In appraising the federal role in education since the "great society" programs got under way in the mid-1960s, Tyler (1974, pp. 181, 182-83) made a number of significant comments about vocational education:

> Vocational education needs to furnish a closer connection between work and education, preferably cooperative education, in which students get actual experience on the job. . . . Yet, only a small fraction, less than two percent, of high school students are in cooperative education or some other form of work-study program. . . .
>
> The goal of the Vocational Education Act of 1963 is still important, but greater and better-directed efforts are essential to attain it. Among the steps likely to improve vocational education are (1) an effort to help children gain a clearer understanding of the highly interdependent world of work in a modern industrialized society—what the functions of important clusters of jobs are, how they contribute to the nation's needs, what their conditions of work are, what abilities they require, what satisfactions they provide, how one prepares for them; (2) the provision of school-supervised work experience for most, if not all, high school students; (3) continuing development, with the aid of advisory committees, of realistic programs of occupational preparation in which the school supplements but does not supplant the training responsibilities of employers.

New Directions

The chief problem with the effort to maintain funding for vocational education, at both the federal and state levels, is that too much of the money goes to preserve the status quo. We believe that the time has come for fundamental changes in the status of vocational education, especially at the high school level, and that these changes can be brought about without a massive new influx of funds. What is required is more effective pooling of funds from a variety of sources, plus a more determined effort to develop alternatives to classroom vocational education. Examples of achievements in several states and areas show that it can be done.

More specifically, we believe that the following changes are needed:

1. Tracking of students in academic, general, and vocational programs at the high school level should cease. All students should be encouraged to participate in combinations of education, work experience, training, and service, though with varying emphases and with a more determined effort on the part of the school to develop an individualized program for each student, as Conant recommended in his first report (1959). Clearly these goals can be more effectively accomplished if there are also changes in school structure along the lines discussed in Section 8.

2. Classroom vocational education at the high school level should be deemphasized in favor of training conducted under employer auspices, apprenticeship, work-experience programs, cooperative education, and other programs that take the student into the community. Interestingly, a recent survey of school officials revealed that one-third of the respondents would shift vocational education entirely to private industry. One of the respondents commented that "voc ed usually has to be relearned on the job, anyway" ("Many School Officials," 1978, p. 4). We have seen in Section 6 how the In-School Placement Project in Wisconsin pools funds from vocational education allocations, the public employment service, and CETA. Other examples of the kinds of innovations that should be encouraged are the following:

    • *The Regional Occupational Program Center in Los Angeles,* under which the Los Angeles Unified School District uses local and state funds to finance a training program that is conducted in facilities of companies (for example, Rockwell International) and in which the teaching is done by full-time company employees who are paid extra to teach, under the supervision of regular teachers employed by the school district. Classes are conducted after school hours and on Saturdays. Students go to the sites for 4 to 15 hours a week, depending on the time needed to learn the particular skill. It was reported in 1975 that 4,000 students were participating in about 223 different classes (Ferrin and Arbeiter, 1975).

· *The schools-as-entrepreneurs program in Hartford, Connecticut,* which was developed because the school system was having difficulty placing students in part-time jobs. Under the program, the schools become entrepreneurs, setting up student-operated businesses. To some extent, the program takes advantage of a "sheltered" market consisting of the school system, students and employees, and the city government. Among the enterprises are an auto repair venture, production and installation of interior storm windows, an advertising agency and printing-copying center, and numerous others ("Hartford, Connecticut," 1978, pp. 6-7).

· *Executive High School Internships of America,* a national program that is designed to cooperate with local school districts in providing opportunities for students to gain work experience at managerial and administrative levels. Eligibility of students does not depend on ability or grade points but rather on stability, independence, and strong interest in a particular assignment. Examples of assignments are assistant on a local newspaper, assistant to a governor or a mayor, and the like. The national office, located in New York City, trains district coordinators. Funds for the national office are provided by various foundations, while local districts are required to provide the salary of at least one full-time coordinator for every 50 to 60 interns and to share in the cost of technical assistance from the national office (Ferrin and Arbeiter, 1975, pp. 52-53).

· *The Experience-Based Career Education program,* conducted by the National Institute of Education, in cooperation with four educational laboratories and communities. The program emphasizes career exploration, with site and job rotation, rather than a single work experience, and the development of general rather than job-specific skills. Demonstration projects were originally conducted in Charleston, West Virginia; Oakland, California; Tigard, Oregon; and Philadelphia. Gradually the program has been extended to other communities. Cooperating in providing assignments for the students are large numbers of community agencies, business firms, colleges, and labor unions. Students are unpaid, and, probably for this reason, the program has appealed chiefly to students from middle- and upper-income families (U.S. National Institute of Education, 1976).

• *City-as-School, Brooklyn, New York,* a program that began with Ford Foundation funds and later was continued with funds from the New York City Board of Education. It is a high school without walls that was planned by students and teachers. Students alternate between work experience and attendance at their home school, usually on a nine-week rotating schedule, with the tenth week of each cycle devoted to guidance and counseling, testing, and preparation for the next cycle (Ferrin and Arbeiter, 1975, pp. 60-61).

3. High school students should have opportunities to enroll in occupational courses at nearby community college and technical institutes, as is happening in some states and areas. As suggested above, the problem of maintaining superior equipment and teachers who are familiar with advancing technology is too costly to be feasible in the typical school district. It appears to be more manageable for community colleges and technical institutes, although much depends on state funding formulas and state-local relationships in the financing of these postsecondary institutions. Moreover, as we note in Section 13, community college programs may have difficulty in keeping abreast of technical developments and frequently can perform more effectively by developing cooperative education programs and apprenticeship programs. In any case,

providing for the participation of high school students in occupational programs of postsecondary institutions can eliminate costly duplicative efforts to maintain adequate equipment and up-to-date teachers in *both* secondary and postsecondary institutions. Moreover, the opportunity to participate in a college-level program in a new and more challenging environment may be just what is needed in many cases to combat the boredom and indifference of high school students.

It probably would not be necessary to amend the federal Vocational Education Act to increase the minimum allocation of 15 percent of a state's federal funds to programs serving postsecondary students. This provision has been a focus of controversy between representatives of secondary and of postsecondary institutions, but in practice the percentage going to postsecondary institutions is often higher. In Wisconsin, 60 percent of vocational education funds go to postsecondary institutions. Moreover, school districts can enter into contractual arrangements with community colleges under which the school district reimburses the community college for the costs of occupational programs for its students.

Some of the more successful examples of links between community colleges or postsecondary technical institutes and high schools were described in a report on articulation prepared by the American Assocation of Community and Junior Colleges and the American Vocational Association (Bushnell, 1978).

Particularly outstanding is the example of the Milwaukee Area Technical College (MATC), with an enrollment of 19,000 and covering an area that includes 21 high school districts. Since 1970 MATC has been providing contract services of various types to these high school districts. High school students may enroll in specialized occupational classes at MATC that sometimes include exploratory work experiences, and in which 945 high school students were enrolled in 1976. There is also an "early leaver" program that enables students who have completed the eleventh grade and have satisfied graduation requirements to enroll in diploma or associate degree training programs at MATC and still graduate with their high school classes. Vocational programs in the high schools are also coordinated with vocational-technical programs at the college, so that high school graduates can bypass introductory courses at the college.

MATC is also one of the postsecondary institutions that is involved in apprenticeship training, as well as CETA training (Bushnell, 1978, pp. 16-19).

4. Wherever feasible, states and localities should pool funds available from CETA, the public employment service, vocational education allocations, and the new high school work-study program that we have proposed to provide more effective combinations of education, training, and work-experience programs to students. The example of Wisconsin shows that it can be done, as do examples in certain communities.

At the federal level, there will always be battles over relative allocations to the U.S. Department of Labor for manpower programs and to the U.S. Department of Health, Education, and Welfare for vocational education appropriations and other allocations, such as the career education program. These battles will be waged by lobbies supporting the various programs and by the two federal departments themselves, and it is probably futile to propose any sweeping measure to combine programs or shift any of them from one department to another.

The probability of success is greater if state and local agencies take advantage of opportunities to combine funds from several sources to achieve more effective programs. One of the most important reasons for urging the development of work-education community councils is to provide a forum in which the advantages of such moves are likely to be perceived.

Yet the federal government can, and should, provide more effective leadership than it has in the past, particularly toward innovations in vocational education. Vocational education funds could become a more effective vehicle for promoting change with only minor changes in the legislation. As the Vocational Education Act now stands, there are provisions for work-study programs, cooperative education programs, placement services, and counseling and guidance services, as well as the more usual vocational education classes—it is a question largely of shifts in the allocation of funds to make the program a more effective vehicle for promoting change.

In the preparation of the Carter administration's 1979-80 budget, Joseph A. Califano, former Secretary of Health, Education, and Welfare, advocated a cut of almost $200 million in the federal allocation for vocational education and wrote to members of the relevant congressional appropriations committees that vocational education was one of HEW's "least effective" programs. Later, in response to protests from vocational educators, Califano disclaimed any intention of criticizing vocational education programs, but said that "HEW funding has little influence or impact on many state programs" because state funding now overshadows federal funding and "80 percent of the funds HEW provides are used primarily as operating subsidies for existing programs" rather than to promote change ("Califano Refuses to Back Away," 1978, p. 4). In response to a flood of letters from vocational educators, however, the administration backed down, despite the vigor of its attempts to restrain the overall budgetary deficit, and restored the allowance for basic state grants to its fiscal year 1979 level ("Yielding to Pressure," 1979, p. 1).

We believe that federal vocational education funds can become a more effective stimulator of change but only through amendments to the legislation, reallocation of funding under the various provisions of the act, and more vigorous and imaginative leadership within the Office of Education in administering the legislation. We urge amending the Vocational Education Act to provide strong incentives for states to promote change. As matters stand, federal matching of funds is, in general, on a 50-50 basis, but the legislation provides for 100 percent matching for cooperative vocational education programs, curriculum development projects, and special programs for the disadvantaged. We believe—on the grounds that it is usually better to use a "carrot" than a "stick" and that there is increasing resentment against too much federal regulation—that federal "over-matching" should be used more vigorously to promote change.

More specifically, we propose:

1. That the legislation be amended to provide for 75 percent (3 to 1) federal matching for (1) state programs aimed at encouraging the development of work-experience and cooperative education programs; (2) contracts for employer-oriented training, including apprenticeships, programs modeled on the lines of the Regional Occupational Programs Center in Los Angeles, and subsidized on-the-job training; and (3) contracts with nearby postsecondary institutions (especially community colleges, technical institutes, and area vocational schools that have postsecondary programs) to provide opportunities for occupational training for high school students. A state program under this provision should call for competitive proposals from local school districts. We note in Section 8 that innovations in school systems tend to be successful if they are planned and initiated by the school personnel who will be involved at the local level.

2. Approximately one-half of the funds currently allocated by the federal government for basic grants for vocational education and for program improvement and supportive services (Table 2) should be made subject to this new federal matching formula, and the proportion should be increased as time goes on. Thus nearly $300 million would be initially provided.[1]

   We do not mean to suggest that every local school district should be required to develop all of these approaches, although all should be expected to develop opportunities for work experience and will be helped in this effort by the availability of work-study funds. By no means do all local communities have large firms using sophisticated technologies like those in the Los Angeles area. Some smaller communities may not have access to appropriate postsecondary institutions, and rural communities are handicapped in developing any of these approaches, including traditional educational education.

---

[1]Although Congress had not completed action on the fiscal 1980 budget when this report went to the printer, there had been action in both houses to increase the allocation for basic vocational education grants by $100 million.

Table 2. Federal allocations for vocational education, by program,
fiscal years 1978 to 1980 (in thousands of dollars)

Program by activities	FY 1978 (actual expenditures)	FY 1979 (estimated expenditures)	FY 1980 (administration budget)
1. Vocational education			
a) State grants and innovative programs			
1) Basic grants	$ 653,154	$571,246	$474,766
2) Program improvement and supportive services	164,497	136,434	112,317
3) Programs of national significance	24,382	42,154	10,000
b) Special programs for the disadvantaged	30,956	24,271	20,000
c) Consumer and homemaking education	63,478	52,241	43,497
d) State advisory councils	4,175	7,031	6,073
e) Bilingual vocational education	2,740	5,600	2,800
f) State planning	—	5,000	5,000
Subtotal, vocational education	943,382	843,977	674,453
2. Adult education	94,564	101,507	90,750
Total obligations	1,037,946	945,484	765,203
Outlays adjusted for obligated balances	692,967	808,014	840,000

Source: The Budget (1979, p. 448). A "permanent appropriation" item of $7,161 thousand
has been omitted.

Nor do we suggest that all classroom vocational education be terminated. In some fields, such as typing and other types of office work, classroom instruction can be quite effective and the cost of maintaining reasonably up-to-date equipment is not very high. We believe, however, that more emphasis on employer-oriented training is particularly needed where equipment is expensive, and where students are bored with classroom programs and truancy is a problem.

3. That all terminology in the legislation that has the effect of confining programs to "vocational" students be deleted, in keeping with the principle of eliminating "tracking."
4. That the concept of "special programs for the disadvantaged" be eliminated except where they are specifically aimed at overcoming language handicaps. We do not believe that economically disadvantaged students should be segregated in special vocational education classes.
5. That no change be made in the minimum percentage of the federal allocation for postsecondary programs (15 percent). We believe that a major need is to encourage school districts to enter into contracts to provide opportunities for high school students to be enrolled in occupational programs in postsecondary institutions and that the funding for this purpose should come from the school districts.

These changes will not, of course, be painless. Deemphasizing classroom vocational education may well mean layoffs of vocational teachers, but, wherever possible, they should be reassigned to provide placement and counseling services. There are provisions in the existing vocational education legislation for training and development services for vocational education personnel which could be used for retraining, where necessary.

Another problem is that, with state appropriations so much larger than federal appropriations, sweetening the federal matching formula may not be as effective as it would be in a situation in which federal and state funds were more nearly equal. Even so, by shifting the use of some of its funds, the state will benefit by receiving more federal funds than it otherwise would.

In addition, if the concept of tracking of students is to be abolished, the name of the vocational education legislation should be changed, even though this proposal may stir up howls of protest from vocational educators. We suggest that the reallocated funds now in the vocational education budget be merged with the appropriation we have suggested for the work-study program in Section 6 and that the new legislation be called the Occupational Skills and Work-Study Act. Clearly the work-study program should be closely integrated with the overall work-experience and cooperative education program and with expanded placement and guidance services.

The Schools and CETA

We earlier called attention to the importance of pooling funds stemming from the U.S. Department of Labor through CETA and funds stemming from the U.S. Department of Health, Education, and Welfare through vocational education and other federal education programs at the state and local levels. As matters stand, although progress is being made in some states and communities in this direction, too often vocational education programs in the schools and manpower training programs at skills centers or other types of training facilities in the community are conducted entirely separately and without any recognition of the fact that a more effective program might be developed through pooling of funds and merging of training projects. Many of the community colleges are now involved in CETA training, usually through special skills centers maintained under the auspices of the colleges, but often these centers have no relationships with the schools and offer no opportunities for high school students to participate.

There are, of course, a number of obstacles to successful pooling of funds and efforts. The definition of "disadvantaged" is stricter under CETA programs for youth than under the Vocational Education Act; training allowances are available for young people in CETA training programs but not usually for students enrolled in high school vocational education programs, and eligibility conditions differ among the various CETA programs for youth. The Department of Labor has recently selected ten prime sponsors in various areas to conduct two-year demonstration projects testing the feasibility of consolidating CETA and other youth programs ("DOL to Test Feasibility," 1979). This is an encouraging move. Moreover, chancellors of big-city community college districts do not find the fact that students in CETA-financed skills centers receive training allowances a special problem, because other students in postsecondary programs can get student aid and, in any case, are usually in a separate program and a separate building from the skills center.[2] The chancellors tend to welcome involvement in CETA programs, because on the whole, the community colleges are reimbursed for the costs of the programs, but they are inclined to bemoan the fact that they are sometimes squeezed in meeting costs, especially if adequate adjustments are not made for inflation. They also are not inclined to complain about restrictions on the duration of training and in some cases have increased their success in placing graduates of skills programs substantially by developing their own placement services.

Recently, there have been indications that the American Vocational Association has become supportive of cooperation between vocational education and CETA programs. The new executive director of the association, Gene Bottoms, testifying before the House Employment Opportunities Subcommittee, called, among other things, for legislative changes requiring that 30 to 50 percent of the money appropriated for vocational education and CETA be spent through jointly developed plans ("Voc Ed Group Calls," 1979).

Recommendation 9: *The federal Vocational Education Act should be renamed the Occupational Skills and Work-Study Act, and its provisions should be merged with those for the work-study program that we have recommended.*

The legislation should be amended to provide approximately $300 million of existing federal vocational education funds for 75 percent matching grants to the states to stimulate the development of programs that move skills training out of the high school classroom and into the workplace or community college.

Recommendation 10: *The U.S. Department of Labor and the U.S. Department of Health, Education, and Welfare should cooperate in developing policies for encouraging coordination*

---

[2]We are indebted to Dr. Edmund G. Gleazer, Jr., president of the American Association of Community and Junior Colleges, for inviting Margaret Gordon of our staff to participate in one of the periodic meetings of chancellors of large-city community college districts, at which this type of issue was discussed, in June 1978.

of manpower and education programs for youth at the state and local levels and in seeking removal of legislative and administrative obstacles, such as differing eligibility conditions, to such coordination.

8

A Fundamental Restructuring of Schools

The Need for Diversity

Among the reforms discussed in Section 5, the most far-reaching and controversial changes concern school structure. Boyer's proposals, especially for transitional schools with varying emphases, are exciting, because of the critical need to overcome the problems of the big-city school, and yet they could increase tracking and segregation if students from middle- and upper-income families failed to opt for the more specialized schools and came to be concentrated in schools with a college preparatory emphasis.

This type of problem could be particularly serious in moderate-sized cities, where a single high school is integrated because it serves all students in the community. Any proposal to create more specialized schools at the high school level in such communities could be extremely controversial and would probably be attacked as a move toward racial tracking. Yet there have been "schools within schools" or so-called "alternative schools" in such communities that create the environment of a smaller and more intimate school.

In fact, the movement for alternative schools has gained momentum in the 1970s, and results of evaluations, indicating predominantly positive impacts on students, are beginning to be available. There were more than 250 alternative public schools in over 40 states by 1974, and by 1977 more than 28 percent of the school districts included in a nationwide survey had alternative schools in operation (Smith, 1974, p. 14; Barr, Colston, and Parrett, 1977, p. 1).

An alternative public school has been defined as "any school that provides alternative learning experiences to those provided by conventional schools within its community and that is available by choice to every family within its community at no extra cost" (Smith, 1974, pp. 14-15). Among the types of alternative schools are:

- *Open schools,* in which learning activities are individualized and organized around interest centers within the classroom or building.
- *Schools without walls,* in which learning activities are carried on throughout the community—in art museums, courthouses, social service agencies, and so on. The first and probably best known school of this type is the Parkway Program in Philadelphia.
- *Learning centers,* which seek to develop distinctive programs, often with a specialized orientation, and which are available to all students in the community. These include magnet schools, educational parks, career-education centers, and technical high schools.
- *Continuation schools,* which provide learning opportunities for students whose education in the conventional school has been (or might be) interrupted. These include dropout centers, reentry programs, pregnancy-maternity centers, and street academies.
- *Multicultural schools,* which emphasize cultural pluralism and usually serve a multicultural student body. Bilingual schools with optional enrollment are included in this group.
- *Free schools,* which emphasize greater freedom for students and teachers than do conventional schools. Most free schools are private, but a few are available by choice within public systems.

- *Schools within schools,* in which a small number of students and teachers are involved by choice in a learning program that differs from that of the conventional school. This group includes minischools and satellite schools. There is overlapping between these schools and the preceding categories, because many of the schools within schools have the distinctive characteristics of one of these categories.
- *Community-controlled schools,* where a group of parents organizes and has power over teacher selection, evaluation of teachers, curriculum, and finances.[1]

A number of the more successful examples of alternative schools in large cities, especially magnet schools, have succeeded in attracting students of varied racial and ethnic backgrounds from all parts of the city. Thus, in some cases at least, they appear to have slowed the out-migration of white families that has left so many inner-city schools racially segregated. There are also schools, both public and private, that have outstanding records because of unique leadership, even though they are in slum locations. And there have been a few successful alternative school programs specifically designed to serve hard-core disadvantaged urban youth—notably the Career Intern program in Philadelphia—which suggest that the appropriate combination of work orientation and intensified learning experience can overcome the drift of such students away from the schools and into patterns of juvenile delinquency (see Section 14).

Admittedly, smaller and more specialized schools may have higher operating costs than larger schools, although they may well escape the heavy security costs facing big-city schools today. To the extent that they reduce social costs associated with juvenile delinquency, they may be well worth the investment. These financing issues are discussed more fully in Section 11.

There is another issue associated with the financing of schools that cannot be evaded, and that is the evidence in the

---

[1]This classification of alternative schools draws on Smith (1974) and *Matters of Choice* (1974).

report of Coleman and others (1966) and a more recent study by Jencks and Brown (1975) to the effect that differences in expenditures per student among school districts make little difference in student performance, once account has been taken of socioeconomic differences in the family backgrounds of the students. These findings have been used very effectively ever since 1966 to combat increased expenditures per pupil on the grounds that it will make little difference in school performance.

A vast literature has grown up around the 1966 Coleman Report (as it came to be called), some of it very critical of the original findings. Among the critics, Bowles and Levin (1968, pp. 8-9) pointed out that the measures of instructional expenditures per pupil used in the Coleman Report related to school districts rather than to individual schools, and yet there is evidence that "the variation in expenditures among schools within a district is likely to follow a systematic pattern" in which schools attended by disadvantaged children are characterized by relatively low expenditures. Perhaps even more crucial was the criticism by Bowles (1968) that the influence of school resources on performance was determined *after* controlling for the influence of social background characteristics, and yet variations in school resources per pupil were highly correlated with variations in socioeconomic characteristics of pupils. The effect of this was greatly to weaken the independent influence of differences in school resources, which, as we noted in the previous section, Conant (1961) had emphasized in his study of inner-city and suburban high schools.

Some of the critics tended to ignore qualifications that Coleman himself made in interpreting his findings. He found, for example, that school factors were more important in affecting the achievement of minority group students than of majority students and that teacher quality was a major determinant of scholastic achievement among black students.

Finally, if changes in school structure are to be effective, they must be accompanied by other changes that we have discussed. The introduction of combinations of work experience and education can be combined with changes in school structure and indeed appears to be an integral aspect of Boyer's proposal for transitional schools. Increased emphasis on more effective contact between schools, parents, and students as an essential aspect of a program to reduce absenteeism must also be an integral part of any move toward structural reform. Innovations in teacher training, to be discussed in Section 10, are just as clearly inseparable from other aspects of school reform.

Moreover, the most effective education and manpower policies, with which this report is concerned, cannot by themselves overcome the impact on children and youths of the influence of slum environments, whether they are urban or rural slums. Welfare reform, housing policies, health programs, and other social policies, which are beyond the scope of this report, must all play a role. And yet we believe that school and employment policies can make a significant difference, as is suggested by examples of promising programs in certain communities.

In many of its reports on higher education, the Carnegie Council, and the Carnegie Commission before it, has emphasized the need to maintain and encourage diversity. The need is no less important at the secondary level. Some of our large cities—notably Boston, New York, and San Francisco—have long had diversified schools. The challenge under present conditions is to promote diversity without encouraging segregation. With enough determination on the part of the community and school leadership, it can be done.

Magnet Schools

In their excellent volume on the future of big-city schools, Levine and Havighurst (1977) place a great deal of emphasis on successful examples of magnet and alternative school programs in some large cities. They also emphasize the extremely important point that the courts and other authorities concerned with school integration have devoted their attention exclusively to racial balance and have failed to recognize that desegregation plans must give equal attention to achieving and maintaining socioeconomic balance if they are to be effective. The more affluent whites are much more likely to move to the suburbs than lower-income whites, and housing policies that will attract middle- and upper-income whites back to central-city areas are just as important in relation to school desegregation as school policies. In addition, desegregation plans should be developed and implemented on a metropolitan or regional basis and should be part of larger, comprehensive, and long-range programs of metropolitan development. The change in the population mix of central-city areas is by now so far advanced that many large-city school districts have too few white students to achieve anything remotely resembling integration. In the central-city school district of Kansas City, Missouri, for example, two-thirds of the pupils are minority students.

The Magnet School Plan in Houston

Influenced by the failure of a court-ordered school integration plan that called for pairing of schools, the General Superintendent of Schools in Houston recommended in November 1974 that the school board appoint a tri-ethnic task force (white, black, and Mexican-American) to promote integration and provide alternatives to involuntary busing. Out of this developed a plan for magnet schools under which individual schools were to submit their own proposals. Initially proposals were submitted by 116 schools, nearly one-half of Houston's public schools. Among criteria for approval of plans were whether each proposed magnet program would increase the number of children attending integrated schools and improve the quality of education. We include some information on magnet schools in Houston at the secondary level, in keeping with the scope of this report, even though many of the magnet schools are at the elementary level:

1. The Foreign Language Academy, which enlarged the number of student places in an already existing school to provide opportunities for students wishing to study Hebrew, Chinese, Italian, or Latin. Other languages are taught on request if a teacher is available. The school does not affect foreign language instruction in other Houston high schools but rather offers the opportunity for individual students to go beyond traditional instruction. Students who enroll in a foreign language class for at least two quarters can follow either a voca-

tional program, training for careers in which foreign language skills would be advantageous, or a college preparatory program.

2. The Contemporary Learning Center, which is located at a junior high school campus, but has places for as many as 500 high school students who may have a history of absenteeism or a record of conflict with classmates. The center emphasizes academic individualization, continuous progress, and various options in learning activities.

3. The Petrochemical Career Institute, at Milby Senior High School, which was established in response to a shortage of skilled technicians in Houston's petrochemical industry. Its vocationally oriented physical science program stresses career information and interaction with persons involved in the petrochemical industry, along with a program to provide on-the-job training for each student.

4. The Aerodynamics Program, at Sterling Senior High School, which emphasizes preparation for aerospace careers, with a background in mathematics and science. Female as well as male students are recruited.

5. The Booker T. Washington School for Engineering Professions, which offers a rigorous college preparatory program centering on mathematics and science.

6. The High School for Visual and Performing Arts, which provides specialized and concentrated work for students talented in art, dance, drama, media, and music. Admission standards are rigorous and are based on an interview and an audition or presentation of a portfolio. Traditional secondary courses are offered, but learning in the arts and in academic areas are closely associated.

7. The High School for Health Professions, which is conducted with the cooperation of the Baylor College of Medicine, is located at the Texas Medical Center and aims to provide entry-level skills to health professions or preparation for more advanced professional training. It was the first secondary school of its type in the nation.

The Houston program has involved substantial additional expenditures for the school district, including staff development costs, lowered student-teacher ratios in the magnet schools, and transportation costs that are difficult to identify precisely, because transportation to magnet schools is coordinated with an already complex busing system. There is some evidence that the program has helped to retain some students who might otherwise have left the district and increased the percentage of whites in some schools. However, it is not a districtwide integration plan but rather an attempt to move toward a more limited integration goal envisioned in the court-mandated pairing arrangements.

The Whitney Young Magnet High School of Chicago

The Whitney Young School is not the only magnet-type school in Chicago. That city has had some specialized vocational and technical schools for decades, and more recently has established some innovative magnet schools at both the elementary and secondary levels. But the opening of Whitney Young in 1975 marked the beginning of an important experiment, in a large new school facility built at considerable expense. It is located just west of the central business district, not far from several major urban renewal projects.[2] Three magnet programs are offered at the school: medical arts, science, and the performing arts. The courses needed for high school graduation are also available, and, in addition, Whitney Young has "a school within a school" for students with hearing impairments.

Each of the three major programs is developed sequentially in the ninth through the twelfth grades, with increasing specialization in the later grades, and all three draw heavily on the resources of major Chicago institutions in science, medicine, and the performing arts.

Admission standards are such that 80 percent of the students read at grade level or above; they are selected to represent a geographical cross section of the city; and the original quota system established by the Chicago Board of Education provided

---

[2]This discussion of the Whitney Young School is based on one of the chapters in Levine and Havighurst (1977) and also on a visit to the school and an interview with Charles Mingo, assistant principal, by Margaret Gordon of our staff in July 1978.

that 40 percent of the students would be black, 40 percent white, 10 percent of Spanish background, and the other 10 percent would be one-half from other minority groups and one-half admitted by the principal at his own discretion. The actual enrollment in 1975-76 was 43 percent black, 34 percent white, 16 percent Spanish, and 7 percent other minorities. Competition to get into the school has been much more intense among blacks than among whites, and yet, considering that many white students commute from other parts of the city, the school's success in achieving racial balance seems substantial. The school has also succeeded in attracting superior teachers from all over the city.

What happens to students who "fail to adjust"? They either drop out or transfer back to their neighborhood school. Whitney Young does not make extraordinary efforts to retain them, on the grounds that, with 4,000 on the waiting list to be admitted, the slot is better filled by a student more likely to succeed.

Some critical observers maintain that, although Whitney Young School is *very* good, it leaves the ghetto schools in a worse position because it attracts the more motivated youngsters. Chicago needs more magnet schools, but it is not entirely clear what the magic number is. If there were too many, the traditional city high schools would become still more of a dumping ground. As matters stand, it seems clear that there are too few.

Perhaps the most promising feature of Whitney Young is that it does provide an opportunity for the more motivated youngsters, white and minority, to get out of inferior ghetto schools and into a school where most students are clearly making good progress and where disciplinary problems seem to be relatively minor. As we shall see in Section 14, there may be other answers for the hard-core disadvantaged.

Skyline Center, Dallas

Skyline Center is not only a magnet school but one of the largest educational parks in the country, and it has a 14-acre building complex on an 80-acre campus. The center is open to students from any high school in Dallas, and its goals include extensive preparation in career education, individualization of instruction, and involvement of community. Among its three main divisions is the Career Development Center, which provides programs that would not be feasible because of space or cost in individual high schools, for example, an aircraft hangar and airstrip, a computer center, and classes in Greek and Swahili (Smith, 1974, pp. 32-33).

Higher Education and Magnet Schools in Boston

Boston's magnet schools are of special interest because each magnet school is "paired" with a college or university in the Boston area (sometimes with several) that helps to guide its program. They are part of a plan mandated by Federal Judge Arthur Garrity in 1975 to bring about school desegregation, in connection with which the judge asked numerous colleges and universities to participate as partners in getting the magnet schools operating (Winkler, 1975). Public agencies and business firms were also asked to become involved, and most magnet schools are paired with business firms as well as with colleges. There are nine magnet schools, seven schools that have magnet cooperative industrial programs, and certain other specialized centers. Three of the magnet schools have special admissions standards. We discuss here a few of the more interesting examples:[3]

1. Boston High School, which has a program designed particularly for students planning to enter the business world, and a "work-study" magnet theme. Students attend classes for half the school day and spend the other half in paid employment in one of more than 100 business firms, universities, hospitals, and public agencies that provide jobs sites for the school. With a student body that includes 41 percent white, 43 per-

---

[3]We are indebted to Jeanne Hardy, acting information officer, Boston Public Schools, for official publications describing the magnet schools, including *Boston Public High Schools* (1979), a guide for parents and students, which includes critical comments on the schools.

cent black, and 16 percent other minorities, the school has a Spanish bilingual program that provides extra instruction in English. It is paired with Boston State College, which offers a tutorial program. Located in an old building in downtown Boston, the school is characterized as a "no-frills" institution, with no amenities such as a gym or a cafeteria, and with emphasis on stern discipline and hard work.

2. Boston Latin School, which was founded in 1635, admits students to grades 7 to 12 on the basis of an entrance examination. It adheres to its long tradition of offering a classical, liberal-arts, college preparatory program. Its student body is predominantly white, but 14 percent are black and 13 percent are other minorities. Qualified juniors and seniors may participate in an advanced placement program in which they have an opportunity to take freshman-level college courses in 13 subject areas. The school is paired with Wellesley College, which has developed summer discovery, tutorial, modern dance, drama, computer, and language lab programs. It is also paired with the Federal Reserve Bank of Boston, which provides computer training and career education, and with Franklin Park and Stoneham zoos and the Boston Symphony Orchestra for cultural programs. Although parents' comments are generally highly favorable, some parents have mentioned inadequacies in the tutorial, counseling, and career education programs.

2. Boston Trade Comprehensive High School, which is located in Roxbury and has a predominantly minority group student body, is a magnet school with emphasis on vocational education but with more of the problems associated with a conventional city high school than some of the other magnet schools. Shop training is provided in a number of blue-collar trades, such as auto repair and basic electronics, but the program lacks "shop-related" instruction in mathematics, science, and drafting. Students enrolled in the vocational education program must meet extensive general education requirements, and the school also offers college preparatory and business programs. The school is paired with Suffolk University, which has cooperated in developing basic skill learn-

ing centers (for reading and math) and a basic skill tutorial program. Although students comment favorably about the shop work, they complain about lax standards, and both parents and teachers complain that the school lacks adequate support from the administration and that the physical plant is in need of extensive renovation.

4. Copley Square High School, which offers a magnet program in communications arts and also features an "extern" program. The extern program is designed to give the students experience in cultural, business, and government institutions. The school is paired with Emerson College, which has developed the communication arts program, including theater arts, media, speech, the humanities, and reading and career education. It is also paired with Suffolk University, which has developed a math lab, providing supplementary math instruction geared to individual needs. The Shawmut Bank of Boston is the school's business partner and provides programs featuring knowledge of the world of work, including a career seminar in banking. Copley High's program is "ungraded," allowing individual students to take courses according to their levels of ability and interests rather than according to grade level. Parent and student comments are generally very favorable, emphasizing the fact that the teachers care about the students.

5. Mario Umana Harbor School of Science and Technology, which offers the only six-year science and four-year technology programs in the school district. Located in East Boston, in a new and modern facility, the school's primary goal is to provide high-quality education for students aiming at technical or scientific careers. The school does not have selective admissions requirements, and some students participate in a special needs program to make up deficiencies. It is paired with the Massachusetts Institute of Technology and with Wentworth Institute, which, along with the Massachusetts Port Authority, have developed programs in reading improvement, math improvement, career awareness, extended computer capabilities, and others. Both teachers and parents comment favorably about the school's unique programs, and

the school has become the most popular of the magnet schools, receiving more new first-preference applications in 1978 than any other magnet school ("Umana School Shows Citywide Popularity," 1978).

6. Cooperative vocational education programs are featured in a number of Boston high schools and are magnet programs in the sense that they are designed to attract students from all parts of the city. The student spends alternate weeks in the classroom studying academic and trade-related subjects and in the shop learning the skills and procedures of the chosen trade. Advanced students have supervised work assignments in local firms during their shop week. An applicant for these programs must select the specific skill he or she wishes to acquire as well as which school is preferred, and shifting to a different program is difficult.

Boston's magnet school program is of special interest, not only because of the unusual pairing feature (which some observers think may be more effective in some cases than in others), but also because court-ordered desegregation brought on a well-publicized crisis, especially in the South Boston area. Thus, the fact that many of the magnet schools have achieved a reasonably balanced racial mix is encouraging, although several of the schools in the ghetto areas (Roxbury and Dorchester) have relatively few white students.

Other Alternative Schools

Magnet schools, as we have seen, are one example of alternative schools, but there are a number of others, of which we include a few illustrations:

Learning Centers

Learning centers may take a variety of forms, but a particularly interesting example is the St. Paul Learning Centers Program, which is a voluntary racial integration model. Learning centers have been developed at elementary, junior high, and senior high levels. All students are assigned to a home school for basic education, but each student may elect to spend part of the school day in one of the learning centers for one quarter during the school year. Examples of specialized learning centers are the Junior and Senior High School Performing Arts Learning Center, the Junior High Automotive Transportation Learning Center, and, at the elementary level, centers that are especially concerned with esthetic environmental issues, foreign languages, career exploration, black minority culture, and others. The centers are designed to attract a cross section of all children in terms of family income level, race or ethnicity, and ability level. All students are bussed from their home schools to the learning centers. By 1975-76 the program was to be fully implemented and available to every family in St. Paul (Smith, 1974, pp. 31-32).

Schools Within Schools

Schools within schools are of special interest because they represent one way of providing a more intimate school environment than that of the typical large high school, and because they can be developed within existing school buildings and thus avoid the expense of new construction.

A well-known example of an attempt to develop a schools-within-schools program, though not within one building, is that of Evanston, Illinois. Its efforts in this direction began in 1924, and in the late 1960s Evanston Township High School was organized as four semi-independent schools, each with its own identity, student body of 1,200, faculty, and physical facilities. The objective was "to ensure the personal understanding of and attention to each student within a small school setting while utilizing fully the assets of diversity and specialization possible only in a very large high school" (Michael, 1969, p. 93). The school had an outstanding record by such measures as the number of students winning National Merit Scholarships and was also notable for having the highest expenditures per student of any high school in the country. However, a cut in the budget in 1976 forced consolidation of the four sub-schools into two sub-schools (Clorfene, 1977).

Evanston has also made special efforts to improve the educational attainments of its black students, who comprise about 25 percent of the student body and include National Merit

Scholarship winners but also a substantial number who are well below grade level. In 1975-76 the school started a new tutoring center, in which low-achieving students were tutored by fellow students, and it has also moved toward making the ability-grouping of students less rigid, with some success, especially in improving the performance of students in the middle-ability range (Clorfene, 1977).

Another example of schools-within-schools, in an environment far less favorable than that of a university town like Evanston, is at Haaren High School, on the west side of New York City. In spring 1970, when the school was experiencing high dropout and truancy rates and low morale, the principal, with the cooperation of the New York Urban Coalition, developed a plan to establish 12 minischools (within a total student body of about 2,000), which was approved by the teachers and by the board of education. Although most of the minischools provide compensatory or basic education programs, some are specialized, including a service station program, conducted in a simulated gasoline station constructed by Mobil Oil Company. After three years, the program was reported to have improved morale and student-teacher relations. A major advantage was the opportunity for each student to spend most of his or her time with a few teachers rather than having brief contacts with many teachers (*Matters of Choice*, 1974, pp. 28-29).

Evaluations

As the alternative school movement has grown and developed, there have been a number of evaluations of such schools or groups of schools. In fact, evaluations have sometimes been mandated by funding agencies, such as the federal government and the Ford Foundation. A thorough review of these evaluations would be beyond the scope of this report, and some of them have been weak in methodology, but the conclusions of a study that analyzed evaluations of six alternative schools are worth quoting (Barr, Colston, and Parrett, 1977, pp. 27-28):

1. Each of the evaluations that measured cognitive achievement found most students to be learning at a rate consistent with or higher than the district norm.

2. The program evaluations consistently found the attitudes of students toward the schools and themselves to be more favorable in an alternative setting.
3. Each of the programs that reported attendance and enrollment data found a decreased rate of student dropout and an increased rate of school and classroom attendance.
4. The three evaluations that included information on graduates of their programs indicated favorable results, with graduates reporting that they had been well prepared for both work and college.[4]

Interestingly, Michael Timpane, senior author of the Rand Corporation review (Timpane and others, 1976) of the three reports on secondary schools discussed at the beginning of Section 5, and now deputy director of the U.S. National Institute of Education, currently has a much more positive attitude toward efforts to achieve smaller school size than was expressed in the Rand report. He has concluded, on the basis of the various evaluations of alternative schools that have been completed, that their favorable impacts are explained to a considerable extent by their typically small size.[5]

Private Schools

About 10 percent of all elementary and secondary school pupils in the United States—or about five million in terms of numbers—are enrolled in private schools. Neither the proportion nor the number has changed greatly in recent years. Some schools—especially among Catholic parochial schools, which account for the majority of pupils in private schools—have lost ground, while others, especially Protestant or nonsectarian private schools in the Southeast and West, have gained ground (U.S. National Center for Education Statistics, 1978b, p. 69).

[4]Included in the evaluation were St. Paul Open School; Learning Unlimited, Indianapolis; Education II, Urbana, Illinois; Walden III, Racine, Wisconsin; the Parkway Program, Philadelphia; and the Chicago High School for Metropolitan Studies.

[5]Timpane expressed this view at a meeting in Washington, D.C., June 1, 1979, which brought together a number of experts on school and labor market problems who had been asked to read and comment on an earlier draft of this report.

The fact that Catholic schools have been having a hard time financially in recent years and that some have had to close has been widely publicized. Much less well known is that a number of Catholic schools are doing an excellent job in the very slum areas in which public schools are meeting their worst problems and that they are doing it with students who are predominantly from disadvantaged minority group families and who are not Catholic.

An article by Hoyt (1977) provided surprising information on Catholic schools in New York City. Of the 368 Catholic grade schools and high schools that operated the preceding year in the New York archdiocese, all but 5 were functioning in 1977, and the drop in grade school enrollment, which had been alarming in the early 1970s, had slowed down. Among the 18,421 students enrolled in 47 inner-city Catholic schools, 78 percent were from minority groups: blacks, Hispanics, Orientals, American Indians, and others. A large proportion of these students came from poor families for whom the tuition (averaging $350 a year) meant a financial hardship. Although costs per student were something like one-quarter to one-third of the cost per student in public schools, children in Catholic inner-city schools generally scored higher on tests than did children in public schools in the same neighborhoods. Hoyt concluded that the success of the Catholic schools was not explained by either selective admissions or getting rid of trouble-making students but rather by determination to make the students succeed, relative autonomy for each school, relatively small size, absence of a centralized bureaucracy, and close relationships of parents with the schools—the latter, no doubt, partly explained by the fact that the parents had deliberately chosen the schools and did not take them for granted, as did some parents of children in public schools.

Rather different was the story of Providence St. Mel High School in a poor, black, and Hispanic area on Chicago's West Side (Sheppard, 1978). This school was quite selective, maintained strong discipline, and had a record of sending 85 percent of its graduates on to college. In summer 1978, however, it was struggling against a decision of the archdiocese to close it.

The success of these Catholic schools in slum areas and on meager budgets tends to lend support to the arguments of those who, like Friedman (1962), maintain that the public schools in the United States would improve in quality if they had to compete on more equal terms with private schools. But are the vouchers that Friedman and others advocate the best way of encouraging such competition—or the tuition tax credits so vigorously advocated by Senator Daniel P. Moynihan of New York and others—or are there other, preferable ways of helping private schools? We consider this question in Section 9.

The Importance of Strong Leadership

Wherever one turns in the literature on reform of secondary education, one finds that the role of local leadership, particularly the school principal, is crucial. This emerges clearly in many of the examples of educational innovation discussed in Silberman's book, *Crisis in the Classroom* (1970). It also is stressed in a Rand Corporation report summarizing the results of evaluations of federal programs supporting innovations (Berman and others, 1975) and suggesting certain policy implications:[6]

* Provide funds only when the people who are going to implement the program want it, design it, and think it will help them address a problem they think is important.
* Concentrate on individual schools as the unit of change and improvement. Stimulate communication and exchange of ideas among principal, other administrative staff, teachers, students, and parents. Provide incentives for these people to come to agreements on purposes and on instructional program focus and strategy.
* Provide opportunities and resources for school staff to seek out sources of new ideas and technical assistance from people whose expertise they respect and with whom they feel rapport, preferably from peers.

[6]This summary also draws on an unpublished paper prepared for internal circulation within the U.S. National Institute of Education, which was kindly provided to us by Michael Timpane, deputy director.

- Help school district staff develop the skills and organizational structure that will enable them in turn to help school staff to make decisions collaboratively, engage in continuous planning, seek out and assess competent and relevant technical assistance, build school-level staff development activities integrated with school programs, and design and implement instructional programs that meet the objectives the school sets for itself.
- Provide incentives and resources to states and localities to help them involve teachers in the organization of staff development programs that meet needs defined by those teachers and that provide opportunities for teachers to learn from one another and to collaborate in the development of school curricula.
- Provide incentives and resources to states and school districts that will help them devise policies and programs for assisting schools to develop quality programs that are not only defined as important by individual schools but are responsive to state and district priorities as well.
- Enable the Office of Education to exercise leadership on important issues in education, not by funding categorical programs on narrow topics, but by supporting the development of new ideas, materials, and approaches that will stimulate and support local program development.
- Enable the states and localities to develop programs for and provide assistance to families that will help parents participate more effectively in the education of their children.

We emphasize these findings because we do not believe that the problem of reform of the secondary schools can be approached on the basis of broad federally initiated policies or massive doses of federal funds. It is one of those situations in which merely "throwing more money" at a problem is not the answer. The federal and state governments and foundations can help by providing support for innovative projects developed through local initiative. The legislative authority for the Office of Education and the National Institute of Education to support innovative projects is in place, and the main question is whether the amount of federal funds available for such support should be increased. In the next two sections, we discuss the case for an increase in federal funding for this purpose.

We have noted that the leadership of the principal is critical in successful innovation, but we have not yet mentioned teachers' organizations. We believe that teachers' organizations could take a much more positive position toward innovation than they typically have in the past and that, in fact, they could often stimulate action where it is lacking. Not only is the role of teachers crucial in bringing about innovation, but, if work experience and on-the-job training are to be given greater emphasis, as we propose in sections 6 and 13, teachers' unions could be effective in bringing about the cooperation of other unions in the community.

Whether or not restructuring of secondary schools is needed—in some cities it is clearly well under way—the school system must make certain that its programs provide opportunities for completion of their education by girls who become pregnant. This is being done in a variety of ways in different communities and should be carried out by the schools in cooperation with other community agencies that are concerned with family planning, child care, and other relevant services. Some programs encourage the girl to continue in her regular school both before and after childbirth, while others operate through special community centers that provide education, child care, and counseling.

Recommendation 11: *School districts throughout the United States should develop local planning efforts, where they have not done so, aimed at determining whether magnet schools, alternative schools, or schools-within-schools are needed.*

Recommendation 12: *Plans for restructuring schools should ensure that racial integration will be encouraged, rather than jeopardized, through the development of new types of schools.*

Recommendation 13: *Boards of education and superintendents should give the principal of each school where change is to occur clear responsibility for planning and carrying out the change, in consultation with teachers, parents, and students.*

Recommendation 14: *Teachers' organizations should support innovation and play an active role in carrying it out.*

Recommendation 15: *Every school district should make certain that its secondary schools have programs, in cooperation with other community agencies, that encourage girls who become pregnant to complete their education.*

9

Toward Greater Equality
of Opportunity
for All Youth

A major theme of this report is the need for greater equality of
opportunity for all youth. The Carnegie Council, and the Carnegie Commission before it, have consistently supported increased
expenditures for student aid in higher education, to make it
more possible for students from low-income and lower-middle-
income families to enroll in college. The increase in federal and
state student aid funds for young people enrolled in postsecondary education in the 1970s has been spectacular—from slightly
more than $1 billion in 1970 to nearly $7 billion in 1979-80
(not including benefits for veterans, for which expenditures
have been declining in the last few years, as Vietnam veterans
have passed beyond the ten-year period of eligibility). If we add
student aid from private sources, the total flow of funds into
aid for students in higher education is even larger (Carnegie
Council, 1979, section 3). We now believe that the need is for
more effective use of these funds rather than for continuing to
increase their amounts.

There has been no comparable movement to provide aid
for students in secondary education. The United States was a
leader among nations in the nineteenth century in moving
toward free public education at both the elementary and sec-

ondary levels, whereas in a number of industrial countries tuition has traditionally been charged in secondary schools and in some cases continues to be charged. Our tradition has been that free public schools would make education through grade 12 accessible to all. Only gradually have we come to recognize that many young people from poor families have felt impelled to go to work to augment the meager subsistence funds available to their families, or in some cases because they could not afford suitable clothes to wear to school or felt embarrassed because their friends had spending money and they did not. In other words, we have come to realize that free tuition is not always enough to keep the doors of secondary school open for youth from poor families, even though financial need is not the most prevalent reason for dropping out. Similarly, we have come to recognize that low tuition in public institutions of higher education is not enough to guarantee access to students from low-income families who cannot afford to give up the earnings needed to provide for subsistence.

In Section 1, we showed how much more federal money was being spent on low-income college students than on low-income youth not attending college. We have already made one proposal for reducing this imbalance—a work-study program at the secondary school level. We shall make other proposals in this and later sections.

Tuition Tax Credits

Undoubtedly the most widely discussed proposal for aid at the secondary level—in this case aid to parents—in the last few years has been for tuition tax credits. Some of the bills introduced into Congress have provided for such credits only at the postsecondary level, while other bills have included credits at the elementary and secondary level as well. Thus far, none of these bills has been approved, although tuition tax credits were defeated in 1978 only at the last minute at the conference committee stage.

We have opposed tuition tax credits at the postsecondary level on the grounds that (1) they are not related to parental need; (2) the amount of parental relief provided under recent proposals has been very small in relation to tuition costs, particularly in private higher education, and therefore there would be continual pressure to increase the amounts of the tax credits, so that the costs in lost tax revenue might ultimately run into many billions of dollars; (3) they are not an effective way of supporting the survival of private institutions of higher education, because they would not reduce the tuition gap between public and private institutions, and, in any case, the bulk of the relief would go to the far more numerous parents whose children attend public colleges and universities; (4) they would probably be self-defeating, because institutions of higher education would tend to raise tuition by the amount of the tax credit, and (5) they could jeopardize appropriations for need-based student aid (Carnegie Council, 1979).

The proposals for tuition tax credits at the elementary and secondary level raise, much more strongly than do those at the postsecondary level, the issue of federal and state constitutional provisions for separation of state and church. This is because the relief would go only to parents of students in private schools, since public schools do not charge tuition, and a large proportion of private school pupils at the elementary and secondary level are in Catholic parochial or other sectarian schools. In 1976-77, more than 60 percent of the 5 million pupils in nonpublic elementary and secondary schools were in Catholic schools (U.S. National Center for Education Statistics, 1978a, p. 47).

Senator Daniel P. Moynihan, sponsor of a tuition tax credit bill that would include elementary and secondary schools and one of the most articulate supporters of such proposals, has argued that the history of relevant judicial opinions does not necessarily indicate that tuition tax credits at the elementary and secondary level would be unconstitutional (Moynihan, 1978, p. C1). On the other hand, Joseph Califano, former Secretary of Health, Education, and Welfare, has argued as spokesman for the Carter administration that the probability that such credits would be declared unconstitutional is great.

Apart from religious and constitutional considerations, the arguments against tuition tax credits at the elementary and secondary level are strong and are much the same as those we have advanced against tax credits at the postsecondary level: (1) they are not related to parental need; (2) they would encourage increases in tuition by private schools; (3) as tuition increased, there would be great pressure to raise the amounts of the credits, with the result that costs to the federal treasury would eventually become much larger than initial estimates; and (4) there are other ways of assisting private schools that we think are more equitable and more justified. Under our proposed work-study program, for example, pupils in private schools could receive work-study grants.

Public schools have always been an important part of the democratic tradition in the United States—more so than in many other countries. The "common school experience" has been an integral feature of American life. If the public schools have fallen on difficult times in some communities, what is needed is a vigorous attack on the evils and not an adoption of financing policies that would consign public schools to an even worse fate.

Recommendation 16: *The Council opposes tuition tax credits at the elementary and secondary level, just as we have opposed them at the postsecondary level, and for many of the same reasons. At the elementary and secondary level, they (1) may well be declared unconstitutional, (2) would help all parents with children in private schools regardless of need, and (3) might encourage a massive shift to private schools.*[1]

Vouchers

It will be recalled that the Coleman Panel report (discussed in Section 5) recommended that young people from age 16 on should be provided with vouchers to use on education or training programs of their own free choice and that institutional subsidization should be discontinued. (The panel, however, also

---

[1]They would not help low-income parents with minimal income tax liabilities unless, as some of the proposals provide, they received cash tax credits regardless of tax liability.

indicated that this approach should be started on a small, experimental scale.)

The idea of vouchers has considerable appeal, and in California there is currently an effort to place an initiative on the ballot at the next state election to authorize shifting to a voucher system of financing elementary and secondary education in the state.

Contemporary discussion of voucher plans stems largely from a proposal made by economist Milton Friedman in *Capitalism and Freedom* (1962) under which institutional subsidization of education would be discontinued and parents would be given vouchers equivalent to the estimated cost of educating a child in a public school, provided that the voucher was used for education in an approved school.

> [This arrangement] would meet the just complaints of parents that if they send their children to private nonsubsidized schools they are required to pay twice for education—once in the form of general taxes and once directly. It would permit competition to develop. The development and improvement of all schools would thus be stimulated. The injection of competition would do much to promote a healthy variety of schools. It would do much, also, to introduce flexibility into school systems. Not least of its benefits would be to make the salaries of school teachers responsive to market forces [Friedman, 1962, p. 93].

The voucher proposal has become controversial and is vigorously opposed by many liberals and civil rights groups on the grounds that it would increase segregation in the schools. Wealthy parents, it is argued, could easily take advantage of the plan by accepting the voucher and then augmenting it with the extra funds needed to send their children to an expensive private school—thereby receiving a sizable public subsidy that such parents cannot now receive. Poor parents would have no such choice, and the public schools would become the "dumping grounds" for the children of the poor.

The California plan, which is spearheaded by John Coons, professor of law at the University of California, Berkeley, has safeguards against this type of effect. In fact, it is what is known as a "regulated voucher plan" (La Noue, 1972). Private scholarship schools participating in the voucher plan could charge more than the basic voucher rate but could not charge the parents directly for the extra amount. A parent wishing to send a child to such a school would have to apply directly to the state for the extra fee. Low-income parents would be granted the extra scholarship for a nominal amount, whereas wealthy parents would have to pay much more. Neither public nor private schools would be obliged to participate in the program, but there would be strong competitive pressures at work to ensure that many of them would. Despite the safeguards, the plan is vigorously opposed by the state's superintendent of public instruction, Wilson Riles, teachers' organizations, and civil rights groups. Riles says, "I'm opposed to vouchers because, either wittingly or unwittingly, the plan would do away with public education in California—that would be the end result" (Moskowitz, 1979).

Proponents of the proposal, on the other hand, argue that some parents are taking advantage of the reduction in property taxes brought about by Proposition 13 (approved overwhelmingly by the state's voters in June 1978) to shift their children to private schools. Meanwhile, Governor Jerry Brown has recently approved a legislative measure that will greatly increase state aid to local school districts on a permanent basis to make up for the severe loss in property tax revenue to the districts resulting from Proposition 13. School districts, along with community college districts and other special-purpose districts, were hit particularly hard by Proposition 13, because, unlike cities and counties, they are authorized to levy only property taxes and not other types of taxes.

As part of the antipoverty program, the Office of Economic Opportunity (OEO) decided, in 1971, to sponsor four experimental voucher programs in selected communities. Three of the communities rejected the opportunity to participate for a variety of reasons, including fears that such an experiment might promote racial segregation. The only school district agreeing to participate in the plan was Alum Rock, an elementary school district in a section of San Jose, California, in which about one-half of the school children were Mexican-American, four-tenths were Caucasian, and one-tenth were black. The experiment was hardly a typical voucher plan, however, because, as a result of negotiation between OEO and the school district, a decision was made to include only 6 of the district's 24 public schools and no private schools in the experiment. The superintendent had been interested for some time in a plan for decentralization of authority within the district and apparently viewed the OEO proposal as a means of getting federal funds to support decentralization. The plan also differed from a true voucher plan in other respects, including its guarantee that no teacher would lose a job because of shifts of children to other schools during the experiment. Among the findings of a Rand Corporation evaluation of the first year of the program were that (1) decision making was decentralized to an important degree, (2) small minischools were developed in which older and younger children were grouped together, (3) parents and teachers were generally well satisfied with the demonstration, (4) teachers were stimulated to greater effort as they took advantage of decentralization to spend more time developing their programs, and (5) fears that parent choice would result in increasing segregation by race or social class were not borne out (Weiler, 1974).

In subsequent years, the experiment did not fare as well. When the district received new funds for compensatory programs from the state, it decided to allocate them to whole schools rather than to minischools. This decision meant that the end of federal voucher funds would also probably bring an end to the extra financial resources the minischools had enjoyed. By the fourth year of the demonstration, a movement was under way to discontinue the minischools—strongly supported by the principals of the schools in which the voucher plan was operating, who felt too much authority had been delegated to the minischools, and by a number of teachers who did not like the added administrative responsibilities and competition involved in the minischools.

In its final evaluation, the Rand team reported that there was little difference in teaching styles or classroom practice between schools that had participated in the demonstration and those that had not but that the voucher schools did enjoy greater availability of instructional materials. Many of the minischools spent substantial sums on books and other classroom aides, but there was relatively little expenditure for staff development. A feeling that decentralization had gone too far developed among both school officials and parents. Parents tended to be confused by the large variety of programs, and the high transiency rate in the district's population made it difficult to inform the parents adequately about choices. However, the district has not reverted to its pre-voucher state entirely. All students in the district are now able to choose which school they will attend, with free transportation provided by the district, and in 1976-77 a significant percentage did attend a school other than the one to which they were geographically assigned. The district has also retained per-pupil budgeting, with the result that compensatory funds follow eligible children from school to school, which is not the practice in most school districts (Bass, 1978).

The Alum Rock experiment suggests that there is a case for a voucher plan that will bring about choice among public schools within a district but that the plan will not operate well unless it has the consistent support of administrators, teachers, and parents. It also suggests that reactions of teachers may be mixed. Some teachers apparently appreciated the greater freedom to use new materials and methods, whereas others either resented the added work or the exposure to competition.

Most discussions of vouchers relate to plans that would facilitate free choice between public and private schools, but we believe that there is a case for at least some experiments designed to encourage choice among public schools, along the lines of the Alum Rock experiment. Such developments would not threaten the future of the public schools, as do proposals for voucher plans involving both public and private schools.

A serious obstacle to adoption of any voucher plan is the opposition of teachers' organizations, which view such plans as a threat to job security. Yet the present situation in which it is often extremely difficult and costly for a school district to dismiss an incompetent teacher is unsatisfactory. Moreover, declining student bodies and financial stringency are forcing layoffs of teachers and transfers of teachers within school districts. Both administrators and teachers are having to learn to live with a situation in which schools are being selectively closed and transfers are inevitable.

We also believe that limited experiments with vouchers that encourage choice between public and private schools should be supported, but we are opposed to any large-scale or statewide move toward a voucher system until more is known about the probable results.

Recommendation 17: *Small-scale experiments with voucher plans should be encouraged, especially experiments that are limited to public schools, but there should be no large-scale or statewide adoptions of voucher plans until the results of such experiments have been evaluated.*

Increasing Resources

We have recommended adoption of a work-study program for secondary school students as one step toward greater equality of opportunity for all youth. We have also recommended shifting the allocation of a portion of vocational education funds, so that they would be directed toward encouraging work experience for secondary school students. The other major need, as far as in-school youth are concerned, is allocation of additional resources to secondary schools, especially those that have large proportions of low-income students.

The secondary schools have received relatively little benefit from the federal Elementary and Secondary Education Act of 1965 (ESEA), which was adopted under the impetus of the "war on poverty," after decades of controversy over any move toward federal aid to elementary and secondary schools—controversy revolving around the issue of whether any portion of proposed federal aid would go to parochial schools. However, by focusing the legislation primarily on the need to improve the education of disadvantaged children, a way was found to bring about acceptance of the legislation and to include some aid to private schools. The bulk of the funds under the act—about $3.5 billion out of a total of nearly $4 billion under the administration budget recommendations for fiscal year 1980—are allocated under Title I, which provides for basic grants to local education agencies to improve the education of poor children, on the basis of a formula that gives extra weight to the number of children aged 5 to 17 in families below the poverty level in the school district.

A special study by the Stanford Research Institute (Larson and others, 1977) provides the best available data on the proportion of Title I funds going to elementary and secondary schools. The study shows that in 1973-74, only 19 percent of Title I funds went to improve educational resources for low-income students in grades 7 to 12, while 71 percent benefited those in 1 through 6 and the remaining 10 percent benefited children in prekindergarten, kindergarten, and ungraded classes. Four factors contributed to the early-grade orientation of Title I: (1) the political and research climate throughout the time of implementation of the legislation and passage of its amendments; (2) the legislation and legislative intent; (3) federal administrative influence, especially through regulations and guidelines; and (4) state and local policies.

The testimony of several social scientists and educators before the congressional committees considering the 1965 legislation emphasized the need to break the cycle of poverty by special educational programs targeted to young children. According to Urie Bronfenbrenner (Larson and others, 1977, p. 34), "we now have research evidence indicating that the environment of poverty has its most debilitating effect on the very young children in the first few years of life. . . ." Therefore, "you change what will be a vicious circle into a benign circle because once [poor children] learn how to learn then they can take over and they start learning anywhere they are." Francis Keppel, then Commissioner of Education, emphasized the same point in a slightly different way: "We rarely succeed in reaching the deprived in later and frustrating school years. . . . We are coming to recognize that our greatest possibility lies in early childhood education" (Larson and others, 1977, p. 35).

Unfortunately, evaluations of the impacts of enriched educational programs for young children have shown that their progress in the early years of school is assisted by participation in such programs but that the effects do not last beyond about the third year of school unless compensatory programs are continued. Furthermore, the gains achieved by junior high school students who participated in compensatory programs were actually greater than those of children in grades 1 to 3 (Larson and others, 1977, p. 72). The authors conclude that there is a strong case for increased federal expenditure targeted toward disadvantaged secondary school students and suggest several different ways in which such increased funding might be distributed among states and local school districts.

We agree that there is a strong case for an increase in Title I funds allocated to secondary education. The federal government has contributed very little to improving the quality of education at the secondary level, and yet, as we noted in Section 2, the need for improvement of quality is particularly critical in inner-city schools and in schools in small towns and rural areas. We discuss the issues in secondary school financing more fully in Section 11, but at this stage we suggest that the federal government needs to take an important step toward overcoming the serious imbalance between funds allocated to college youth compared with noncollege youth—not only through the work-study program and reallocation of vocational education funds that we have already recommended but also through an increase in funding for Title I under policies that will ensure that the increase flows to secondary school students.

We believe that the increased funds should benefit both junior and senior high school students, and on this particular issue depart from our general rule of confining the scope of this report to the 16- to 21-age group.

Recommendation 18: *The federal government should modify its policy of allocating meager funds to secondary schools under Title I of the Elementary and Secondary Act by increasing funding under the act specifically for the purpose of benefiting secondary schools. We suggest an initial increase for this purpose of $500 million in 1980-81.*

10

The Responsibilities
of Postsecondary
Education

As we note in the Preface, institutions of postsecondary education have an important stake in national policies aimed at overcoming the educational deficiencies of youth. Talent is lost to
higher education when able young people leave school early.
Colleges and universities, moreover, have had to devote increased resources in recent years to remedial courses aimed at
overcoming deficiencies, especially in the use of the English language, of their entering students.

In this section, we consider policies under which institutions of higher education could make a greater contribution
toward meeting the problems of youth than they are now making.

Partnerships with Secondary Schools

The Boston program in which each magnet high school is paired
with a college or university in the area is a model that could
well be adopted in other areas. No doubt, as some observers in
the Boston area comment, not all institutions of higher education take their obligations equally seriously, but the evidence
indicates that some of the magnet schools have benefited substantially from the partnership arrangement. At the same time,
the Boston program suggests that a college or university should

not make its contribution on a hit-or-miss basis but as part of a communitywide plan, in which the particular strengths of individual institutions of higher education are paired with the specialties emphasized in the secondary schools, as in the case of the Massachusetts Institute of Technology and the Mario Umana Harbor School of Science and Technology.

Recommendation 19: *Colleges and universities in large metropolitan areas should seek opportunities to contribute to improving the quality of secondary school programs in their areas, preferably through joining in a communitywide pairing plan like the one in Boston.*

New and Expanding Roles for Community Colleges

Community colleges are playing a more important role in most communities than other institutions of higher education in relation to the disadvantaged, through their role in CETA programs and through providing opportunities in some cases for high school students to enroll in occupational programs in community colleges. They can become even more involved in other ways:

1. Developing some middle colleges that combine the last two years of high school with the first two years of college. The purpose would be twofold: to create a more challenging environment for high school juniors and seniors who are bored with their schools or on the verge of dropping out, and to eliminate the overlapping that now often occurs between the curricula of the last two years of high school and the first two years of college.
2. Experimenting, in some cases, with admission at age 16. Some of the experiments might require a high school diploma or performance certificate for admission, while others might not. The objectives would be much the same as for middle colleges.
3. Contracting with local school districts to provide occupational programs for high school students.
4. Placing greater emphasis on the development of cooperative

education and apprenticeship programs that, in some cases, would be open to high school students.

5. Taking the leadership in promoting the development of work-education councils in their communities, if such councils do not exist.

6. Maintaining close ties with both CETA and school authorities, with a view to making a maximum contribution to the development of education, work-experience, and training opportunities for disadvantaged youth.

In communities that lack a community college, or in which the resources of community colleges are deficient, comprehensive colleges should undertake at least some of these functions.

Recommendation 20: Community colleges should (1) cooperate with CETA and school authorities in the development of training and work-experience programs, (2) experiment with admitting students at age 16 and with the development of middle colleges, (3) provide opportunities for high school students to participate in their occupational programs, and (4) develop more opportunities for cooperative education and apprenticeship for both secondary and postsecondary students.

Comprehensive colleges should assume these responsibilities in communities that lack a community college.

The FIPSE Program

In spring 1979, the Fund for the Improvement of Postsecondary Education (FIPSE) announced a program that resulted from an interagency agreement between the U.S. Department of Labor (DOL) and the U.S. Department of Health, Education, and Welfare (HEW), under which $1 million of discretionary funds would be transferred from DOL's Office of Youth Programs to HEW's FIPSE to fund projects that would apply the resources of institutions of postsecondary education to meeting the pressing needs of disadvantaged youth. FIPSE indicated its intention to support 16 to 20 projects that would demonstrate postsecondary approaches for serving CETA youth. The projects would operate for 16 to 17 months beginning in September or October 1979 at funding levels between $40,000 and $60,000. The program would have the immediate goal of identifying and learning about promising models emerging from postsecondary agencies as educational providers for CETA youth. The program specifically addresses youth aged 16 to 21 who are qualified for participation in the CETA program (Fund for the Improvement of Postsecondary Education, 1979).

We commend this development, not only as an encouraging case of interagency cooperation but also as a step toward the urban grant program that was suggested by the Carnegie Commission in its first report (1968, p. 45), when it said:

> The land-grant college movement had a significant effect on the nature of the public and, to some extent, the private university. Today the pressing problems of the city are calling for a new evaluation of the university's relationship to the city.
>
> If universities and colleges are to aid in the solutions of the complex problems of the inner city, they will have to develop new curricular programs and new concepts of public service.

In fact, FIPSE—established under the Education Amendments of 1972—is designed to carry out the purposes envisaged by the Carnegie Commission when it recommended a national foundation for the development of higher education and, in its six years of activity, has funded many promising innovations in curricula and teaching methods. We believe that the present experimental program will provide valuable guidance as to the types of projects that colleges and universities can carry out to aid disadvantaged youth and that funds allocated to FIPSE should be increased for the specific purpose of supporting projects aiding disadvantaged youth, including both in-school and out-of-school youth in rural as well as in urban areas. Such projects should include some pairing plans, as in Boston.

Recommendation 21: *The annual appropriation for FIPSE should be increased from the $14 million included in the admin-*

istration's fiscal year 1980 budget to $20 million in fiscal year 1981, under provisions that would allocate the additional $6 million to projects designed to serve disadvantaged youth.

The Trio Programs

An important link between secondary and postsecondary education in serving disadvantaged youth is provided by the so-called "Trio" programs or "special programs for the disadvantaged"— Talent Search, Upward Bound, and Educational Opportunity Centers. Under these programs, promising students from disadvantaged families are sought out and helped to prepare for college through summer seminars and other special programs. In addition, some colleges and universities have developed similar programs financed by institutional or privately raised funds, such as the faculty-supported Committee on Special Scholarships at the University of California, Berkeley.

We urge continued and gradually increased federal support for these programs.

Recommendation 22: *The federal government should continue to support the Trio programs and gradually increase their funding. We suggest an increase from $130 million in 1979-80 to $150 million (in constant 1979 dollars) in 1980-81.*

College Students as a Resource

College students can play an important part in programs for disadvantaged youth by serving as tutors, "big brothers," teachers' aides, assistants to organizers of community services, and in other ways. We envisage this type of activity as an important aspect of the youth service program recommended in Section 17. In fact, a good deal of this activity does go on in various colleges and universities. A good example was the "One-to-One" program sponsored by the University YMCA associated with the University of California, Berkeley (Stiles Hall), under which university students served as tutors to disadvantaged students in Oakland ghetto schools. This program has been discontinued, but Stiles Hall now has a "big brother" program under which disadvantaged youngsters are referred by various community agencies and are eventually paired with university students who serve as big brothers, taking them to sports and cultural events, showing an interest in their problems, and so on.

Some of the college students who are assisted by the College Work-Study (CWS) program participate in community agencies as their assignment under that program, but the great majority of CWS jobs has always been on campus. In its recent report, *Next Steps for the 1980s in Student Financial Aid* (1979), the Carnegie Council recommended increasing the appropriation for the CWS program from $550 million in 1979-80 to $900 million in 1982-83 (in constant 1979 dollars). One of the objectives we had in mind was increased emphasis on useful off-campus jobs in community agencies. We recognize that, to accomplish that objective, colleges and universities should be permitted to allocate an adequate percentage of funds received under the program to the student aid office, so that more staff resources can be devoted to job development in the community.[1]

Particularly in larger colleges and universities located in urban areas, we believe that an office of community services (of which the student aid office might be a part) should be established to coordinate activities of the institution relating to the community, including participation of students in activities directed to assisting disadvantaged youth. In the development of our proposed youth service program, such an office could play a very important role. As we point out in Section 17, moreover, offices of community services in colleges and universities could cooperate on a regional basis in developing opportunities for youth service.

Recommendation 23: *Especially on larger campuses, colleges and universities should coordinate participation of students in community service by establishing offices of community service.*

---

[1]Since 1976 institutions have been permitted to use 10 percent of CWS funds, or $15,000, whichever is less, for job development in the community, and the administration has recently proposed that CWS participants be sent to junior and senior high schools to inform pupils about federal student aid programs and to tutor needy students ("Administration Proposes," 1979, p. 4).

The Training of Teachers and Administrators

The most important single contribution that universities and colleges can make to overcoming the problems of the schools is through radical changes in teacher training. There is widespread agreement that schools of education have not kept abreast of the changing problems of the schools, have not trained teachers to cope with the education of disadvantaged youngsters, and have not maintained influence on the teacher training that goes on in arts and sciences departments, where potential secondary school teachers get much of their higher education.

It can be argued, of course, that innovations in teacher training are irrelevant since the job market for teachers is in the doldrums, but this is not entirely true. There is a significant replacement demand for teachers, ranging from 100,000 to 170,000 a year in the early 1980s according to alternate projections (U.S. National Center for Education Statistics, 1978b, table 19). There are also continuing shortages of teachers with specialized skills, such as bilingual teachers and teachers skilled in remedial work; and enrollment in masters programs in education continues to be very large, because many employed teachers enroll to upgrade their training and status and because some disappointed recipients of bachelor's degrees seek more advanced training to improve their job prospects in education.

Over the years there have been excellent proposals for reform of teacher training, notably those of Conant (1963), Silberman (1970), and the Study Commission on Undergraduate Education and the Education of Teachers (*Teacher Education,* 1976), and yet the recommended changes have not occurred to any great extent. The explanations appear to be chiefly inertia and insulation of schools of education from the problems actually encountered in the schools, particularly secondary schools with disadvantaged student bodies. As we shall see when we consider the experience of the Teacher Corps—a special program sponsored by the federal government as part of the war on poverty to train teachers for ghetto schools—there have been instances when schools of education have adopted innovative methods for training members of the Teacher Corps, without changing their regular teacher training programs at all.

We propose the following reforms in teacher education:

1. Changes in teacher education must parallel changes in the schools. First of all, students preparing to teach in secondary schools (and also in elementary schools) must have a thorough understanding of the changes that are occurring in the youthful population—especially the growth in the relative importance of minority groups—and must have practice in teaching in varied types of schools, including suburban and inner-city schools. Second, students must understand the various reasons for the growing trend toward alternative schools and must have training and practice in the more informal teaching methods that characterize those schools.

2. As nearly all proposals for reform of teacher training have emphasized, practice teaching under carefully administered procedures for supervision and evaluation of performance should be given much greater emphasis than is now the case in many schools of education.

3. Secondary school teachers should be trained for more versatile roles. Schools of education should recognize explicitly that some secondary school teachers will be primarily concerned with the classroom and with an academic subject, whereas others will be more concerned with extracurricular activities, administration of work-experience programs, counseling services, and placement services. The former will be specialists and the latter will be more in the nature of generalists. This suggests two differing lines of emphasis in secondary teacher training, but we do not believe that the split should be complete. All secondary school teachers should have both subject matter competence and an understanding of the kinds of problems encountered in managing programs outside the classroom.

4. In view of the scarcity of job opportunities for newly trained teachers, these changes must be emphasized, not only in undergraduate teacher training but also in the master's programs that cater to employed teachers. As has been widely recognized, in a period of declining school enrollment, there must also be much greater emphasis on in-

service training. Moreover, much of this in-service training should take place not in the academic setting of the school of education but in teacher training centers jointly sponsored by schools of education and local school districts in the area (Carnegie Commission, 1973a, p. 93). School districts must be assisted in allocating adequate funds to the costs of in-service training by both the federal and state governments. In fact, this may be one of the most important paths to improving the quality of secondary schools and needs to be given very high priority. Funds should be used to make possible periodic part-time assignments for teachers so that part of their time is released for in-service training or even for full-time sabbaticals in some cases.

5. Increased emphasis on an understanding of the problems of the inner city and on the expansion of the role of community colleges that we are recommending in this report is also a critical need in relation to the training of community college faculty. This training occurs largely under master's programs and often does not involve practice teaching—a serious weakness in the training of community college teachers. Clearly, also, community college faculty—especially those who will be involved in occupational education—need an understanding of the world of work, of the relationships between educational and manpower programs, of cooperative education, and of apprenticeship.

6. It is time to end the divorce between the courses in arts and sciences taken by students training for secondary school teaching and the courses of education taken by those students in schools of education. This should be accomplished by establishing faculty committees that include representation from both schools of education and arts and science departments, by joint appointments, and other ways of integrating the student's program.

7. The needs of students training to be teachers should be given special attention in plans for general institutional curriculum reform.

8. All faculty members who are concerned with teacher education, in the faculty of arts and sciences and in the school of

education, should be involved in relations with representatives of school districts in the area and also should be in close touch with faculty members and administrators who have special responsibilities for supervising practice teaching.

9. Young people who plan on teaching careers should be particularly advised to spend a year or two in youth service (to be discussed in Section 17) in an activity that involves teaching experience (abroad in the Peace Corps or in this country). The best time for this would probably be after the sophomore or junior year in college.

10. Standards for the licensing of teachers should cease to give so much emphasis to courses taken and should give much more emphasis to practice teaching requirements and to the performance of students in practice teaching. A provisional license should precede the regular license, with requirements during the provisional period for additional training and evaluation of teaching ability.

11. Universities and colleges involved in teacher training should emphasize recruitment and admissions policies that will encourage cultural pluralism among students pursuing teacher training. They should also consider giving preference to young people who have had some work experience and who have an understanding of the relationship between education and the world of work. A work-experience requirement is being considered in several European countries and was recently recommended by the 1974 Swedish Commission on Teacher Education (*Teachers for a School in Transition,* 1979).

12. Schools of education should not only participate in Teacher Corps training but should also incorporate techniques and procedures used in such training into their regular curricula, where appropriate.

13. Most important of all, the president of a university or college should take the leadership in "shaking up" the school of education if the dean is not changing traditional methods.

Recommendation 24: *The time has come for colleges and universities involved in teacher training to take decisive steps to reform that training to meet the changing needs of the schools in the 1980s. The president of the institution should take the lead in ensuring such changes if the school of education is resisting change.*

The Teacher Corps

The Teacher Corps is a "Great Society" program originally suggested by economist John Kenneth Galbraith (1964) in an article in *Harper's,* in which he called on the federal government to enlist the aid of teachers in the war against poverty. Modeled after the Peace Corps, a corps of teachers should be trained to serve in urban or rural poverty areas. At about the same time, a similar idea was being discussed informally in Congress in connection with proposals for the Elementary and Secondary Education Act of 1965. As it turned out, however, the provision for a Teacher Corps was included in Title V of the Higher Education Act of 1965.

As stated in the legislation, the purpose of the Teacher Corps is "to strengthen the educational opportunities available to children in areas having concentrations of low-income families and to encourage colleges and universities to broaden their programs of teacher preparation. . . ." The program is intended to attract and train (1) qualified teachers who will be made available to local education agencies in poverty areas, (2) inexperienced teacher-interns who will be made available for teaching and in-service training to local education agencies in teams led by an experienced teacher, (3) volunteers to serve as part-time tutors or full-time instructional assistants, and (4) educational personnel to provide relevant remedial, basic, and secondary educational training (*A Compilation,* 1975, pp. 361-362).

The program operates through contracts with institutions of higher education or with local educational agencies. Appropriations for the program rose from $9.5 million in fiscal year 1966 to $37.5 million in fiscal year 1973 and have remained at that level since then (National Advisory Council on Education Professions Development, 1975, p. 11; *The Budget,* 1979, p. 453). Plans for fiscal year 1980 call for 121 projects providing training for 26,200 educational personnel, as well as for a few demonstration projects. Although the emphasis in the early years of the program was on attracting and training new, young teachers who would be prepared to serve in poverty areas, the legislation was amended in 1974 to add retraining of experienced teachers as a major aim, whereas experienced teachers had formerly been involved only as leaders of groups of inexperienced interns. In explaining this change the Senate Committee on Labor and Public Welfare stated:

> While the overall teaching shortage may no longer be the severe problem it was in the past, there continue to be special needs, particularly in poverty area schools. The Teacher Corps has effectively utilized such techniques as individualized instruction, team teaching, and competency-based teacher training in poverty area schools. The Committee believes that the Teacher Corps should have the authority to support demonstration projects retraining present educational staffs in these techniques, in addition to supporting the teacher-intern program in such schools [National Advisory Council on Education Professions Development, 1975, p. 3].

As an experimental program, not always viewed with favor in professional teaching circles, the Teacher Corps has been the subject of a number of evaluations (see especially National Advisory Council on Education Professions Development, 1975; Corwin, 1973; and Comptroller General of the United States, 1972). The program has been successful in attracting trainees from minority populations (in 1972, for example, 61 percent of interns were members of minority groups). Moreover, most of the trainees stay in the field of education and take teaching positions in poverty areas. Some evaluations have shown Teacher Corps graduates to be more effective than control groups of teachers both in terms of teaching skills and the progress of their pupils. In other respects, however, the results have been less encouraging, especially in bringing about reform in teacher training. Several studies found that institutions of higher education tended to isolate their Teacher Corps projects from normal teacher training programs and to be inflexible in their curricula and procedures.

The positive results of the Teacher Corps program, however, have been sufficiently impressive to warrant, not only its continuation, but also a gradual increase in funding for the program in the coming years.

Recommendation 25: *The federal government should continue to support the Teacher Corps, and the appropriation for the program should be increased from $37.5 million in 1979-80 to $40 million (in constant dollars) in 1980-81.*

The Training of Administrators

If there is one thing that comes out clearly in studies of problems in the schools, it is that the leadership of the principal is probably the most important single factor in explaining whether the schools are meeting their problems successfully or not. The studies tend to be less informative on just what qualities go to make an effective principal or on what kinds of training effective principals have had.

Other administrators are also important, of course, especially the superintendent, but the principal is the one who is in a position to stimulate or discourage high motivation on the part of the teachers and to know just where to draw the line between firmness and permissiveness in handling discipline problems and disruptions.

We believe that administrators should have had teaching experience and should normally come back to institutions of higher education for advanced training in administration after some years of teaching experience, as is the prevailing practice. We also believe that the training of administrators should include a combination of training in an academic subject matter field, educational philosophy, and management. At the stage of advanced training, management should be emphasized and should not take place exclusively in a school of education. Joint programs should be developed between the school of education and the school of business administration or a school of public administration or public policy.

An understanding of the changing social environment of schools, especially in large cities, is just as crucial for administrators as for teachers.

Recommendation 26: *Schools of education should give special attention to improving the training of school administrators, especially by giving preference to candidates for advanced degrees who have had varied types of teaching experience, and by developing programs in school management in cooperation with schools of business or public administration.*

Training Community Coordinators

If work-education councils are to be effective and if communities are to surmount the many obstacles to coordination of efforts, especially in large cities, trained community coordinators are needed. These persons should understand the economics and sociology of poverty, should know enough about industrial relations to work effectively with employer and union groups, and should know enough about problems of contemporary secondary schools to work effectively with school officials. Institutions of higher education, especially larger universities, should consider developing special interdisciplinary programs at the master's level for such training.[2]

Recommendation 27: *Universities should develop interdisciplinary programs at the master's level for training community coordinators of programs for youth.*

---

[2]We are indebted to Stephen K. Bailey, professor of education, Harvard University, for this suggestion.

11

Notation on
Costs and Methods
of Financing

Needs of Secondary Schools

School finance in the United States is in trouble. The traditional reliance on the local real property tax as the main source of financing of public schools is breaking down as a result of (1) court decisions following the lead of *Serrano* v. *Priest* (California Supreme Court, 1971), which declared that heavy reliance on local property taxes was unconstitutional because it denied equal protection of the law to children living in poor school districts; (2) revolts of local taxpayers who have refused to vote for school tax measures and who voted in large majorities for the property-tax-slashing Proposition 13 in California and some similar measures in other states; (3) the ills of the central cities, which have forced the schools to fight a difficult and frequently losing battle for local funds in competition with welfare and law enforcement costs; (4) the unionization of teachers, which, especially in an environment of rapid inflation, has resulted in the flow of a large proportion of any increases in school district funds into increased compensation for teachers and administrators; and (5) other impacts of inflation on school costs.

The declining school enrollments, which might have been expected to help free funds for increased expenditure per pupil, have not had that result in many communities, because state support and some federal allocations are based on Average Daily Attendance (ADA) and tend to decline, at least in constant dollars, when enrollment falls.

Figure 18 shows how sources of school financing have changed since 1919-20. The periods of greatest increases in the share of the states were the depression decade of the 1930s, when local finances were in deep trouble; World War II, when state aid was desperately needed to meet the problems of localities that experienced explosive population growth because of the presence of war industries or military installations; and the

Figure 18. Percentages of revenues of public elementary and secondary schools from federal, state, and local sources, United States, 1919-20 to 1977-78

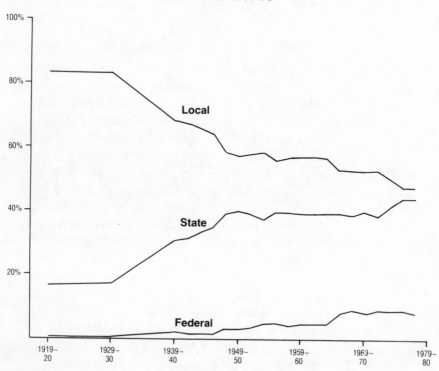

Source: U.S. National Center for Education Statistics (1978a, p. 67; 1979, table 4.3).

mid-1970s, when the most important influence was probably the judicial decisions calling for greater state equalization. Many of the states have also allocated sizable proportions of federal general revenue sharing funds to support of the schools. The federal share, which historically was practically nonexistent, went up somewhat after World War II and again in the mid-1960s, but in the 1970s it has leveled off at around 8 percent.

Despite these broad trends, there is enormous variation from state to state in the distribution of sources. The southern states, with their low-income populations, tend to receive the largest shares from the federal government, reflecting the fact that the main thrust of federal aid to elementary and secondary education is to encourage increased expenditures on the disadvantaged. State shares vary enormously, with the highest percentage (87.2 percent) in Hawaii, which requires no local contribution, and the lowest (9.5 percent) in New Hampshire, which has a long tradition of reluctance to impose state taxes. In between these extremes, there is great variation, with some tendency for the state share to be relatively high in the South. The local share is well above the national average in a number of states in the Northeast and Middle West (U.S. National Center for Education Statistics, 1978a, p. 66).

If state effort is measured in terms of state and local expenditures (combined) as a percentage of state personal income, differences among the states are also very wide, ranging from 2.9 percent in the District of Columbia to 6.9 percent in Alaska in 1976-77. The relationship between the comparative affluence of a state and the percentage of personal income spent on the public schools, however, follows no consistent pattern. As the National Center for Education Statistics points out in the caption on Figure 19 one-half of the states with above average state-local expenditures as a percentage of personal income are below the average in per capita personal income. Figure 19 also shows the comparatively larger federal contribution in such poor states as New Mexico, South Carolina, Louisiana, Alabama, Mississippi, and the District of Columbia (here treated as a state).

Despite the movement toward disproportionately large

**Figure 19. Revenue of public schools as a percentage of
personal income, by state, 1976-77**

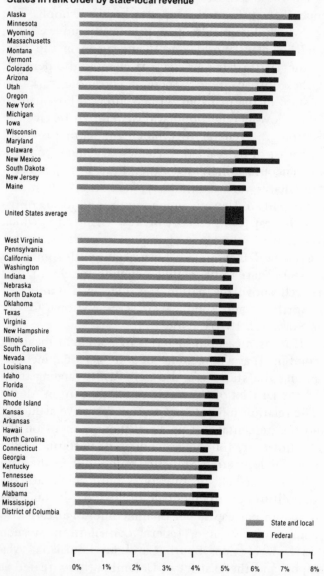

States in rank order by state-local revenue

Alaska
Minnesota
Wyoming
Massachusetts
Montana
Vermont
Colorado
Arizona
Utah
Oregon
New York
Michigan
Iowa
Wisconsin
Maryland
Delaware
New Mexico
South Dakota
New Jersey
Maine

United States average

West Virginia
Pennsylvania
California
Washington
Indiana
Nebraska
North Dakota
Oklahoma
Texas
Virginia
New Hampshire
Illinois
South Carolina
Nevada
Louisiana
Idaho
Florida
Ohio
Rhode Island
Kansas
Arkansas
Hawaii
North Carolina
Connecticut
Georgia
Kentucky
Tennessee
Missouri
Alabama
Mississippi
District of Columbia

▨ State and local
■ Federal

0%   1%   2%   3%   4%   5%   6%   7%   8%

Note: Of the 20 states above the U.S. average in public schools revenue receipts from
state and local sources, one-half are below the average in per capital personal income.

Source: U.S. National Center for Education Statistics (1979, chart 4.5).

state aid for poorer local school districts, disparities in expenditures *within* states also remain pronounced. In 1977, the range was from no disparity in Hawaii, where the system is wholly state-financed, to an index of 2.2 in Massachusetts, indicating that a school district near the top in terms of expenditures per pupil spent more than twice as much as a district near the bottom. Other states with large disparities (indexes ranging from 1.81 to 1.97) were Nebraska, South Dakota, New Hampshire, Maine, Ohio, Delaware, New Jersey, Illinois, Georgia, Vermont, New York, and Tennessee (U.S. National Center for Education Statistics, 1979, table 4.13).

It is not as true today as when Conant wrote *Slums and Suburbs* (1961) that funding of inner-city schools is woefully inadequate compared with funding of schools in the suburbs. Data comparing the situation in 1967-68 with that in 1974-75 show that the ratio of per-pupil revenues in large-city school systems to average per-pupil revenues in their states increased from 0.95 in the former year to 1.13 in the latter. The change was in large part attributable to a relatively big increase in the flow of federal funds to large-city school systems through Title I of the Elementary and Secondary Education Act (ESEA) and through the school lunch program (U.S. National Center for Education Statistics, 1978c, p. 78).

However, there are several reasons for believing that elementary schools have benefited more than secondary schools from the change. For one thing, the bulk of Title I funds goes to elementary schools. For another, in view of the evidence of more serious problems of violence and related problems in secondary schools, it seems probable that security costs absorb larger proportions of school funds at the secondary level. Experts on school finance tend to believe that secondary schools, which have higher costs per pupil than elementary schools, are relatively squeezed.

Redressing the Balance

We have noted that college youth have been assisted by federal initiatives in the 1970s far more than noncollege youth and that it is time to redress the balance. There has been a tendency in the 1970s, and especially in the last few years, to increase fed-

eral expenditures on manpower programs for youth administered by the U.S. Department of Labor more than on support
to schools administered by HEW. Total federal expenditures on
manpower programs increased from about $1.5 billion in fiscal
year 1971 to about $7 billion in fiscal year 1979 and a recom-
mended $6.8 billion in the administration budget for fiscal year
1980 (The President, 1972, p. 261; *The Budget,* 1979, p. 644).
Largely as a result of the enactment of YEDPA in 1977, more
than $2 billion of the $7 billion spent in fiscal year 1979 was
for special programs for youth, and a certain proportion (perhaps 30 percent) of the balance flowed to young people.[1]

Of course, all of these increases were much less pronounced in constant dollars. For example, the increase in federal undergraduate student aid expenditures was about 500 percent in current dollars, compared with 250 percent in constant
dollars. But all of the appropriations were affected similarly by
inflation.

It is not the purpose of this section to undertake a thorough discussion of all of the issues in school financing. The
comprehensive study by Reischauer and Hartman (1973) for
the Brookings Institution shows how varied the options at the
federal, state, and local institutions are for reform in school
finance. We shall confine our discussion to certain general prin-
ciples and to a recapitulation of certain specific suggestions for
new or adjusted expenditures made in preceding sections.

Social Cost-Benefit Considerations

Despite the tax revolt and the numerous instances of defeat of
school tax measures, a nationwide public opinion survey by the
National Opinion Research Center in 1978 indicated that 51.6
percent of the respondents thought too little was being spent on
education. About 33 percent thought expenditures were "about
right," while only 11 percent thought too much was being spent

---

[1]We refer here only to funds allocated for the Comprehensive Employment and
Training Administration (CETA). Under a broader definition of federal manpower
programs, including the public employment service, occupational health and safety,
and so on, the total would be larger.

for this purpose. The percentage who thought too little was being spent on health was slightly larger (55.4 percent), but only 15 percent thought too little was being spent on foreign aid and defense, and only 13 percent thought too little was being spent on welfare. The proportion who thought too much was being spent on welfare was large (58.2 percent) and had increased considerably since 1974 (U.S. National Center for Education Statistics, 1979, table 4.1). These results are consistent with surveys conducted shortly after the passage of Proposition 13 in California, which indicated that welfare expenditures were particularly resented by the voters. It seems likely that most of the Californians who voted for Proposition 13 did not realize that the chief losers would be the school districts (along with the community college districts). The campaign in favor of the measure placed its chief emphasis on the "waste and fat" in government that could be cut out if taxes were reduced.

Clearly, there is a critical need to call attention to the heavy expenditures for property damage, personal injury, and law enforcement that are associated with failure to meet the problems of the secondary schools, especially in the inner city. We also noted in Section 3 the large proportion of AFDC recipients who had experienced teenage pregnancies.

Adequate estimates of the savings that might result from pronounced changes in school structure are, of course, not available, particularly since the efficacy of such changes on costs associated with juvenile delinquency or welfare dependency cannot be estimated with any degree of precision.

Probably the most promising and direct way in which certain types of expenditures could produce benefits that would more than offset their costs would be through a more effective attack on chronic truancy. The study by the Economic Development Council of New York City (1977), discussed in Section 2, showed that a large majority of the Youth Division-1 citations (YD-1 are juvenile criminal activities other than felonies, unlawful assembly, or serious misdemeanors) in the city were issued during school hours, when the offenders should have been in school. Other evidence has indicated that many of the acts of violence committed in and around the schools are the work of nonstudents—dropouts, chronic truants, and others. The Economic Development Council estimated that school-age youths in the city stole or destroyed property worth $234 million and that the public and private costs of controlling youth crime came to another $277 million in 1976.

That absenteeism can be greatly reduced when a sustained effort is made, the council's report showed, is illustrated by the experience of Brandeis High School, a predominantly low-income, minority group school. In 1970, when its efforts began, about 26 percent of its students were reported absent each day. One of the problems its program had to face was that some students who did not show up in their homerooms where daily attendance was taken did attend one or more recitation classes on the same day, a phenomenon that greatly complicated adequate record keeping. Thus, the school adopted a system of record keeping under which each teacher recorded the absence of any student from a homeroom or a class on a special form, which was turned in and fed directly into a computer each day. The following morning all teachers were given a report on each class listing absentees and cuts from the previous day, and, in addition, a weekly report of cuts and absences was provided to the attendance and deans' offices, who notified the parents. The result was an 11 percent increase in average daily attendance from 1969-70 to 1975-76, as well as increased support from the parents for the school's efforts to improve attendance.

It is not clear, however, that these efforts had a positive effect on what was being learned by the chronic truants. Merely enforcing attendance in big-city high schools, without other changes, may reduce juvenile delinquency without greatly improving the probability that the young people involved will graduate with an adequate education and a better chance to escape lifetime patterns of unemployment and crime.

Thus, the changes in school structure discussed in Section 8 seem important, *along* with efforts to overcome the problem of chronic truancy.

That reforms in school structure will eventually reduce the prison population is a proposition that is not capable of proof, especially in view of the fact that the size of the prison population depends a great deal on criminal justice policies (National Council on Crime and Delinquency, 1978; Silberman, 1978). Even so, it is instructive to consider the relative costs involved, because they give some idea of the order of magnitude of the savings that *could* result from giving more young people a better start in life. According to Hoyt (1977, p. 50), the average per-pupil cost in the New York City school system was $2,647 in 1977—he was unable to get a breakdown for elementary and secondary schools. Data for the nation as a whole indicate average per-pupil expenditures on public schools of about $1,700 in 1975-76, with state-by-state expenditures ranging from $1,072 in Mississippi to $2,580 in New York (U.S. National Center for Education Statistics, 1978a, table 73). (Alaska, however, with expenditures far above those of any other state, was actually at the top, with an average of $3,710.)

Costs of maintaining an inmate in an adult state prison vary greatly from one state to another. The average for adult state prisons in 1976 was $9,439 a year per prisoner, but in some states the cost exceeded $20,000 per prisoner (National Council on Crime and Delinquency, 1978, p. 7).

According to experts on juvenile delinquency, costs of juvenile institutionalization tend to be higher than prison costs, because more is spent on rehabilitative services for juveniles. An Arthur D. Little (1977) report covering ten states showed costs on an annual basis in correctional facilities ranging from $12,500 in Florida to $26,000 in New York, while costs in other types of detention facilities were in some cases lower and in some cases higher, and costs in so-called "residential alternatives" were uniformly lower. Interestingly, however, Illinois data for 1978 showed direct costs in relatively informal community-based programs for juvenile delinquents of $13,000, compared with $14,000 in institutions maintained by the Department of Corrections; but, when costs were adjusted to allow for costs when juveniles had to be transferred from community-based programs to correctional facilities and for costs of processing offenses, the community-based annual costs turned out to be $19,500 compared with $17,500 for the correctional facilities. We have used an annual figure of $18,000 in Section 1 as a reasonably representative cost estimate.[2]

Incarceration costs are by no means, of course, the only social costs resulting from dropping out, failure to graduate with basic skills, and patterns of juvenile delinquency. Other social costs include:

* Costs associated with unemployment of the young people involved and with patterns of unemployment that persist through life, particularly unemployment insurance.
* Costs of welfare dependency.
* Lost tax revenue.
* Costs of damage to property and injury to persons.
* Law enforcement costs.

The Federal Role

There is a strong case for increased federal expenditures on secondary schools, even though massive new programs are unlikely to receive support in the present climate of tax revolt. As we have pointed out in earlier reports in discussing the case for federal aid to higher education: (1) the federal government, for constitutional and other reasons, has a special responsibility for encouraging equality of opportunity; (2) the federal tax structure is more equitable and more capable of generating increasing revenues with rising income than are state and local tax structures (though the contrasts are less glaring than they were a few years ago, as more states adopt income taxes and as state fiscal systems generate budgetary surpluses); and (3) federal expenditures can contribute to equalization of expenditures among the states, with their wide disparities in income levels. Beyond these

---

[2]We are indebted to Diana R. Gordon, vice president, and Mary Ann Zimmerman-McKinney, research associate, National Council on Crime and Delinquency, for providing data and reports on costs of adult prisons and juvenile institutionalization. The Arthur D. Little report gave costs on a daily basis, while the Illinois report gave them on a monthly basis. We have converted the data to an annual basis, but it should be recognized that juveniles are frequently placed in institutions for only short periods.

considerations, federal initiative can be framed in such a way as to stimulate changes in school policies and structures in an environment in which strong forces tend to maintain and preserve the status quo in school systems.

In the preceding sections, we have recommended certain immediate increases in federal expenditures to benefit secondary education, while also proposing that these amounts be increased in some cases as administrative structures develop and state and local school systems become adapted to them. These increases are summarized in Table 3.

Recommendations for certain other budgetary allocations will follow in later sections.

The State Role

The state role in the financing of secondary schools will, of course, continue to be important, and the state share in overall financing of the public schools is likely to increase under the influence of the various forces mentioned earlier that are contributing to the crisis in school financing.

We believe that the states should exercise strong leadership in bringing about the kinds of changes that have been discussed in this report. In fact, without strong state leadership, the changes, especially as they relate to school structure, are unlikely to occur. The states will play a particularly important role in implementing the changes in the allocation of vocational education funds that we have recommended. In fact, since state vocational education funds are far larger than is required by federal matching formulas, the states can move much farther in the direction of reallocation of vocational education funds than our recommendations for changes in federal matching policies would require.

Many of the states have enjoyed budgetary surpluses in the last few years, and, while the fiscal position of the states may weaken during the present recession, the long-term fiscal outlook for the states for the 1980s is favorable for several reasons: (1) some of the states that had regressive tax structures have recently adopted income taxes that bring in relatively more revenue with rising incomes; (2) federal general revenue sharing

Table 3. Selected federal youth programs: Carnegie Council
recommendations for new or reallocated expenditures, 1980-81
compared with 1979-80 (in millions of constant [1979] dollars)

Programs	Administration budget for 1979-80[a]	Council recommendation for 1980-81
U.S. Department of Health, Education and Welfare		
Increased funds for secondary schools under Title I, Elementary and Secondary Education Act	$3,478.0	$3,978.0
Vocational education—change name of act to Occupational Skills and Work-Study Act; add $300 million for work-study and reallocate $300 million for 75 percent matching grants for work experience, cooperative education, and related programs	682.0	982.0
Fund for the Improvement of Postsecondary Education—increase allocated for programs of colleges and universities to aid disadvantaged youth	14.0	20.0
Teacher Corps	37.5	40.0
Push for Excellence	1.0	2.0
Trio Programs	130.0	150.0
Total for selected programs	$4,342.5	$5,172.0
Net increase		$ 829.5

[a]In some cases, the final budget figure may differ from that recommended by the administration, as a result of congressional action.

Source: *The Budget,* 1979; Carnegie Council recommendations.

has helped and will probably not be cut off completely, although Congress has lately shown a disposition to reduce amounts going to the states; (3) not only support of education, but also other types of state expenditures are population-related and will benefit from a declining rate of population growth.

Therefore, we believe that there is a strong case for increased state support for the public schools and for particular attention to improving the quality of the secondary schools. At the same time, we urge that state aid not be given in such a way as to impair local control of the schools.

Recommendation 28: *The states should take advantage of declining enrollment growth by increasing state aid to local school districts, with particular attention to the needs of secondary schools. States that are below the national average in the percentage of personal income flowing to the public schools have a special need to review their school financing policies.*

Part III

Employment

12

Current
Reform Proposals

During the past two decades, the United States has gradually placed increasing emphasis on an array of what used to be called "manpower" programs but now usually are called employment and training or labor market programs. Prior to 1962 such programs had been neglected, except in time of war, although a number of other industrial countries, notably Sweden, had been emphasizing labor market policies throughout most of the postwar period. The high unemployment rate that prevailed in the first few years of the Kennedy administration, however, led to demands for more active labor market policies, and then Secretary of Labor Arthur Goldberg, with other Labor Department officials, went abroad to investigate programs of retraining the unemployed in several countries of western Europe. There followed enactment of the Manpower Development and Training Act of 1962 (MDTA) that authorized a program of training and retraining programs for the unemployed.

At the time, a major debate was under way about the causes of the persistent unemployment problem. Was it attributable primarily to a deficiency of aggregate demand, as the Council of Economic Advisers maintained, or to structural changes in the economy, as some labor economists, notably Charles Killingsworth (1966), argued? Concern about the labor displacement effects of automation was widespread and figured prominently in explaining the position of the structuralists. As time went on, especially after the tax cut of 1964 appeared to have decisive results in stimulating the economy and bringing down the unemployment rate, participants in the debate came closer to a consensus that recognized the overriding importance of policies to maintain aggregate demand, but at the same time they appreciated the need for manpower programs to meet the special needs of workers whose skills were obsolescent and to hold down the rate of inflation by overcoming bottlenecks in the economy attributable to shortages of workers with needed skills. Meanwhile, the fear of automation abated somewhat, as various case studies of the impact of introduction of automated equipment showed that total employment in the enterprises was often maintained or even increased, even though shifts occurred in the types of skills needed.

As the Vietnam War escalated, however, and the overall unemployment rate fell to the lowest levels since the Korean War, the persistence of severe pockets of unemployment, especially in inner-city areas, gave rise to growing concern. The U.S. Bureau of Labor Statistics conducted intensive surveys in ghetto areas in the latter half of the 1960s, which revealed a persistent and serious problem of unemployment and underemployment in those areas. Meanwhile, the unemployment rate of youth and of new entrants to the labor market without previous work experience had risen sharply since the early 1960s, and the rates were particularly alarming among minority group youth.

All of this led to a gradual change in policies that gave the primary emphasis to the disadvantaged in the MDTA program— a change that, in fact, was stimulated not only by the changing patterns of unemployment but also by the war on poverty.

In 1973, MDTA was replaced by the Comprehensive Employment and Training program (CETA), under which the federal government would largely replace federally administered programs by grants to states and local communities that would be responsible for designing and administering their own employment and training programs for the disadvantaged. In other words, the 1973 act inaugurated a policy of decentralization.

Although program participants in MDTA and in CETA

programs, prior to enactment of the Youth Employment and Demonstration Project Act of 1977 (YEDPA), were predominantly relatively youthful, the programs were not aimed to any large extent at teenagers. From 1963 to 1973, only 14 percent of enrollees in MDTA institutional training programs were under 19 years of age, while about 25 percent were aged 19 to 21 and 38 percent were in the 22- to 34-age bracket—in other words, more than three-fourths were under 35 (The President, 1974, table F-5). Two of the MDTA programs, however, were largely or wholly intended for teenagers. One of these was the Job Corps, a comparatively small program that was specifically designed for severely disadvantaged school dropouts and in which 79 percent of the enrollees in fiscal 1973 were under 19 years of age (The President, 1974, table F-10). The other was the Neighborhood Youth Corps, which, as we noted in Section 6, provided summer employment for a large number of predominantly high school youth but also served relatively small numbers of both in-school and out-of-school youth during the school year.

On the whole, prior to the 1977 act, the youth served by both MDTA and CETA were primarily school dropouts. It was assumed that most vocational education for youth would take place under regular school programs. Under CETA, however, the emphasis on in-school youth gradually increased somewhat, and a school-to-work transition program was inaugurated, involving a number of pilot projects, including the Vocational Exploration Program, which began in summer 1976 in cooperation with a number of large corporations (The President, 1977, p. 53).

Even though both the overall unemployment rate and the youth unemployment rate fell as the economy recovered from the 1974-75 recession, a disturbingly high youth unemployment rate continued, especially among minority-group youth in inner cities. It was concern over this persistent problem that led to enactment of YEDPA. The act embodied a number of ideas that had been proposed by groups concerned with employment policy and provided for four programs. We have already discussed the Youth Incentive Entitlement Pilot Projects and the

218   *Giving Youth a Better Chance*

Youth Employment and Training Programs in Section 6. The legislation also provided for the Youth Adult Conservation Corps, with an initial allocation of $233 million, and the Youth Community Conservation and Improvement Projects, for which $115 million was appropriated. The total initial allocation under YEDPA amounted to nearly $1 billion. Total expenditures on youth programs by the Employment and Training Administration (ETA) of the U.S. Department of Labor rose from $1.4 billion in fiscal year 1978 to $2.2 billion in fiscal year 1979. However, expenditures on all programs administered by ETA also rose sharply—from $4.7 billion to $7.1 billion (*The Budget,* 1979, p. 644). Thus, the increase in the percentage spent on youth programs was quite moderate—from 29 to 31 percent.

A thorough review of all of the existing labor market programs for youth and of the large and proliferating literature evaluating those programs would be beyond the scope of this report. In this section, we summarize the recommendations of several important recent reports on labor market policies, and in the next section we recommend certain changes or new emphases in policy that we favor. The reports that will be reviewed are as follows:

* Committee for Economic Development (CED). *Jobs for the Hard-to-Employ: New Directions for a Public-Private Partnership.* New York: 1978.
* National Child Labor Committee and National Urban League. *Toward a National Youth Development Policy (A Call to Action).* New York: 1978.
* National Commission for Manpower Policy. *An Employment Strategy for the United States: Next Steps.* Second Annual Report to The President and the Congress. Washington, D.C.: 1976.
* Organization for Economic Cooperation and Development (OECD). *Education and Working Life in Modern Society.* A Report of the Secretary-General's Ad Hoc Group on the Relations Between Education and Employment. (Clark Kerr, Chairman.) Paris: 1975.
* Work in America Institute, Inc. *Job Strategies for Urban*

Youth: Sixteen Pilot Programs in Action. Scarsdale, N.Y.: 1979.

Some of these reports cut across school and employment policies, but they are included here, rather than in Section 4, because the reports summarized in Section 4 are concerned much more with school policies. Unlike the school reports, these labor market documents differ substantially, especially with regard to their relative emphasis on job creation in the public sector versus greater involvement of the private sector in employment and training programs for youth. We therefore summarize the most important recommendations in each report separately, since any attempt to present a consolidated summary would be misleading.

The CED Report

The CED report, as its title implies, emphasized greater involvement of the private sector in programs to train and employ the disadvantaged, who are defined as:

- Undereducated, unskilled, or inexperienced.
- Considered too young or too old.
- Unable to work full time.
- Subject to discrimination or restrictive labor market practices.
- Lacking the basic work disciplines and abilities necessary to get and hold a steady job.

The major recommendations (including only those that are applicable to youth) were as follows:

1. New and expanded use, on a nationwide basis, of programs in the private sector that already work effectively, and creation of a clearinghouse for disseminating information about successful and innovative programs.
2. Strengthening of organizational mechanisms to mobilize private-sector involvement, including wider use of
   —Direct government manpower contracts with private nonprofit organizations created by consortia of business firms

(as exemplified by a program in Chicago that was described
in an accompanying report summarizing case studies of private-sector programs—Robison, 1978).

—Other types of intermediary organizations that can help
business handle job development, training, and placement
activities.

—Jobs corporations to provide training and jobs for the hard-
to-employ.

—Cooperative community efforts, involving businesses, nonprofit organizations, unions, schools, and governments, to
increase training and job opportunities.

3. Increased incentives and reduced disincentives for private employment of the hard-to-employ, including additional experiments with categorical tax credits, with stipends for trainees
and apprentices, and with selective exemptions from the
minimum wage and from increased social security earnings
ceilings.

4. Improved approaches to the problems of particular groups of
the hard-to-employ, including

—Increased stress on business involvement in skill training
and upgrading of the disadvantaged.

—Improved transition from school to work for youths as well
as for other age groups, including increased use of apprenticeships and cooperative education programs.

—Increased and wider use of alternative work patterns to
make more employment available to the young, the old,
and other workers who cannot conform to a full-time work
schedule.

5. Greater business use of alternatives to outright layoffs in recessions, including skill upgrading and work sharing.

6. Improved management and closer integration of government
programs that facilitate the employment of the hard-to-
employ, particularly the U.S. Employment Service and the
CETA programs.

The National Child Labor Committee
and National Urban League Report

With major emphasis on a National Youth Development Program, this report calls for the most comprehensive set of poli-

cies of any of the reports reviewed here, with estimated expenditures when fully developed of $12 billion by the federal government and $6 billion by private employers. The report, however, estimates offsets to the federal government of $9 billion in savings on existing education, employment, training, and income maintenance programs, and in increased tax revenues. Thus, the net costs of the youth development programs to the federal government would be $3 billion. There would also be offsets to private employers in the form of goods and services produced by employed youth, but no estimate is made of these offsets.

The most important features of the youth development program would be as follows:

- A program open to all youth from the ages of 14 to 21 to prepare them for employment in the primary labor market by providing integrating work experience, occupational training, and associated education, generating the needed jobs, and providing individual counseling and placement. The program would operate under existing state educational systems and could be melded into the traditional local educational structure when that structure is able to administer the proposed program.
- Compensation of the youths at rates meeting or exceeding the minimum wage, with employers receiving partial reimbursement for their training costs.
- Provision of most of the funds, along with technical and other assistance by the federal government, but with administration of the program by state and local governments.
- Emphasis on real and productive work, geared to meeting the standards and opportunities of the private sector.
- A cooperative federal-state-local system to serve as the overall coordinating agency for the entire program and as the primary linkage to the labor market, providing employment opportunities for in-school youths and a voluntary work interlude between high school and college.
- Gradual phasing-in of the program, starting in metropolitan areas that need it most and are able to undertake it and extending it to the entire nation over an 11-year period.

The National Commission for Manpower Policy

The National Commission for Manpower Policy was established under the provisions of the Concentrated Employment and Training Act of 1973. It has issued four annual reports and a number of special reports, but its second annual report is selected for discussion here, because it included a set of recommendations on youth employment policy, as follows:

* The conversion of the Youth Conservation Corps program from an eight-week summer program to a year-round training and work program for 50,000 young people from low-income families, particularly but not exclusively those from rural backgrounds.
* Establishment for 400,000 in-school youths of a year-round, skill-training, and work-experience program that can pay training stipends to disadvantaged youths who otherwise would be unprepared to obtain and keep jobs when they leave school.
* The expansion of training and employment programs for out-of-school unemployed youths between the ages of 18 and 24 who are so discouraged that they have ceased looking for work. The commission recommended a program that would serve 250,000 youths.
* Establishment by The President of an interagency committee to plan training and manpower services for young veterans, especially those from minority groups, and appropriation by Congress of funds that would be required by the Department of Defense to help prepare prospective returnees for the transition to civilian life.

The OECD Report

In addition to a group of general recommendations calling for improvements in the quality of working life, special assistance for the disadvantaged, equal access to education and training opportunities for both sexes, and a bill of rights for migrants, the OECD report made, among others, the following recommendations:

- A fund for continuing education, with contributions by government and private enterprises.
- Reduction of social security payments for young employees.
- Student aid for low-income, upper-secondary students.
- Arrangements that strengthen the rights of young workers to educational leave, both for vocational and educational purposes.
- Development of a modern form of apprenticeship, which overcomes the weaknesses associated with traditional apprenticeship and is so organized that there are possibilities for apprentices to proceed to higher education.
- Development in Europe of more opportunities for publicly supported, part-time work for students, along the lines of the College Work-Study program in the United States.
- Liberalization of entry into higher education in European countries where only graduates of academic secondary schools have been admitted, as well as policies that permit deferral of entry until young people have gained work or social service experience.
- Development of more opportunities for students in upper-secondary schools to gain work experience through incentives for industrial, commercial, and administrative enterprises, public and private, to develop practical projects with pedagogical value for students.
- More opportunities, also, for alternation between school and work.
- Endorsement of the concept of recurrent education.

The Work in America Institute Report

As its subtitle, *Sixteen Pilot Programs for Action,* indicates, the Work in America Institute report is entirely concerned with proposals for pilot projects in selected communities that are intended as demonstration projects to be replicated on a broader scale if they are successful. The proposals have been presented to the Secretary of Labor, who has expressed enthusiasm for them and has the authority to approve at least some of the individual projects under provisions of existing CETA legislation that gives him discretionary funds for certain purposes and provides for experimental and demonstration projects. The pilot projects are as follows:

- To increase incentives for employment in entry-level jobs, a sample of youth and employers would be exempted from social security taxes for up to six months.
- To increase the incentive to work, disadvantaged youth earning less than $3.00 an hour would be exempted from all income taxes in a selected city during one calendar year.
- As an incentive for youth to seek and hold entry-level jobs, a sample of young people would be granted taxfree cash awards for staying on the job, at three intervals within the first six months of employment.
- To help connect inner-city youth with jobs available throughout the metropolitan area, a pilot project would eliminate cost disincentives and arrange transportation services, through such devices as free passes on existing routes, shuttle services to areas with large factories or other large establishments outside of the city, and the like.
- A pilot youth development corporation would be established to find ways to create youth-operated enterprises.
- A contract-service organization would be created to provide full-time jobs to young people through regularizing odd jobs and providing opportunities for upward mobility to youth who were given practice in managing the program.
- A temporary employment service, modeled on Manpower, Inc., would enable employers to hire disadvantaged youths on a test basis for up to three months without an immediate permanent commitment and/or hire them for strictly short-term assignments.
- Jobs for Youth and Vocational Foundation, Inc. (two programs that specialize in placing severely disadvantaged youth) would share their know-how with other agencies that want to follow suit. (We discuss Vocational Foundation, Inc., in Section 14.)
- Youthful exoffenders would be assisted in the transition to

private employment through a program modeled on that of the Safer Foundation in Chicago, which has an astonishingly low rate of recidivism.

- A strategy would be developed for more widespread replication of industrial skills-training centers like the particularly successful Training and Technology program at Oak Ridge, Tennessee, and the Hampden District Regional Skills Center in Springfield, Massachusetts.

- In a middle-sized industrial city, an experiment would be carried out involving pooling of the resources of a variety of community agencies to develop training and placement programs for disadvantaged out-of-school youths.

- A community-based experience reference service would compile for youthful jobseekers an experience report that summarizes and certifies the youth's developmental experiences during high school and afterward.

- Pilot programs would be created within the community-college structure that combine private employment and education for out-of-school, inner-city youth as a step toward career opportunities.

- The job-development strategies followed by ten highly effective agencies would be analyzed and compared.

- A program that would recruit, select, train, and employ between 100 and 200 disadvantaged urban youth would be organized in each of the ten federal regions in a variety of federal agencies.

- Several programs in which inner-city youth would be given internships in the civilian sector and others would be given a preparatory period in the military sector of the U.S. Department of Defense.

- Small groups of young people from the inner city would develop public-service projects to be performed in their neighborhoods and receive funding to carry them out from a public service initiatives board that is broadly representative of the community.

As we have listed them, there are 17 pilot projects, rather

than the 16 indicated by the title of the report, because the first two projects that we have listed are treated as a single project by Work in America Institute.

Mention should also be made of *The Boundless Resource* by Willard Wirtz and the National Manpower Institute (1975), with its emphasis on the formation of work-education councils, which we discussed in Section 6.

13

Better Paths
into Labor Markets

Broad Strategies

Until recently, most of the emphasis in labor market policies for youth, as we have seen, was on programs for disadvantaged out-of-school youth. Under YEDPA, we are beginning to see the development of programs that are primarily or partially concerned with in-school youth. If such programs are successful in preventing dropping out and decreasing the number.of youths who leave school without basic skills, it should be possible to reduce the emphasis on programs for out-of-school youth gradually as time goes on. Thus, we favor a long-term strategy that places increasing relative emphasis on in-school youth *and* that strengthens the ties—until recently almost nonexistent—between education and labor market policies for youth. Both education and labor market policies should also be integrated with a youth service program, to be discussed in the last portion of this report.

Some of the specific policies carried out under YEDPA, particularly the Youth Incentive Entitlement Pilot Projects, are being evaluated, and the final results of evaluations will undoubtedly have an important bearing on the future development of labor market policies for youth. Meanwhile, in preparation for renewal of YEDPA, a White House task force under the chairmanship of Vice-President Walter F. Mondale is scheduled to complete its report in October 1979.

Because the economy is currently moving into a recession, it may be essential in the short run to increase expenditures on programs for out-of-school youth, even though that may not be the most desirable long-run strategy. For this reason, we recommend a range of expenditures on labor market programs for youth in Section 15, with the actual appropriation for 1980-81 to be related to the youth unemployment situation in 1980.

Measures to Increase Labor Market Demand

In Section 2, we discussed barriers to the employment of youth. These include the high costs of employing youth, labor-protective measures, shifts in employment toward trade and service jobs that are often low paid and "dead end," and the movement of industry out of central cities. We believe that there are measures that can be taken—some new and some already in existence to some extent—that will increase the demand for youth.

Exempting Teenagers from Social Security Coverage

One means of decreasing the cost of employing youth—and *also* increasing their take-home pay—would be to exempt teenagers from social security coverage. The method would probably be politically more acceptable than adoption of a subminimum wage for youth, because it would not interfere with the principle of the standard wage, to which organized labor attaches great importance. Teenagers would not lose valuable benefits through exemption, because they would have the rest of their working lives to accumulate contributions toward retirement. The only potential loss would be in case of permanent and total nonoccupational disability, which is unlikely at this age, and for which in any case there is protection in the public assistance program. Occupational disability, which is a more serious hazard for youth, would still be protected under workmen's compensation laws.[1]

---

[1]The social security provision for benefits to children of eligible deceased, retired, or disabled workers who have been permanently and totally disabled since before age 18 would not be affected by the exemption, since these benefits derive from a parent's coverage.

The saving to the employer would be (under 1979 contribution rates) 6.13 percent of the wage paid to the teenager. This is not a large percentage, but could be significant in inducing employers to hire youth, especially small employers to whom marginal savings in wage costs are important and also larger employers if accompanied by other savings, such as exemption from pension plans.

The saving to the teenager would also be 6.13 percent of gross pay, or slightly more than 10 percent of net take-home pay. Increasing the take-home pay of teenagers would (1) possibly increase his or her job tenure by making the pay more attractive, (2) increase the amount that might be available to tide the young person over between jobs, and (3) reduce the alternative attraction of illicit earnings.

As the Work in America Institute has pointed out (1979, p. 17), under the National Pact for Employment launched by the French government in 1977, employers were granted exemption from social security taxes for up to a year for each employee under age 25, and the exemptions were tied to training programs. A year later, it was reported that youth unemployment had decreased by more than 5 percent, and aggregate unemployment had also decreased. However, a more recent report suggests that the policy resulted in little net job creation.[2] Whatever the actual results, the benefit to French employers was relatively large, because social security costs in France are paid chiefly through an employer payroll tax, which amounts to about 35 percent of wages and covers more types of social insurance than does the social security tax in the United States.

Under our proposal, there would be a net cost to the social security fund, because contributions on behalf of teenagers would no longer be paid, while teenagers seldom become eligible for benefits and thus cost the fund very little. However, since earnings of teenagers tend to be small, the loss to the fund would not be great—the increase in the taxable earnings base in

[2]This more recent report comes from the helpful comments on an earlier draft which we received from Beatrice Reubens and is based on her interview with a special assistant to the French prime minister in March 1979.

recent years to an amount far above typical annual earnings of teenagers tends to reduce the percentage of annual contributory payments that would be lost through exemption of teenagers. Data for a recent year indicate that teenagers (workers under age 20) earned only about 2 percent of the total estimated earnings of covered workers. Contributions on behalf of teenagers (if data were available) would amount to an even smaller percentage of total contributions, since earnings above the maximum taxable amount are included in total earnings (U.S. Social Security Administration, 1977, pp. 74-75).

The exemption should apply to all workers under the age of 20.

Recommendation 29: *Teenagers should be exempted from social security coverage.*

Involving the Private Sector

Ever since the Manpower Development and Training Act was adopted in 1962, there has been a program of federal subsidies to pay the *costs of training* incurred by employers who hire unemployed persons for on-the-job training under the program (now continued under CETA). The provisions were gradually liberalized to allow employers partial wage subsidies. On-the-job training (OJT) has played a fluctuating role in federal manpower programs, because employers have tended to increase their participation in the program during business upswings and to decrease it in downswings, when they tend to do little hiring. Thus, although OJT has certain advantages over institutional manpower training programs—lower subsidies and a greater likelihood that the trainee will be taken on as a permanent employee at the end of his training period—proposals to do away with institutional training and rely entirely on OJT have not gotten very far, because such a policy would be ineffective in recessions, when manpower programs are particularly needed as a countercyclical tool. Moreover, there is considerable evidence that employers "cream" by hiring the most qualified applicants in OJT programs, and thus it is frequently argued that OJT is not adequately targeted toward the disadvantaged.

Wage subsidies, under which the government picks up part of the cost of wages paid to an employee, are more controversial than training subsidies, especially if they are targeted on youth, because there is a danger that youths hired under the provisions will displace adults.[3] Organized labor tends to oppose wage subsidies payable for hiring youth for this reason, although it is not opposed to wage subsidies that are not so targeted.

In the 1970s and especially in the last few years, we have moved gradually toward wage subsidies for private employers, and the administration has indicated its intention of increasing emphasis on this approach under CETA in the future.[4] Yet past experience does not provide a basis for a high degree of optimism about the results.

The first full-fledged use of employment subsidies was introduced as part of the Revenue Act of 1971 and provided tax credits (equal to 20 percent of wages) for employers hiring welfare recipients enrolled in the WIN program (a manpower program for welfare recipients). The use of the program by employers has been minimal. More recently, Congress has approved a number of new types of wage subsidies, some of them targeted toward youth or other specified disadvantaged groups. The economic stimulus package of 1977 included a New Jobs Tax Credit designed to subsidize net nontargeted increases in private sector employment. The Youth Employment and Demonstration Projects Act of 1977 contained authorization for several new experiments to encourage the private sector to participate more actively in training and employing young people with labor market handicaps, including, as we have seen, a provision for 100 percent subsidization of wages under the Youth Incentive Entitlement program. The CETA amendments of 1978 contained a provision for a new Title VII designed to encourage more private sector involvement, including a mandatory provi-

[3]See, especially, the illuminating debate on the displacement issue in Rockefeller Foundation (1977).

[4]See, for example, a statement of Vice-President Mondale, May 19, 1978, quoted in National Commission for Manpower Policy (1978, p. 28).

sion for formation of private industry councils by prime sponsors. Finally, the 1978 Revenue Act included a new Targeted Jobs Tax Credit under which employers would be entitled to a tax credit of 50 percent of the first $6,000 of wages during the employee's first year of work and 25 percent in the second year (with limits on the total subsidies any employer could receive). The targeted groups are: (1) vocational rehabilitation referrals, (2) economically disadvantaged youth, (3) economically disadvantaged Vietnam-era veterans, (4) Supplemental Security Income recipients, (5) general assistance recipients, (6) youths participating in a cooperative education program, and (7) economically disadvantaged ex-convicts.

The fourth annual report of the National Commission for Manpower Policy (1978) included an authoritative evaluation of the effectiveness of public versus private sector jobs creation, drawing on much of the research that has been done on the CETA program. The report showed that federal spending (including "tax expenditures" or revenue losses) had been far greater for public sector than for private sector job creation. The subsidy level for the private sector programs is much lower than for the public sector programs, although the private sector target groups are somewhat more disadvantaged. The experience with the New Jobs Tax Credit was somewhat more encouraging than with the WIN program. Even though many firms were apparently ignorant of its existence, it has been estimated that the program produced several hundred thousand additional jobs during 1977-78.

Both public and private job creation programs suffer from the problem of displacement. In the public sector, the subsidies may be used to hire people who would have been hired anyway or who displace existing employees. This can also happen in private employment. It has been estimated that there is (probably as a minimum) about a 20-percent displacement rate in the public sector and that there was an 80-percent displacement rate in the private sector under the New Jobs Tax Credit program. Even so, private sector job creation is still the cheaper alternative because the average subsidy level prevailing in CETA public service employment is much higher than the subsidy level in the private sector, according to the commission.

It is certainly true that an employee who is hired under a program providing a wage subsidy to a private employer is likely to move into permanent employment in the firm if his or her performance is satisfactory, whereas public service employment under CETA is limited in duration and may not improve an individual's capacity to find employment in the private sector. Even so, it must be remembered that wage subsidies are not likely to be very effective in inducing private hiring in a recession. The importance of encouraging employment in the nonprofit sector, where community service is often involved, should also be kept in mind, as the commission has noted in other reports.

Among the various evaluations of OJT and related programs to induce employers to hire the unemployed, including the JOBS program under the National Alliance of Businessmen (NAB) in the late 1960s, an aversion of employers to becoming involved with government red tape stands out as a reason for nonparticipation. Even the widely admired program of the Chicago Alliance of Business Manpower Services (CABMS) under which this nonprofit organization, associated with NAB, centralizes negotiations with the federal government for OJT contracts, has involved primarily smaller employers and minority business firms (Robison, 1978, pp. 51-52). Large firms resist becoming involved, partly because they have their own training programs that do include the disadvantaged.[5]

Probably the chief underlying reason for the difficulty in drawing large firms into wage subsidy programs is their skepticism about the prospective productivity of the disadvantaged as employees. Nevertheless, there are some outstanding examples of successful and imaginative efforts, including the IBM plant in Bedford-Stuyvesant.

We fully agree with the aim of the administration to draw private employers more extensively into participation in programs for disadvantaged youth, but we do not believe that wage subsidies should be a primary part of that effort. The move to form private industry councils under CETA is a commendable

[5]Interview of Margaret Gordon with staff members of the National Alliance of Businessmen and the Mayor's Office of Manpower Programs, Chicago, July 1978.

step, provided emphasis is placed on participation of all the relevant groups, including school officials, in the councils, along the lines of the work-education councils sponsored by the National Manpower Institute. Moreover, we agree with a number of the recommendations in the CED report (discussed in Section 12) for greater involvement of the private sector.

Recommendation 30: *Federal government programs for training and employment of youth should place strong emphasis on efforts to involve private employers, especially through encouraging participation of employers in work-education councils and through provision of training subsidies, but wage subsidies should be limited to modest experimental programs.*

The Public and Nonprofit Sectors

During the 1970s, especially in recession periods, emphasis on public service employment as a means of combatting unemployment increased. The nonprofit sector also became involved under CETA programs in a good many communities. Even if an effort to involve the private sector more extensively is successful, there are advantages in continuing a certain degree of emphasis on jobs and training positions in the public and nonprofit sectors. Experience has indicated that public service employment can be increased quite promptly in a recession, when few OJT positions are likely to be offered in the private sector.

We believe, however, that in the future much of the emphasis in involvement of the public and nonprofit sectors should be placed on development of the youth service program that we recommend in Section 17. We also believe that apprenticeship programs should be expanded in the public sector, including military service—a movement that has, in fact, been under way for several years.

Apprenticeship

In contrast with the situation in certain western European countries, especially Austria, West Germany, and Switzerland, apprenticeship has long played a minor role as a method of training in the United States (Table 4). The failure of appren-

Table 4. The incidence of apprenticeship in selected OECD countries, 1974

Country	Number of apprentices (thousands)	Apprentices as a percentage of total civilian employment
Australia	131	2.3%
Austria	164	5.4
Belgium	18	0.5
Canada	67[a]	0.7
Denmark	32	1.4
Finland	3	0.2
France	197	0.9
Germany	1,130	5.2
Ireland	15	1.4
Italy	670	3.6
Netherlands	70	1.5
New Zealand	32	2.7
Norway[b]	10	0.7
Spain	8	0.1
Sweden	1	c
Switzerland	143	4.9
United Kingdom	463[d]	2.1
United States	291	0.3

[a]Excluding apprenticeship in Quebec.

[b]1970.

[c]Under 0.1 percent.

[d]Great Britain: *1971 Census, Economic Activity*, part II, tables 2, 10. Number of apprentices in Great Britain estimated from category "Apprentices, articled clerks and formal trainees."

Source: Organization for Economic Cooperation and Development (1979).

ticeship to assume importance in this country has frequently been attributed to the rapid growth and high rate of geographical mobility that characterized our economic development historically. In such an environment there were chronic scarcities of skilled craftsmen, and workers tended to pick up their skills on the job.

The chief feature that distinguishes apprenticeship from other forms of training is the existence of a contract between the apprentice, or his parent or legal guardian, and the employer. The apprentice agrees to work for the employer at a wage that begins at a rate well below the skilled journeyman's rate in the trade and gradually increases during training, while the employer provides instruction and practice leading to the acquisition of a recognized qualification as a skilled craftsman. The training traditionally tended to last for four or five years, but in recent years there has been a trend toward shortening the duration of apprenticeship. In the United States, the Bureau of Apprenticeship and Training in the U.S. Department of Labor identifies and sets standards for apprenticeable trades, but detailed regulation is largely left to the states. In practice, the determination of such matters as standards of admission is a subject for collective bargaining between labor and management, and representatives on joint apprenticeship boards established in specific occupations administer the agreement. Although apprenticeship training historically took place entirely on the job, there has been a tendency in recent decades to add requirements for accompanying classroom training.

American unions have been notoriously restrictive in their policies for admission to apprenticeship, partly because of their interest in holding down the supply of skilled workers and partly because of a natural interest in granting admission to relatives and friends of union members. It used to be said that "you have to be the son or son-in-law of an electrician to get into the electricians' apprenticeship program," and, in fact, sons of skilled craftsmen often follow in their fathers' footsteps via the apprenticeship route.

All of this augured poorly for the admission of youth who had no relatives in the union, and especially for minority groups. Indeed, the almost complete absence of blacks from apprenticeship programs has been a subject of great bitterness in the black community and also the subject of extensive research by labor economists, including Secretary of Labor Ray Marshall (Marshall and Briggs, 1967).

Until very recently, apprenticeship programs in the United States continued their historic pattern of small numbers and presence primarily in the building and metal trades. Between 1958 and 1976, the number of registered apprentices grew very slowly, along with a modest upward trend in the total number of skilled craftworkers (Figure 20). Fluctuations in growth in the number of apprentices and in the number of skilled craftsmen tended to coincide, as employers adjusted their employment upward or downward over the course of the business cycle.

Under the impact of the civil rights movement, however, significant changes began to occur in the latter half of the 1960s, as civil rights groups and the government exerted pressure toward opening the doors of apprenticeship programs to blacks and members of other minority groups. The U.S. Department of Labor provided financial support for the Apprenticeship Outreach Program (AOP), conducted by the Recruitment and Training Program and several other organizations, and aimed at recruiting minority youths for apprenticeship and, if necessary, providing preapprentice training to prepare them for the admissions tests. The AOP program marked the first use of federal government funds to support apprenticeship, beyond the funds required for administration of the Bureau of Apprenticeship and Training.

The efforts to increase the percentage of minority groups in apprenticeship programs have been quite successful. The percentage of members of minority groups among registered apprentices rose from 6 percent in 1967 to 18 percent in 1977 (The President, 1972, 1978).

In the past few years, the movement to increase opportunities for apprenticeships, especially by extending apprenticeship training to occupations for which it has not existed before—and thus making apprenticeship less dependent on uncertain and fluctuating employment in the building and metal trades—has been stepped up. Under the Department of Labor's New Initiatives in Apprenticeship programs, inaugurated early in 1977, $12.3 million in CETA funds were allocated for contracts that would ultimately provide more than 30,000 apprenticeships in such fields as health, auto repair, mining, petroleum, and the civil service (including police forces). Of special interest was the allocation of nearly $2.5 million to organizations in Cleveland, Houston, Nashville, and New Orleans to place approximately

Figure 20. Registered apprentices, craft and kindred workers, and
apprentices as a percentage of craft and kindred workers, 1958 to 1976

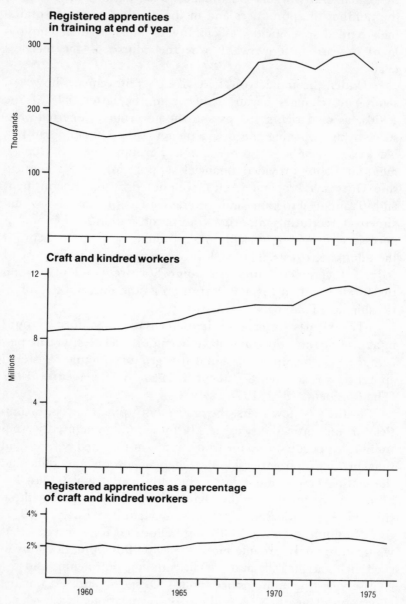

Source: The President (1978, pp. 205, 320).

1,100 high school students in apprenticeship programs during their senior year. In addition, grants totaling $1.2 million were made to nonprofit organizations and community colleges in ten selected cities to establish multitrade apprenticeship committees that would provide assistance to small employers to continue or start apprenticeship programs.

In July 1977, an agreement was signed by the Secretary of Labor, the Secretary of the Navy, and the Marine Corps Commandant establishing national standards for apprenticeship for the Marine Corps under which marines could complete Marine Corps qualifications and at the same time complete a formal apprenticeship program in a nationally recognized apprenticeable occupation. A similar agreement was signed with the U.S. Army in July 1975 (The President, 1978, pp. 56-57). Apprenticeships for prison inmates were also being developed.

Another important development has been the growing involvement of community colleges in providing the classroom training required under apprenticeship regulations. According to a national survey conducted by the American Association of Community and Junior Colleges in 1977, community and junior colleges offered more than 1,200 apprenticeship training programs and were increasingly offering associate degrees for apprentices ("Community Colleges Offer," 1977, p. 4).

Only a few years ago, a good many labor market experts were pessimistic about the outlook for increasing the role of apprenticeships. Employment in traditional apprenticeship occupations was relatively stagnant, and this was true not only in this country but in a number of countries in western Europe as well (Organization for Economic Cooperation and Development, 1979). More and more questions were raised about the suitability of apprenticeship training under the impact of advancing technology, which tended to increase the demand for more highly educated and therefore more mature workers, for whom apprenticeship was not appealing.

Now there is a new attitude in discussions of the future of apprenticeship in the United States, well expressed by Donald Vial, director of the California Department of Industrial Relations, when he called for vast expansion of "apprenticeship training to occupations which lend themselves to cost-effective methods of integrating progressive skill development on the job with classroom training in community colleges and other vocational education centers" (Vial, 1978, p. 529). Pointing out that community college classroom programs for training electronic technicians were regarded as insufficiently in touch with industry requirements at a time when employment in the electronics industry was expanding, and there was an acute shortage of electronic technicians in California, Vial has been spearheading a movement to develop new apprenticeship programs in cooperation with community colleges—not only in electronics but also in health and other growing occupations. Not only has the number of apprenticeships increased significantly in the state in the last few years, but the number of women apprentices increased from 312 at the end of 1975 to 1,328 at the end of 1978.[6]

We welcome these promising developments in apprenticeship and believe they should be continued and strengthened. When well conducted, apprenticeship programs have great advantages over most other types of vocational training available to young people:

- On-the-job and related classroom training are combined.
- Apprenticeship provides a pathway to jobs in the primary labor market and eventually, in many cases, to supervisorial positions. A recent study of skilled construction workers showed that those who learned their trades through formal apprenticeship programs had steadier jobs and were more likely to become supervisors than those who gained their skills in other ways ("Construction Union Apprenticeships," 1975, p. 9).
- Compensation of apprentices is often above the minimum wage and far superior to wages earned by youth in secondary labor market jobs. For example, in 1975, in New York City, where journeymen sheetmetal workers earned $11.67 per

---

[6]We are indebted to Dr. Sara Behman, deputy director, California Department of Industrial Relations, for extensive information about these new programs in the state.

hour, the union's first-year apprentices began at $4.67 per hour, or twice the federal minimum wage (Green, 1976, p. 208). Thus, apprenticeship holds promise of enticing youth away from the life of the street and illicit earnings.

- Training tends to be prolonged but, if well conducted, is much more thorough than most other types of training and provides security of employment.
- Although apprenticeship training is now more likely to be publicly subsidized than has traditionally been the case, and subsidies are particularly essential to achieve the purposes of the Apprenticeship Outreach Program, costs continue to be met in large part through funds provided by unions and management under joint apprenticeship agreements, and the public subsidy per trainee is likely to be much less than for most other types of training. However, we favor the use of subsidies to cover training costs and possibly a portion of wages in situations where this will encourage the introduction of apprenticeships in occupations or industries that have not had them or will encourage small employers to participate.

To achieve substantial expansion of apprenticeship and continued progress in bringing women and minorities into apprenticeship programs, current efforts to increase the number of apprenticeable occupations must continue, as must the Apprenticeship Outreach Program. In addition, we believe that the age for admission to apprenticeship programs should not exceed 16 (it frequently does under existing joint apprenticeship agreements), a rigid requirement for high school graduation should be avoided (at least the alternative of a GED should be permitted), and apprenticeship opportunities should be made available in the last several years of high school (a movement that is beginning).

Recommendation 31: *Federal and state programs to increase the number of apprenticeable occupations, to include more women and minorities in apprenticeship programs, to develop apprenticeship programs in the civil and military services, to seek the cooperation of community colleges in apprenticeship*

*training, and to open up apprenticeship opportunities for sec-
ondary school students should continue.*

Premilitary Training

Even though we do not believe that the military draft should be
resumed (see Section 16), it will clearly be somewhat more difficult for the armed forces to maintain the voluntary army at
full strength in the 1980s in the face of a decline in the size of
the youthful population. Many young persons are rejected for
induction because of poor performance on tests or for other
reasons. We believe that opportunities for premilitary training
should be expanded, so that young people who fail to meet the
standards for induction can overcome their deficiencies and at
the same time gain useful experience. Premilitary training might
be conducted as an apprenticeship program by the U.S. Department of Defense or under contract with community colleges or
other appropriate institutions. Such training should be available
from the age of 16.

Recommendation 32: *The U.S. Department of Defense, in cooperation with the U.S. Department of Labor, should stimulate
the development of premilitary training.*

Occupational Orientation Centers

In both Great Britain and Belgium, occupational assessment or
orientation centers have been developed to assist young people
who have not made a career choice to try out their work apti-
tudes and occupational preferences through a variety of tests
and orientation programs (Maclure, 1979, p. 122; Janne, 1979,
p. 21). In Britain the centers are sometimes located in colleges
of further education but more frequently in employers' establishments, and the programs typically last two weeks. In Belgium, the centers are geographically distributed throughout the
country and are an outgrowth of a long-established program of
training centers for the unemployed.

In the United States, occupational orientation is sometimes included in the skills centers that are funded through the
CETA program and often located in community colleges, but it

could be developed on a more generally available basis. As the discussion in Section 6 makes clear, career education programs in high schools also include occupational orientation in some cases, but such programs are not accessible to dropouts. We believe that CETA programs aimed at out-of-school youth should uniformly provide opportunities for occupational orientation, preferably under the auspices of community colleges but planned by CETA prime sponsors in conjunction with both secondary schools and community colleges.

Recommendation 33: *CETA prime sponsors, schools, and community colleges should cooperate in making certain that opportunities for occupational orientation programs are available for both in-school and out-of-school youth.*

Regularizing Odd Jobs

As we saw in Section 12, the Work in America Institute (1979) has developed proposals for pilot programs designed to test various methods of stimulating the employment and training of youth. These programs all deserve serious consideration for financial support from the federal government, foundations, or other sources. We select two of them for special consideration: (1) regularizing odd jobs, and (2) job retention awards.

For many young people in large cities, "odd jobs" that provide little pay and no benefits are the only job opportunities available. A pilot program of Contract Service Organizations (CSO) that would offer full-time work to inner-city youth, while providing homeowners and business firms with a regular means of contracting for odd jobs, including maintenance and repair, cleaning, painting, gardening, temporary office services, and others should be established. The CSO would recruit and select employees, providing training, assessing, transporting, and supervising. The employees would form a full-time, year-round pool of young workers receiving steady salaries and benefits from CSO, while homeowners and business firms hiring them for odd jobs would pay set hourly fees. The institute estimates that a program of four demonstration projects would cost between $1 and $2 million, which should be provided by a combination of public and private sources. The program would be modeled after the experience of Manpower, Inc., and similar organizations that supply temporary workers.

Recommendation 34: *The U.S. Department of Labor should encourage the development of a program that would provide fulltime work to inner-city youth, through contract service organizations that would regularize the odd-job labor market, using a combination of public and private funds.*

Job Retention Awards

A common complaint about many disadvantaged young people is that they do not stay on the job very long. Dual labor market theorists contend that high job turnover in the secondary labor market results not only from a high propensity of disadvantaged workers to quit jobs that are low paid and offer poor working conditions but also from the fact that employers in secondary labor markets do not want to incur the obligations normally associated with long-term employment (seniority rights, fringe benefits, and so on) but prefer to take on workers for short periods at low pay. The proposal for job retention awards is aimed at providing an incentive for young workers to stay on the job and would probably be more attractive to employers in the primary labor market than to many of those in the secondary labor market. The plan would provide for taxfree cash awards to youths earning the minimum wage at three critical points during their first six months on the job. The awards would be issued directly by CETA prime sponsors to youth, following certification by the employer, and would provide a lump-sum payment of $150 after 30 days, $300 after 90 days, and $450 after 180 days. The institute suggests that there would be no need for additional awards, because a young person who had held a job for six months would be likely to continue without further special inducement and might even have qualified for promotion.

Recommendation 35: *The U.S. Department of Labor should provide support for pilot projects under which CETA prime* *sponsors would provide lump-sum payments to disadvantaged youth who stay on the job at several intervals during the first six months of employment.*

Protective Legislation

Employment of young people is hampered by protective labor legislation, compulsory school attendance laws that require full-time attendance and interfere with the possibility of work-experience and cooperative education programs, and other types of legislation. The National Committee on Employment of Youth (1975) published a most useful analysis of these laws and recommended many changes. Among the changes that are particularly in line with policies recommended in this report are revision of state laws that are barriers to work-experience programs. The committee also called attention to the fact that many apprenticeship programs have minimum age requirements as high as age 18 and recommended that these should be modified so that 16- and 17-year-olds have access to apprenticeship.

Recommendation 36: *The states should review protective legislation, compulsory attendance laws, and other legislation to remove unnecessary barriers to employment of youth.*

Toward Increased Flexibility

In our review of the literature on the impacts of CETA programs and earlier MDTA programs, we have been impressed with the continued existence of certain rigidities, traceable to federal policies and regulations, even though the 1973 CETA legislation was designed to provide for greater flexibility in the management of programs at the local level. In particular, federal regulations and funding formulas tend to limit the duration of training programs. In CETA institutional training, for example, generally conducted in skills centers, the duration of training is ordinarily limited to about 26 weeks. This means that at best certain entry-level skills can be provided. The policy can be defended on grounds of economy, but it may well be at least in part responsible for the fact that participants who complete such training usually experience improved earnings, compared with control groups, in the short run, but that such benefits tend to disappear after a period of several years. Limits on duration of training also tend to restrict the number of skills for which training can be provided (Mangum and Walsh, 1978, p. 88). Training programs for the unemployed in western Europe have tended, on the whole, to be more flexible (Gordon, 1965).

Such considerations as these influence our recommendation in favor of increased emphasis on apprenticeship. Within the existing framework of CETA training programs, however, we believe that greater flexibility and a wider range of types of training should be sought and that the decline in the size of the population of young people should gradually facilitate programs that may cost more per individual trainee but that yield more effective and more lasting results.

Recommendation 37: *In the future development of training programs for out-of-school youth, greater emphasis should be placed on flexibility in the duration of programs and in the types of training provided.*

14

The Most Difficult
Issue of All: Policies
for the Deprived

Trow's Typology of Youth

Sociologist Martin Trow has developed a four-way classification of youth that is useful in determining the different policies that are needed for groups with quite different problems:

A TYPOLOGY OF YOUTH

		Early education and socialization	
		Adequate	*Inadequate*
Family financial resources	*Adequate*	The advantaged	The alienated
	Inadequate	The disadvantaged	The deprived

Briefly, Trow (in Gordon, forthcoming) describes the four groups as follows:

The Advantaged

These young men and women have both the personal and financial resources to move toward adult roles that are roughly commensurate with their talents and ambitions.

The Alienated

These are young people who have not been deprived economically, but who are having difficulty in their transition to adult roles because of other problems relating to their earlier socialization, education, or both. . . . Many are psychologically and emotionally outside the society in which they live; their behavior is governed by their feeling apart from and often hostile to the dominant culture and social institutions. Some of these young people are in fact seeking and creating alternative socializing communities—in communes, in religious sects (Eastern or fundamentalist Christian), or in political communities that embody distinctive philosophies and life-styles. Others seek further education outside the traditional educational system that many in this category have found punishing. Some are simply downwardly mobile for complicated reasons that involve their natural abilities and energies, their aspirations and values, their family dynamics and relationships to their parents, and various combinations of these forces.

The Disadvantaged

These young men and women have personal and academic skills, motivations, and in most cases family encouragement. They need financial aid, counseling, and in some cases publicly supported programs of employment to translate their potential into adult achievement. It is this group that provides the "new" students in postsecondary education, and whose members profit most from state scholarship programs and Basic Opportunity Grants, low-cost loans, and inexpensive community and state colleges. Young people in this category are perhaps the best candidates for various kinds of nontraditional education, such as work-study programs. . . .

The Deprived

In this category are to be found the young men and women who have the most severe and difficult problems of growth and maturation, who are at once most in need of help from public and private sources and are least able to seek it out or profit from such help when it is offered. For these youth, a combination of poverty, inadequate education, and weak psychological resources result in a litany of human and social disaster: high rates of criminal activity, drug and alcohol addiction, chronic unemployment, physical and mental illness, dependence on public welfare, and institutionalization. Society currently spends large sums on these youth—on the police, the courts, jails and prisons, and systems of probation and parole; on drug abuse programs; and on other forms of support. The real costs of deprivation are infinitely greater. The threat to urban life that lies in the high rates of violent street crime, much of it committed by deprived youth, and the loss to the society of their potential contributions, are only the greatest of those hidden costs. . . .

Trow then points out that deprived youth are a source of much of the national anxiety about the problem of "youth." They are particularly difficult to reach through public programs, and the special programs that have been developed for them have not been especially successful. This, Trow maintains, is partly because public agencies have not recognized important differences between disadvantaged and deprived youth. Whereas the disadvantaged can profit from additional resources for gaining skills and getting adult jobs, the deprived often have trouble using such resources because of a combination of personal difficulties, cultural attitudes toward work, and a poor educational background.

In addition, local agencies that administer federally funded programs are more likely to give the available jobs to disadvantaged rather than to deprived youth.[1] Disadvantaged youth are more likely to get to work on time and in other ways to meet the needs of employers, and, in addition, are likely to be the sons and daughters of the " 'respectable' ethnic community members—the people who vote, belong to ethnic organizations, and serve as orientation for the ethnic organizations which distribute much of this federal support."

Reaching the Deprived

Although we believe that most youth programs should not be heavily targeted toward the disadvantaged but should serve all youth, we agree with Trow that many existing programs do not reach the deprived. In this section, we discuss several examples of programs that have been specifically designed to serve severely disadvantaged or deprived youth.

For purposes of measuring the relative size of the groups, we developed in Section 1 a modification of Trow's classification under which the category of the deprived includes young persons who do not finish high school for reasons (a) of personal ability, or (b) of social circumstances. In this section, we shall be concerned with youth who are deprived because of social circumstances, and we recognize that not all dropouts have the characteristics of Trow's deprived group. Some of those who drop out of school do so because they have opportunities to get reasonably satisfactory jobs. They are not likely to become social problems. We shall also not consider those who drop out for reasons of personal ability, because considerable progress has been made in the last several decades in developing programs for youth who are mentally retarded or severely disabled. The young people who are deprived in Trow's sense are those who develop patterns of delinquency, alcoholism,

[1]These remarks are based on studies of CETA-funded youth programs in the San Francisco Bay Area carried out by Trow and a group of graduate students in summer 1978, with support from the Carnegie Council.

drug addiction, or inability to hold a steady job because of various irregular patterns of living or lack of motivation.

The Job Corps

A number of sociologists believe that at least some deprived youth who have developed serious patterns of delinquency or deviant behavior would benefit from removal from their home environment and placement in a special type of boarding school or residential program designed to motivate and train them for participation in the labor force and in normal social life. The Job Corps, which was created under the Economic Opportunity Act of 1964, comes close to such a model, although it was planned for severely disadvantaged youth, not specifically for the deprived. To a large extent, the Job Corps has been a residential program designed to provide training and education for disadvantaged men and women aged 16 through 21. Job Corps centers have been operated both by government agencies and by private industry. Among the services available at the centers are counseling, basic education, high school equivalency instruction, skill training, work experience, and placement.

In 1969, the structure of the Job Corps was changed when the U.S. Department of Labor assumed responsibility for its administration, as part of a broader move of the Nixon administration to shift functions away from the Office of Economic Opportunity. The emphasis also shifted from rural to urban residential centers and to greater emphasis upon skill training as compared with nontraining supportive services. This reorientation tended to narrow the difference between the Job Corps and other urban-based labor market programs. Even so, the heavy concentration of the highly disadvantaged in the Job Corps limits the range of jobs for which skill training is feasible in a limited period of time (an average of six months is spent in the program). Much of the training period must be devoted to remedial education and attention to personal characteristics that prevent enrollees from holding a job.

All participants in the Job Corps are out of work and out of school and in need of additional education, vocational training, counseling, and other services to help them obtain employment, return to school, qualify for other training programs, or enlist in the armed forces. In 1977 the program included 27 civilian conservation centers administered by the U.S. Departments of Agriculture and the Interior in national parks and forests; 31 centers operated under contract with business firms, nonprofit organizations, or government agencies; and several were operated by unions. Increasing emphasis was being placed on greater union involvement in vocational training, inclusion of women in the program, and development of coeducational facilities. Union programs, some of which offered preapprenticeship training, were being conducted by the various skilled building trades; by railway, airline, and steamship clerks; and by marine cooks and stewards. At the Atlanta Job Corps Center, AFDC mothers were receiving basic education, skill training, and other services, while day-care services were provided for their children (The President, 1977, pp. 55-57).

Until recently, the Job Corps enrolled about 40,000 youths at some point every year, or about 20,000 at any given time. Its limited size was at least partly explained by the fact that costs per trainee were considerably higher than in other training programs, largely because of its residential character. Thus, there has been reluctance to expand the program, because more enrollees could be served at the same total cost in other programs. However, early in the Carter administration, a decision was made to double the size of the Job Corps, increasing its capacity to about 44,000 enrollees and thereby serving about 88,000 youths a year. The newer centers are both residential and nonresidential, and among the skills taught are electrical appliance repair, building maintenance, automobile repair, food service, health care, cosmetology, clerical skills, and sales skills.

In April 1978, it was announced that top professional athletes from a variety of sports would assist the Job Corps in expanding its size by appearing on radio and television spots, visiting the centers for morale purposes and physical training programs, establishing liaison with business firms and labor unions, and other activities (U.S. Department of Labor, 1978).

There have been a number of evaluations of the Job Corps,

with somewhat mixed results. From the beginning, it had a relatively high dropout rate, as might be expected in a program
enrolling the severely disadvantaged—much as the least selective
colleges tend to have the highest dropout rates. The residential
character of the program also played a role—some youths just
got homesick. Moreover, the training stipends were low, and enrollees sometimes left to enroll in other programs with higher
training allowances. On the other hand, especially in recent
years, the Job Corps has had a high placement rate for those
who complete the program. In a Ph.D. thesis comparing samples
of youth enrolled in the Job Corps, MDTA institutional training, and MDTA on-the-job training, Rawlins (1969) found that,
on a strict cost-benefit basis, on-the-job training with its low
subsidy costs came out ahead, but in terms of lasting tenure on
jobs and gains in earnings for those who completed the program, the Job Corps came out well.

In one of the more recent evaluations, Levitan and Johnston (1975, pp. 103-109) came to a number of significant conclusions:

1. There is merit in the basic concept of separating
   youths from their home environments and providing them with a comprehensive package of support
   and services in addition to education and training. . . .
2. The potential size of the hard-core disadvantaged
   population who can be attracted to enroll in centers is much smaller than original projections. . . . Large numbers either are disinclined to
   remain away from home or are not interested in
   the disciplined and demanding training program. . . . Overall, it is doubtful that the real universe of need is more than 250,000. . . .
3. Better screening is required to ensure that those
   who can best benefit from the training receive it.
4. The Job Corps itself has not fully resolved the
   question of whom it aims to help. Evidence has
   accumulated that young enrollees, and those with

the greatest disadvantages, do not benefit as much as others from enrollment in a center. . . .

5. The linkage to unions for screening, training, and placement has been a signal success. Whether this record has been a result of union control over jobs or of educational expertise, there can be little doubt that enrollees fortunate enough to be in union-run programs have a better chance of landing well-paying jobs than those who are not. Union power to place youth in apprenticeable occupations is limited, however, and alternative linkages of Job Corps to employment have not been explored adequately.

6. The quality of training and the chances for enrollees' success have depended less on the type or size of center, or on the characteristics of enrollees, than on the quality of administration and staff. . . . Neither private nor public contractors have shown consistent superiority in providing these essential ingredients.

7. The value of Job Corps training seems to depend less on the specific skills or knowledge acquired than on a reorientation toward productive work or school roles.

Looking toward the future, Levitan and Johnston (1975) recommend: (1) new linkages to unions, employers, or other organizations in a position to place corpsmen; (2) raising the limits on cost-per-man-year; (3) restructuring the training allowance system to provide greater incentives to complete the program, perhaps making lump-sum payments for completion of various phases of training; (4) strengthening the linkage of the Job Corps to CETA and other community-based programs, in order to provide more effective placement services for enrollees who have been away from home for training; and (5) aiming at a better match between the racial and ethnic characteristics of enrollees (predominantly minority group) and staff (with much lower percentages of minority group members). The authors conclude by pointing out that the defenders of the program are those who have been directly involved and are impressed by the human success stories they have witnessed, whereas the critics have been outside examiners who have questioned the cost-benefit results.

These results are of interest for several reasons. First, they suggest that programs for the deprived are beset with inherent difficulties and should be deemed successful if they reorient a significant portion of the enrollees, even though they may also fail with a substantial fraction. Second, the finding that the quality of management and staff was more important in explaining success than other factors is similar to the finding that the leadership of the principal is the most important factor in innovations in schools. Once again, we find that what actually happens on the local scene is crucial and that uniform national success cannot be expected even with the best designed program.

The Career Intern Program

The Career Intern Program (CIP) was developed by the Opportunities Industrialization Corporation of America, Inc., under the leadership of Reverend Leon Sullivan in Philadelphia, and has been supported by National Institute of Education funds.[2] It is designed to encourage both career preparation and high school completion for severely disadvantaged youth and includes three phases. Phase I is directed at improving students' career awareness and lasts 21 weeks. The students study English, mathematics, social studies, and science, but the instruction is keyed to the world of work. Phase II may last from four months to a full year, depending on the student's previous preparation and progress. Courses that combine academic and career information are continued, while the students are also exposed to several job experiences. In Phase III, students concentrate on the transition from school to work or to more advanced education. Students who go on to vocational or on-the-job training are assisted by counselors for six months after leav-

[2] Earlier the program was supported by the Office of Education.

ing the program; college-bound students receive counseling for a full year after leaving.

From the fall of 1972 to the end of 1975, the program in Philadelphia served 502 young people, all of whom were black and most of whom were either in academic trouble or had dropped out of school. In addition, almost all students applying to the program came from neighborhoods characterized by gang activity and drug use. A majority came from families in which the primary wage earner was a woman in a low-status occupation.

A followup study of 286 young people who entered the program between January 1974 and September 1975, compared with a control group chosen at random from CIP applicants, yielded impressive results. By December 1975, about 67 percent of the CIP students, but only 13 percent of the control group, had graduated or were still attending school. About 44 percent of the CIP students had received high school diplomas, compared with 7 percent of the control students. Although levels of reading and mathematical achievement were low for both groups, the CIP interns "were showing very high levels of career planning and development skills" (Gibboney Associates, 1977, p. 3). In the fall of 1975, 77 of the graduates who had been out of CIP for six months to a year were followed up; 42 percent were employed compared with 39 percent of the control group. Of the CIP graduates, 29 percent were in college or technical school, contrasted with none of the control group.

The success of the program was attributed to (1) the active leadership role of the principal, who spent a great deal of time in the classroom, (2) the "supportive" atmosphere as perceived by the students, (3) the clear identification of the program with the formulation and pursuit of career objectives, (4) constant feedback on students' progress, (5) actual work experience, and (6) small student-faculty ratios. Although the cost of $248 per student was considerably higher than those of regular academic and general programs in Philadelphia high schools at the time ($170), they were less than monthly costs of a high-quality private school in the city ($293) and only slightly more than vocational education programs in the city's high schools (Gibboney Associates, 1977).[3]

This program is particularly significant because it indicates that substantially increased school resources, including a low student-faculty ratio, can be effective, in spite of the findings of the Coleman Report and other negative evidence. Among others, Radner and Miller (1975) have argued that a pronounced reduction in the student-faculty ratio might have a significant effect on learning, whereas a modest reduction might have no effect.

The Harbor Learning Center

The Harbor City Learning Alternative Program in Baltimore is designed to encourage both high school completion and preparation for employment for dropouts and potential dropouts. Jointly sponsored by the Baltimore CETA program—considered one of the most effectively administered CETA programs in the nation—and the city's school district, the bulk of the funds come through CETA. A modest amount of funding is also received from the Law Enforcement Assistance Administration to cover the costs of ex-offenders who participate in the program.

The in-school component provides part-time, after-school work experience for vocational curriculum students aged 14 to 19 who have been identified as potential dropouts and recommended for the program by their school counselors. Usually, students are recommended because of poor attendance, low grades, financial problems, or other difficulties that lead to dropping out. Students in this component work on jobs involving cafeteria service, housing rehabilitation, painting, auto repair, musical instrument repair, and horticulture.

The second component of the program offers dropouts a combination of services, including work experience and job-related academic studies in nontraditional courses. Students can choose from four occupational clusters—business, health, com-

[3]Our discussion of the program is based partly on an interview with Michael Timpane, deputy director of the National Institute of Education, in February 1978.

munications, or community services. Each former dropout admitted to the program chooses one of four minischools according to his or her occupational interests and abilities. Every two weeks the students move from the nontraditional classrooms to related public sector worksites where they can sample jobs in the cluster they have chosen. The program, which leads to a high school diploma or high school equivalency certificate, is designed for completion in two years, but it may be completed in less time.

Among the support services offered is a parent-infant center that provides day care and an educational program for children of the enrollees, which requires that the parent (or parents) participate in child-rearing classes. There is also a student resource center that provides job counseling, vocational assessment, and placement.

The out-of-school program has a reasonably satisfactory retention rate (about 60 to 62 percent on an annual basis) and considerable success in attracting dropouts who hear about the program through their friends. Although work experience is predominantly in the public sector, a strong effort is being made to place students completing the program in jobs in the private sector through a network of labor market advisory committees in ten occupational areas. Most terminations are attributable to failure to fulfill academic requirements, and increasing emphasis is being placed on development of more individualized academic programs that are closely related to job experience (National League of Cities and United States Conference of Mayors, n.d.; Mayor's Office of Manpower Resources, Baltimore, 1977).

The chief problem with the program, as viewed by city officials, is that it does not begin to reach all the dropouts. The in-school program can serve 700 youths, while the out-of-school program has a capacity of 1,300. As against these numbers, 8,200 youths left high school in a recent year, while an additional 40,000 were classified as chronic truants.[4]

---

[4]Our discussion of the Harbor City program is based partly on interviews with staff members of the Mayor's Office of Manpower Resources, Baltimore, in July 1978.

Vocational Foundation, Inc.

Vocational Foundation, Inc., is a private agency in New York City that specializes in finding jobs for unemployed youths, about half of whom have a drug or correctional background and are referred by various city agencies concerned with juvenile delinquency. Most of the young people served are aged 16 to 19, with an average educational attainment level of 10.3 grades and an average reading level of 6.7 grades. Almost all are either blacks or Hispanics, about 37 percent have had no previous work experience, and 18 percent are receiving public assistance.

Before young people are referred for jobs, they are tested and provided with counseling about behavior on the job. Some are referred for training in CETA programs, while the foundation conducts some training programs of its own. A staff of job developers works intensively on locating jobs, but most of those in which they achieve placements are low-level and temporary. The average stay on a job is about three months. The program emphasizes encouraging youths to return for additional counseling and placement efforts when a job terminates, and about 25 percent of their clients do eventually return for additional help. A significant percentage succeed in settling in permanent jobs eventually, but the organization has no way of knowing just what this percentage is.

In an interview with the deputy director of the program, the necessity of ancillary services, such as preplacement and postplacement counseling, was stressed as essential to success.[5]

The foundation receives its funds from a combination of private foundations and community agencies and from the federal government. Federal funding, according to the deputy director, is less satisfactory than the private sources, because its timing and amount are uncertain.

National Demonstration of Supported Work

The National Demonstration of Supported Work was started about four years ago with funds from a consortium of federal

[5]Interview of Margaret Gordon with Jerry Ornstein, deputy director, Vocational Foundation, Inc., December 1977.

agencies and the Ford Foundation to test the effects of the "supported-work concept" on four groups of people—welfare mothers, ex-offenders, ex-addicts, and dropout youths—who have had long histories of severe unemployment and resistance to traditional manpower efforts. The supported-work concept emphasizes peer-group support and graduated stress. By providing groups of supported workers with close supervision and by gradually increasing the performance standards required of them, the program aims at preparing enrollees for the transition to regular, unsubsidized jobs. It also aims at achieving reductions in drug use, criminal activity, and welfare dependency. It is conducted in 13 localities, including both rural and urban settings.

The first evaluations of the program were published in fall 1977 and showed results that were, on the whole, quite favorable. The findings were presented in two reports. The first of these covered a sample of 691 ex-offenders, ex-addicts, and youths at seven sites, of whom 356 were program participants and 335 were members of a control group. The second report covered a sample of 303 AFDC women recipients at six sites, 147 of whom were participants and 156 were members of control groups (Manpower Demonstration Research Corporation, 1977a, 1977b).

In terms of earnings, the results were particularly positive for the AFDC women in the program, who had earnings averaging $3,673 in a nine-month period, compared with $532 for the control group, and received only 60 percent as much in AFDC payments. For the other three target groups, the difference in earnings between participants and control groups was not quite as large but still substantial. These large differences in earnings were, of course, to some extent explained by the fact that participants were offered supported-work jobs, while controls were not. Even so, the substantial earnings of participants reflected willingness to work on the part of persons whose earlier records suggested little work effort.

Differences in other aspects of behavior were much less pronounced, but in most cases were statistically significant. In the three target groups other than AFDC, for example, it was reported that 29.3 percent of the members of the control group were arrested, compared with 21.6 percent of the participants. Among youth, the percentage reporting any drug use was much lower (14.3 percent) for participants than for members of control groups (33.3 percent). On the other hand, among adults in these groups, differences in percentages reporting drug use were not significant—for example, 22.8 percent of participants compared with 22.1 percent of the members of control groups reported use of cocaine. Differences in percentages reporting illegal activities (youths and adults combined) were also not significant—18.1 percent for participants and 20.1 percent for members of control groups.[6]

General Comments

Even though our general view is that programs for youth should not be heavily targeted on the disadvantaged, it is clear that an exception needs to be made for the deprived, many of whom simply will not be reached by most manpower and educational programs. Programs for the deprived must be especially designed to reach the target group, must be intensive, must have low ratios of participants to teachers and other staff members, and must anticipate a significant attrition rate. They are almost certain to be more costly per participant than programs aimed at youths with less severe problems.

A particularly encouraging aspect of several of the programs we have described is the blending of public and private funds in their financing. This is true of Vocational Foundation, Inc., and of the Supported Work Program. The Career Intern Program, while funded largely from public funds, was started under the initiative of a privately organized agency. There is a particularly strong case for blending of private and public efforts in this type of program, because each program must be tailored to meet the needs of the particular group it is trying to reach and cannot be fitted into a rigid national model. At the same time, a private group can approach a government agency

---

[6]Discussion of this program is based partly on an interview of Margaret Gordon with Mitchell Sviridoff, vice-president of the Ford Foundation, December 1977.

for support of a carefully designed program and substantially augment the funds that can be provided from its own resources.

Recommendation 38: *Public and private agencies should cooperate in sponsoring and funding programs for the deprived, expanding program designs that have been successful and discontinuing those that have failed or shown limited success.*

15

Notation
on Financing

With the enactment of the Youth Employment and Demonstration Project Act of 1977 (YEDPA), the level of federal expenditures on manpower programs for youth administered by the U.S. Department of Labor (DOL) was substantially increased. About one billion dollars was appropriated to carry out the specific provisions of the legislation in its first year of operation. These funds augmented the allocations already available to carry out existing special programs for youth, such as the Job Corps, the Youth Conservation Corps, and the Summer Program for Economically Disadvantaged Youth (SPEDY). Actual expenditures by DOL for special programs for youth rose from $1,364 million in fiscal year 1978 to $2,242 million in fiscal year 1979, and the administration recommended $2,131 million for these programs in fiscal year 1980 (*The Budget*, 1979, p. 644). Additional sums are spent on youth under CETA programs that are not especially targeted on youth, but it is not easy to determine from published data just how much these expenditures are.

Congress was particularly careful to mandate evaluations of the new or augmented programs authorized under YEDPA. Until those evaluations have been completed, it will not be possible to reach sound decisions on the outcomes, especially in the case of the Youth Incentive Entitlement Projects, discussed in Section 6.

Thus, additional sharp increases in funds expended on such programs are not likely until more is known about the results. However, as we noted in Section 1, augmented funds may be needed for youth programs if the unemployment rate rises as much in 1980 as some economists are now predicting, for, if that happens, youth unemployment rates will also rise. We have expressed our preference for quick action on four types of programs:

1. Financing needy students in high school.
2. Targeting student financial aid more toward low-income students.
3. Creation of civil service and military apprenticeships.
4. Creation of a multifaceted voluntary youth service.

The first of these should be carried out through the work-study program that was recommended in Section 6, with federal funding of $300 million and matching state funds of $100 million. The second was recommended in the Council's recent report, *Next Steps for the 1980s in Student Financial Aid* (1979). The third would call for increased expenditures by the U.S. Department of Labor to subsidize apprenticeship programs in the civil service and the armed forces. We did not recommend increased expenditures for such programs in Section 13, where they were discussed, because the Department of Labor has been placing considerable emphasis on development of such programs in the past several years. However, in the event of a pronounced rise in the unemployment rate, there would be a strong case for accelerating these efforts with expanded funds to make possible complete subsidization of apprentices employed in the civil service. The program could be extended through CETA to finance apprenticeships in state and local government agencies as well. However, under conditions of a recession, there would also be a need for expanded public service employment for youth, because it would probably not be possible to complete arrangements for apprenticeship programs quickly enough to meet the emergency. We believe that there would be a need for at least an additional $500 million for special youth programs.

The fourth priority, creation of a multifaceted voluntary youth service, is discussed in Section 17.

Recommendation 39: *In the event of a substantial rise in the unemployment rate in 1980, funds allocated to the U.S. Department of Labor for special youth programs should be augmented by $500 million, to be expended primarily on civil service apprenticeship programs at all levels of government and on public service employment.*

Recommendation 40: *Nevertheless, the long-run goal should be to increase the percentage of funds expended on in-school youth in CETA youth programs, as success is achieved in reducing school dropout rates and unemployment rates of out-of-school youth.*

Part IV

Service

16

Current Proposals
for Youth Service

For many years there have been proposals for a comprehensive national youth service that would provide opportunities like those available in the Peace Corps and VISTA but on a much larger scale. Recently, interest in such proposals has intensified, not only because of persistently high youth unemployment rates but also because there is growing concern that it will not be possible to maintain an adequate military service on a voluntary basis in the 1980s, when the number of 18-year-olds will decline. Because reinstitution of compulsory military service would be strongly opposed, especially by student and other youth groups, the need for providing the option of civilian service is viewed as a way of making the return of the draft more palatable. Proponents of this broad approach also recognize that the plan would have to include certain financial advantages for those who opt for military service in order to maintain an adequate flow of young people into military as opposed to civilian service.

We believe that there is a strong case for a large-scale youth service program quite apart from military considerations. The period of dependence and lack of involvement of young people in society's problems has become more prolonged, even while the gradual reduction of the age of puberty has meant earlier maturity. Young people need "a piece of the action." Largely as a result of extensive exposure to TV, they tend to know more about social problems than did earlier generations, but they have little opportunity to do anything about them.

Numerous studies and surveys have shown many unmet needs in our society that could be met at least partially through youth service programs. Needs are particularly critical in social service—in programs for the aged and handicapped; in programs for people who have limited access to services because they live in rural or suburban areas where they are not available;[1] and, of course, as we have stressed in this report, in tutoring, counseling, placement services, and other services for disadvantaged youth. Other needs are critical in conservation and preservation of the environment.

We shall later discuss, as examples of existing youth service programs, those in Seattle and Syracuse. However, we should also call attention to special surveys that have been conducted in other communities to determine needs for services. One such study, completed as part of the National Association of Secondary School Principals' study, "American Youth in the Mid-Seventies," surveyed agencies in the central-city area of Portland, Oregon; in part of the metropolitan fringe area of Washington, D.C.; and in a nonmetropolitan area, Sheboygan County, Wisconsin (Havighurst, Graham, and Eberly, 1972). The results indicated that schools, hospitals, waste-recovery projects, day care centers, sanitariums, and other local agencies were able to identify hundreds of volunteer jobs that could be filled by young people. Still more jobs would open up if the schools or some other agency could provide transportation to and from work, could cover costs of insurance and supervision, and could prepare students, in advance, to meet entry-level skill specifications. "Under these circumstances," the authors pointed out, "there would be enough jobs to provide every 15- through 20-year-old in the areas surveyed with almost three hours of service-learning opportunities a week, some in jobs that require only a few hours each week, others in full-time work for a half year or more" (p. 7).

Recently, a report was issued by a distinguished group, the

---

[1]This point is developed especially by Petersen (Rehn and Petersen, forthcoming).

Committee for the Study of National Service, established under the auspices of the Potomac Institute, and headed by Jacqueline G. Wexler and Harris Wofford. Funds for the study were provided by the Ford Foundation, along with additional assistance from other foundations.

The committee came out strongly for a national youth service, but on a voluntary basis. In the introduction to its report (Potomac Institute, 1979, p. 1) it said:

> Until the spirit of service is restored among American citizens, the most pressing human problems of our society will not be solved. The full participation of youth in national service could be a powerful force in meeting the needs of the nation and in strengthening the spirit of service. Today, little is asked of young people except that they be consumers of goods and services. A vast industry serves youth with schooling, entertainment, and goods of all kinds, but there are limited opportunities for the young themselves to produce goods and serve others.

The committee called for the country to move toward universal service by stages and by incentives but without compulsion. At least a year of service after leaving secondary or higher education should become a common expectation of youth. Young people should be involved in service programs in the home community, in national parks, in other parts of the country, and overseas. The system should aim to enlist at each stage a representative cross section of American young people. The administrative structure should emphasize decentralization and result in the smallest feasible government bureaucracy with the strongest possible ties to the private and voluntary sectors of American society. All the present government programs, such as VISTA, the Peace Corps, and the Youth Adult Conservation Corps, should be included among the options in the program. Another option could be individual or small-team arrangements with public or private agencies in local communities along the lines of the ACTION project in Seattle.

Following the precedents of the Peace Corps and VISTA, the general rule during service should be a reasonable living allowance. One of the incentives for participants should be appropriate postservice educational and employment benefits along the lines of the G.I. Bill of Rights and the Peace Corps adjustment allowance, apportioned according to the length of service. Not all such postservice benefits need to be provided by the government. Private business, for example, should give weight to an applicant's national service in hiring decisions. Participants should also be encouraged to continue their education while in the national service through evening classes and the like.

On the issue of the possible need for a mandatory service, the committee stated that "it is not necessary now to decide whether the nation should require such service. During the gradual development of a voluntary system, the idea of mandatory service can be carefully considered. If it should be determined that the needs of national defense call for the restoration of the military draft, at that point the case for mandatory universal service, including nonmilitary options, would be very strong" (pp. 4-5).

In the meantime, military enlistment should be recognized as a form of national service, and service should be reemphasized as "the central mission" of the military. A growing expectation of service "should improve the climate for all volunteering, and thus aid the armed forces in attracting young people without having to offer ever-higher compensation and benefits" (p. 5).

The committee recommended that the national service system be established as a public corporation, chartered and funded by Congress but drawing its leadership largely from the private sector of American society. The system should be empowered to set overall guidelines and criteria for funding and monitoring the various programs in which young people may serve, and to establish a network of local service councils for information and counseling. Various estimates of total cost for programs with differing numbers of participants were presented, drawing on previous proposals by other groups or individuals. The committee pointed out that there could be savings in amounts spent on military recruiting (through consolidation with national service recruiting), federal employment and training programs, unemployment compensation, food stamps, and student aid that might otherwise be received by persons enrolled in the national service. Economist Charles Killingsworth, a member of the committee, argued that "taking a portion of funds which would otherwise be lost through a proposed federal tax cut and using them instead in support of national service will have a greater stimulating effect on the national economy than the return of those taxes" (p. 127).

As the Potomac Institute report points out in the detailed background section of its report prepared by Roger Landrum, a long line of distinguished citizens and groups have proposed youth service programs. They include:

* William James, when he called for a "moral equivalent of war" (1910).
* The Coleman Task Force, as we noted in Section 5 (1973).
* The Carnegie Commission on Higher Education, in its report, *Toward a Learning Society* (1973c).
* Willard Wirtz and the National Manpower Institute in *The Boundless Resource* (1975).
* Margaret Mead, who felt that a "national institution of universal youth service would be an instrument of social integration" (1967).
* Reverend Theodore M. Hesburgh, who believes that the experience of service to others should be accepted as part of our whole educational system (1965).
* Senator Hubert H. Humphrey, who coupled a proposal for a nationwide community service jobs program for youths with improved counseling and placement services for them (1976).
* Former Congressman and Ambassador to the United Nations, Andrew Young, in testimony before the Joint Economic Committee (1976).
* Donald J. Eberly, executive director of the National Service Secretariat, who has written many articles and papers over the years (for example, 1976), presenting proposals that do not differ greatly from that of the Potomac Institute.
* The Congressional Budget Office, which explored several dif-

ferent proposals for a national youth service (1978) but did not make any recommendations, in accordance with its practice.

Seattle

Certain community programs that might serve as models for activities within a national service framework should be mentioned at this point in our discussion. One of these is an ACTION program in Seattle, which was launched in 1973. The program was open to everyone aged 18 to 25 living in a specified area in or near Seattle. It offered full-time, one-year community service positions for a stipend of $50 a week plus complete medical coverage and other fringe benefits. Each volunteer was also to receive a lump sum of $300 at the end of the year's service. Those selected for the program included an above-average proportion of women, minorities, and persons from low-income families, with an above-average educational level. About 70 percent were unemployed and looking for work. Sponsors, including both public agencies and private nonprofit organizations, contributed to program costs and assumed responsibility for supervision and in-service training. An evaluation prepared by a private research organization indicated that the benefits from the volunteer service far outweighed the costs. The average volunteer was providing service valued at an annual rate of $7,000 compared with an annual service cost of approximately $4,000 per volunteer (Control Systems Research, 1973).

Syracuse

A second community program that is being closely watched by youth and manpower experts is being conducted in Syracuse under the auspices of ACTION with funds made available by YEDPA. In February 1979, ACTION submitted an interim progress report to the U.S. Department of Labor on this National Youth Community Service Demonstration Project (ACTION, 1979). It reported the formation of a new nonprofit corporation to operate the Youth Community Service/Syracuse (YCS/S) program. Applications were received from 2,700 youth out of the estimated 3,500 to 6,000 unemployed and out-of-school young people (aged 16 to 21) in greater Syracuse. In January 1979 there were 789 volunteers in service, of whom 54 percent were women, 72 percent were aged 16 to 19, 57 percent were black, 3 percent were Hispanic, and 35 percent were high school dropouts. Most of them were from lower-income families, but perhaps one-fourth were from middle-income families. The report stated (p. ii) that "the profile gives a preliminary indication of the willingness of minority youth and lower-income youth to participate in stipended community service. Skepticism about the appeal of this alternative to these groups of young people may be overblown."

Projects in which volunteers participate include: neighborhood revitalization, emergency home repairs, recreation supervision, evening and home crisis day care, and the like. The YCS/S participants work more as interns than as employees and receive a VISTA-level stipend (basically a food and living allowance) as opposed to a wage. The participants play an active role in working with sponsors to identify an appropriate service "match" rather than being assigned to a particular job or project.

The Outlook for Military Service

Much of the current discussion of a national youth service program, as suggested earlier, is related to concern that a voluntary military service will not work well in the 1980s, in the face of a decline in the youthful population. Recently, Representative Paul McCloskey, Jr., of California, joined by 14 colleagues, introduced a bill (H.R. 2206) to create a "National Youth Service System as an alternative to the draft" (McCloskey, 1979, pp. 1070-1071). The main features of the bill are as follows:

1. The Selective Service System will be replaced by the National Service System and all persons, men and women, will be required to register within ten days after their seventeenth birthday.
2. Information on service opportunities will be made available to all persons between their seventeenth and eighteenth birthdays.
3. All registrants will have the option of serving in a civilian

capacity for one year or in the military service for two years or more and will be allowed to defer such service until the age of 23.

4. At the age of 18, persons will have the right to elect:
   a. Two years of military service, which will entitle them to four years of educational and training benefits.
   b. Six months of active duty, followed by five-and-one-half years of Reserve obligation.
   c. One year of service in a civilian capacity.
   d. None of the above, in which case they will be placed in a military lottery pool for six years of draft liability. If military manpower requirements are not filled during the period, these individuals might be required to serve two years of active duty and would also incur a four-year Reserve obligation. They would be entitled to two years of educational and training benefits.
5. If voluntary enlistments are not adequate, then and then only would one be subject to possible conscription.
6. The Civilian Services Corps will be operated by a National Service Foundation (for which details are provided, resembling those outlined by the Committee for the Study of National Service).

Although Congressman McCloskey stated, in introducing the bill, that it "does not provide universal conscription for military service," it provides for a quasi-mandatory rather than an entirely voluntary national youth service. Another feature of the bill is a reduction in the military pay for junior enlisted personnel (those with less than two years of service) to a subsistence level. The all-volunteer force (AVF) concept, McCloskey stated, "is too expensive."

It seems clear that a controversy over continuation of a voluntary military service is developing into a major congressional issue. Various bills have been introduced that would call for resumption of registration or other versions of a semireturn to the draft, and a subcommittee of the House Armed Services Committee recently approved a bill to reinstate military registration of 18-year-old men. However, a bipartisan group of 39 congressmen announced their opposition to any move to bring back the draft ("39 Congressmen Warn," 1979). Any such move is vigorously opposed by student groups and by such organizations as the American Civil Liberties Union.

Despite all of this activity, which seems predicated on the assumption that the voluntary military service is not working, two authoritative reports issued in the last few years have concluded emphatically that this is not the case. One of these is a report based on a two-year study by a task force of the U.S. Department of Defense (*America's Volunteers*, 1978), and the other is a comprehensive report prepared in connection with this study by the Rand Corporation (Cooper, 1977).

The report on *America's Volunteers* pointed out that the growth of the population of eligible young men in the 1960s and 1970s reduced the percentage of eligibles who were required to provide the officer and enlisted strengths needed by the active and reserve forces—from about 60 percent in the mid-1950s to 25 percent in 1978. "The supply of young men decreases by about one-fourth over the next 15 years; however, recruiting requirements do not exceed 30 percent of the eligibles in any future year. These requirements are lower than the percentages of young men required when the AVF decision was made" (p. 2). The report added that, although the population of young men will decline in the 1980s, circumstances will remain favorable because the youth population will remain well above the low levels of the 1950s and 1960s (apparently here the early 1960s was meant, see Figure 21).

Other important conclusions of this report were as follows:

1. Since the end of the draft, the active forces have remained within 1.5 percent of congressionally authorized levels.
2. The quality of those serving on active duty, as measured by the education levels of active duty personnel and the average test scores of new recruits has not declined as popularly believed but has markedly and steadily improved since the end of the draft. In this connection, the educational levels of the force are much higher than in the pre-Vietnam era, and the

Figure 21. Supply and demand for young men

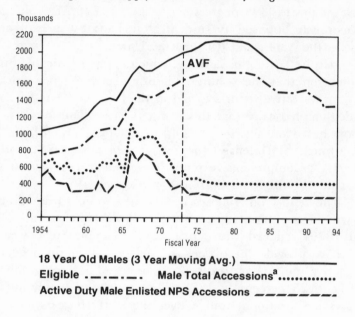

Thousands

18 Year Old Males (3 Year Moving Avg.) ——————
Eligible . —. —. —.   Male Total Accessions[a]...............
Active Duty Male Enlisted NPS Accessions ————————

[a]Officer and enlisted, active reserve.

Source: America's Volunteers (1978, p. 1).

recruit class of fiscal year 1979 contains the highest percentage of high school graduates of any year in our history.

3. The costs of the AVF are within 20 percent of the cost levels
predicted by the Gates Commission in 1970.

4. Retention of enlisted personnel has increased under the AVF
and is well above pre-Vietnam rates.

5. Disciplinary incidents have shown a steady and in some cases
dramatic improvement since the early 1970s, returning to
about the pre-Vietnam level.

6. The all-volunteer force appears to offer better opportunities
for women and minorities, a choice of training and occupations to new recruits, and improved living standards for
junior personnel once on active duty.

The report, however, pointed out that these favorable results did not mean that there were not problems here and there,

including declining test scores of recruits for the Army since 1975-76, disciplinary problems in the Navy, and high first-term attrition rates. However, efforts were being made to reduce attrition and to recruit more women. Meanwhile, the Army Reserve and the National Guard had sagged below authorized minima, but action was being taken to improve incentives, including reform of the reserve compensation system.

The Rand report (Cooper, 1977, pp. vi-x) arrived at very similar conclusions but also shed additional light on certain issues:

1. The key AVF issue is not manpower supply, but accession requirements. Service policies such as limiting the flow of manpower into the career force (which is due in part to congressional limitations on the numbers of personnel in senior pay grades) have resulted in accession requirements that are actually higher under the volunteer force than under the draft—the reverse of what would have been expected. The long-run success of the volunteer force depends on reducing enlisted accession requirements by reducing personnel turnover rates.
2. The rise in the proportion of blacks in the armed forces is largely unrelated to the volunteer force; it is instead due mainly to the increasing numbers of blacks found eligible for the military service and to the unusually high unemployment rates experienced by black males of military age. Although blacks continue to score lower than whites on mental aptitude tests, the proportion of blacks failing to qualify for military service has decreased significantly over the past 20 years. Because of this, the black proportion of the prime manpower pool—that is, military-age males of average and above-average mental aptitude—has increased from a little under 3 percent in 1960 to more than 7 percent in the mid-1970s.
3. The attribution of increased costs to the volunteer force is "plainly incorrect." The factors leading to the considerable growth in manpower costs can be traced to events that began nearly three decades ago. Whereas the military career historically consisted of 30 years of service, the immediate post-World War II period saw the widespread implementation and

use of the 20-year military career. Similarly, the 1960s marked the implementation of comparability pay for civilian employees of the U.S. Department of Defense, the beginning of annual pay increases for military personnel, and other similar changes. In fact, the total cost of personnel amounts for those in their first two years of service is only about $6 billion, or just a little over 10 percent of the total defense manpower outlay. Military retirement is part of the compensation system that is particularly in need of thorough review. Retirement costs are among the largest and fastest growing components of manpower spending, having increased from $477 million in 1956 to more than $9 billion projected for 1978. Now that military pay equals or exceeds civilian pay, the retirement system should be reexamined in terms of its basic purpose (Cooper, 1977, pp. vi-x).

A report by the Comptroller General of the United States (1978) is sometimes cited as contradicting the view that increased costs associated with the volunteer army have not been heavy, but, in fact, that report shows that the additional costs (over 1970) that could legitimately be attributed to the volunteer army by 1977 amounted to about $3 billion in current dollars a year and to $2 billion in constant (1970) dollars. This does not seem to invalidate the general position of the Rand report appreciably, and it should be pointed out that the Comptroller General's report made no allowance for certain offsets that were associated with the higher pay standards for the volunteer army, such as increased tax revenues and reduced welfare payments to dependents of members of the armed forces.

17

Youth Service:
Voluntary for All

We favor the development of a comprehensive youth service on a gradual scale. It will take time to develop appropriate community projects, and political support for sudden authorization of a large-scale and, therefore, expensive comprehensive youth service would not be likely to be forthcoming. As the youth service grows in size, there will be an opportunity to measure the size of the offsets attributable to reduced unemployment and other costs and to apply these savings to the financing of the youth service program.

We also believe, as does the National Committee for the Study of Youth Service, that the service should be voluntary, at least for the time being. The evidence that we are facing a crisis in our capacity to maintain a voluntary military service does not seem convincing, and the emphasis on the excessive costs of the volunteer service is, in the light of the Rand report, decidedly misleading.

However, one of the problems with a voluntary youth service, as opposed to a mandatory service, would be to make certain that those in the service were broadly representative of all youth. There may be a danger that college or college-bound young people would be more likely to be attracted by the appeal of a service program than young people from disadvantaged families. If this happened, the service would fail to achieve two of its major purposes—(1) to provide valuable experience to young people plagued by unemployment and the other problems associated with the environment of the ghetto, and (2) to bring together young people from many different environments.

We believe that the evidence from the Seattle and Syracuse experiences (preliminary though the latter are) suggests that vigorous leadership and active recruitment of unemployed and other disadvantaged youth in a community are likely to be successful in combatting the danger that a national youth service would be overloaded with highly educated youth. But this is another reason for gradual development of the program. Such efforts clearly need to be based on grassroots activity at the community level.

We propose that young people aged 16 to 24 be eligible for the service and that they should be expected to participate for a minimum of one year and a maximum of two years. However, we believe that 16- and 17-year-olds should usually be involved in education, work experience, and training programs in their own communities and that active recruitment for the comprehensive youth service should preferably begin at age 18. All young people should be counseled and urged to participate at some point from age 18 to age 24. The liberal policies that colleges and universities have adopted to encourage stopping out will be particularly helpful in this connection.

Recommendation 41: *We recommend establishment of a National Youth Service in which participation would be voluntary, and all young people aged 16 to 24 would be eligible. Although a National Youth Service Foundation would be responsible for development of the program, projects would be initiated and administered on a decentralized basis.*

Local Initiative and Matching Funds

We stress the importance of local initiative in the development of youth service programs. Rather than a national program with uniform requirements and regulations, we urge maximum flexibility at the local level. Moreover, although federal funds should be available for much of the financing, we believe that the program should operate principally through project proposals developed in local communities or, in some cases, by state agencies.

Approximately one-half of the federal funds allocated to the program, furthermore, should be made available on a matching basis. The community agency initiating the proposal might put up a portion of the matching funds and seek an additional portion from the state or from a foundation. We believe that foundations would be prepared to support well-developed youth service programs in local communities.

Some communities with large college or university populations—such as Cambridge, Massachusetts; Berkeley, California; or Ann Arbor, Michigan—could not be expected to develop community projects large enough to accommodate all of the university students who would want to participate. Therefore, we suggest consortia of institutions of higher education, operating through the offices for community services that we suggested in Section 10, for the purpose of developing service projects that would attract youth on a broad regional basis or on the basis of a particular type of concern, such as conservation. Such consortia would be in a particularly good position to attract foundation support, but it would be important for them to include plans for recruitment of noncollege as well as college youth in their projects.

The program should also include provision for initiation of some projects by state government agencies, which would be expected to contribute part of the funding in such cases. In addition, a portion of the funds should be allocated for discretionary use by the National Youth Service Foundation for a limited number of projects that would not be feasible at the local or state level.

Recommendation 42: *One-half of the federal funds allocated for the program should call for 50 percent matching by the agency initiating the program. Such an agency would typically be a local community group, but it might also be a state agency or a consortium of institutions of higher education.*

The initiating agency might seek a portion of the matching amount from state agencies or foundations.

Scope and Funding

To implement our proposal for gradual development of the program, we suggest an initial federal allocation of $600 million. Allowing for the provision for matching funds, and also for a contribution of 10 percent of the cost at the local or project-initiating level for those projects not subject to the 50 percent matching requirement, we estimate that an allocation of $600 million would accommodate about 135,000 to 140,000 civilian participants initially, including the number now in ACTION programs. This assumes that compensation at the project level would be somewhat flexible, but that, in all cases of compensation below the minimum wage, the federal government would deposit the difference between actual compensation and the minimum wage on behalf of the participant in the National Educational Fund proposed in the next section.

Military service would always be compensated at a somewhat higher level than civilian service, at least for the foreseeable future, in order to encourage an adequate flow of youth into the voluntary armed services, and it is not included in our cost estimates, because it does not involve additional funding. We envisage a gradual increase in the numbers involved in the civilian youth service to about one million by the end of the 1980s. The net costs would not necessarily increase commensurately, if the combined result of all of our proposals in this report reduced existing societal costs for juvenile delinquency, unemployment compensation, and so on. Moreover, we do not suggest automatic increases of a predetermined number each year. We believe that the service should be expanded on the basis of careful evaluations of needs and impacts.

Recommendation 43: *We suggest an initial federal allocation of $600 million in 1980-81, which we estimate would accommodate 135,000 to 140,000 volunteers initially, including those already in ACTION and allowing for augmentation of funds through the matching provisions.*

In general, our proposal agrees quite closely with the Potomac Institute proposal. The chief difference is that we place greater emphasis on initiation of proposals at the local level. We also develop an explicit proposal for matching funds, which should result in somewhat less reliance on federal funding and provide incentives for foundations and state agencies to provide partial funding.

18

A National Education Fund: A Path to Self-Help

Linked with our proposal for a National Youth Service is a related proposal for a National Education Fund. The link would be in the form of educational credits that would be deposited in the National Education Fund on behalf of participating youths. The National Education Fund, however, could be established independently of a National Youth Service plan, and vice versa. Sources of funds for the National Education Fund would be:

1. Voluntary saving by participants in youth service programs.
2. Federal credits for youth service, including more generous credits for those in military service.
3. Employer deposits on behalf of employees—these could be made as employer-initiated fringe benefits or as part of a collective bargaining agreement. Employer fringe benefits might take the form, wholly or partially, of an agreement to match voluntary savings deposited in the fund by employees.
4. Voluntary savings by employed persons at any age up to 55.
5. Contributions by parents on behalf of a child at any age from birth on.

Each individual with deposits in the fund would have an individual account, as in the Teachers Insurance Annuity Association (TIAA), but the benefits would take the form of educational credits rather than retirement annuities. Compound interest would be credited to each account at the maximum rate obtainable on long-term savings accounts. Withdrawals could be made only for educational purposes (in institutions approved for other federal student aid programs). However, there would be a right of withdrawal after five years, or in emergency situations, but only with the approval of special advisory committees (which might be attached to regional offices of the fund). Only the individual's own contributions, with accumulated interest, could be withdrawn. Educational credits stemming from government contributions could not be withdrawn. Individual credits could also freely be withdrawn at age 55 for transfer to a retirement plan.

Educational credits should be related to those available for members of the armed forces in such a way as to provide larger benefits for those opting for military service. Under the provisions of the Post-Vietnam Veterans' Educational Assistance Act (October 15, 1967), each person entering military service has a right to enroll in an educational benefits program. Those enrolling must agree to monthly pay deductions of $50 minimum to $75 maximum. The Veterans Administration provides matching benefits on a $2 for every $1 basis. The Secretary of Defense is authorized to contribute an additional amount if it is deemed necessary or appropriate to encourage persons to enter or remain in the armed forces.

Under our proposal, the federal government would match voluntary monthly pay deductions for those in the civilian portion of the National Youth Service on a one-to-one basis. There would also be stipulated federal credits unrelated to individual saving. However, both those in the military and those in civilian service could make additional voluntary unmatched contributions to the fund.

Persons leaving the armed forces receive monthly benefits (under the provisions of the Post-Vietnam Act) for a maximum of 36 months on the basis of the individual's accumulated fund divided by 36. Although this differs from provisions for Vietnam-era veterans, the monthly benefits are similar.

We believe that the policies relating to educational credits should be closely integrated with the Council's student aid policies, as most recently revised and issued in its report, *Next Steps for the 1980s in Student Financial Aid* (1979). While recommending improvements in the Basic Educational Opportunity Grant program, a pronounced expansion of the federal-state State Student Incentive Grant program, and other changes, we also recommended that eligibility for student grants should normally include a requirement for a self-help contribution from applicants for student aid. Under our recommendations, the Basic Educational Opportunity Grant program would be designed to provide for subsistence, and students would ordinarily be expected to provide $600 a year at the lower-division level and $1,000 a year at the upper-division level either through earnings or borrowing, as a condition of eligibility for a grant. To be eligible for a tuition grant in the State Student Incentive Grant program, the student would be expected to contribute the first $250 of tuition plus any amount over the tuition grant itself (which could not exceed $1,500) and the expected parental contribution.

Another important feature of our recommendations—also made earlier by the Council and its predecessor, the Carnegie Commission—was adoption of a greatly improved student loan program through establishment of a National Student Loan Bank, which would be a nonprofit private corporation chartered by the federal government and financed by the sale of governmentally guaranteed securities.

A student completing civilian service and not eligible for student grants (under family income eligibility conditions) would be free to use his or her educational credits quite flexibly, although withdrawal from the fund would be permitted only for attendance at an approved educational institution (under federal regulations currently applying to student aid programs, which involve chiefly a requirement that the institution be accredited), and the total amount withdrawn in any given year could not exceed the student's educational expenses (including tuition, subsistence, necessary expenditures for books, and so on).

A student qualifying for student grants on the basis of

family income would not lose his or her eligibility but could use the educational credits to meet our self-help requirements and also to avoid borrowing.

We believe that the National Education Fund (NEF) should resemble the National Student Loan Bank in that it should be a nonprofit private corporation chartered by the federal government. Although it might be set up as part of the National Student Loan Bank, under the same board of directors, we do not believe its establishment should be dependent on establishment of the National Student Loan Bank. The NEF would be self-sustaining (earning interest through investment in government securities), but it would need very modest initial funding to begin operations.

Looking toward the future, we believe that one of the problems that may be developing, as a result of pressure to provide student aid to students from middle- and middle-upper-income families, is the trend toward universal eligibility for student aid. Under these circumstances, qualifying for aid through a youth service program, regardless of family income, seems preferable to further liberalization of family income eligibility standards.

Adults with accumulated credits in the National Education Fund could arrange with their employers for leaves of absence for educational purposes. Thus, the proposal is related to European paid educational leave systems, but we believe that the plan should leave the employee free to choose his own educational program (assuming it is in an approved institution), whereas under some of the European plans the employer tends to approve only work-related types of training.

The National Education Fund differs from ordinary saving in that it is closely associated with a program of educational credits, and withdrawals for purposes other than education would be subject to scrutiny and would not normally be expected. It would constitute one of the attractions for participation in the National Youth Service.

Recommendation 44: *We favor the establishment of a National Education Fund in which credits could be established for indi-*

vidual youths and adults from five sources: (1) voluntary savings by participants in youth service programs, (2) federal educational credits for youth service, (3) employer deposits on behalf of employees, (4) voluntary savings by employees up to age 55, and (5) contributions by parents on behalf of their children.

Part V

Summation

19

A Balance Sheet
of Costs and Benefits
to Society

The total increase in federal expenditures recommended in this report is $1.4 billion to $1.9 billion (Table 5). The recommendations for immediate increases in federal funding do not represent the ultimate cost of full development of the programs we propose, which would be much larger. Over the years, however, there should be substantial offsets in reduced social costs for youth. Thus, an estimate of the ultimate costs of new or augmented programs that we propose would be misleading, because it would not take account of these offsets, which cannot be estimated in any exact way. We have given illustrative figures in Section 1 of such costs as unemployment insurance and juvenile incarceration on a per-person basis.

In this section, we develop an illustrative estimate of the immediate social savings that might result from the $1.4 to $1.9 billion increase in federal expenditures involved in our recommendations. The estimate is based on what might seem to be "reasonable offsets," but they should be regarded as suggestive rather than precise.

We estimate that approximately 3.5 million youths would be aided by our proposals in a given year in the early stages of the program. The largest number would be those affected by

Table 5. Selected federal youth programs: Carnegie Council
recommendations for new or reallocated expenditures,
1980-81 compared with 1979-80
(in millions of constant [1979] dollars)

Programs	Administration budget for 1979-80	Council recommendation for 1980-81
U.S. Department of Health, Education, and Welfare		
Total for selected programs included in Table 3	$4,342.5	$5,172.0
National Youth Service Foundation (incorporating ACTION)	105.0 (ACTION)	705.0 (NYSF)
U.S. Department of Labor		
Employment and Training Administration		
Special programs for youth	2,131.0	2,131.0 to 2,631.0[a]
Total for selected programs	6,578.5	8,008.0 to 8,508.0
Net increase		1,429.5 to 1,929.5

[a]The higher amount would be appropriated in the event of a sharp increase in the unemployment rate in 1980.

Source: The Budget, 1979; Carnegie Council recommendations.

work-experience programs and shifting vocational education out of the classroom. Of the 3.5 million assisted:

1. Perhaps 2.9 million would have remained in school in any case.
2. 100,000 would have dropped out or become chronic truants and committed acts of vandalism costing their communities an average of $500 per truant.
3. 50,000 would have been placed in juvenile incarceration facilities at a cost of $18,000 per youth a year.
4. 120,000 would have experienced unemployment during the

year, of which one-half would have qualified for unemployment benefits averaging $800.

5. 100,000 would have been responsible for law enforcement costs averaging $1,000 even though they were not placed in a juvenile facility.

6. 100,000 would have become pregnant, and, of these, 50,000 eventually would have qualified for AFDC at an average cost of $4,000 per year, while 75,000 would have qualified for Medicaid at an average cost of $1,000.

7. 100,000 would have dropped out and qualified for manpower programs, at an average cost of $5,000.

8. The remaining young people would have gotten jobs and not have experienced unemployment.

On this basis, total immediate social savings would be about $1.9 billion. However, those who stayed in school rather than dropping out or becoming involved in juvenile delinquency, pregnancy, and the like would have cost the schools about $2,500 per student. Thus, the immediate effect is somewhat higher expenditures, despite social savings. In the long run, there would clearly be social savings as a rising proportion of these young people finished school, achieved stable employment, and avoided crime.

Another consideration in support of the increased expenditures for which our proposals call, as we noted in Section 1, is the declining size of the total youthful population in the 1980s. This will make possible somewhat reduced costs of supporting schools (in real terms) and lower numbers involved in dropping out and joblessness, even in the absence of the reduction in dropout and unemployment rates toward which our proposals are aimed.

20

Who Should Do What?

The Congress

- Amend the Vocational Education Act, which comes up for renewal in 1981, changing its name to the Occupational Skills and Student Services Act, incorporating in the legislation the new work-study program for low-income secondary school students that we propose, and shifting $300 million of the existing allocation to support a new program designed to stimulate the states to move high school vocational education out of the classroom and into the workplace or community college.
- Increase the appropriation for Title I of the Elementary and Secondary Education Act by $500 million, to be allocated entirely for programs in junior and senior high schools.
- Increase the appropriation for the College Work-Study program, in accordance with the Council's recommendation in its recent report, *Next Steps for the 1980s in Student Financial Aid* (1979), including provisions designed to stimulate allocation of most of the increased funds for tutoring and teacher's aide jobs in secondary schools and for jobs in nonprofit community agencies.
- Increase the appropriation for FIPSE by $6 million, including provisions that would allocate the additional funds to projects of colleges and universities designed to serve disadvantaged youth.
- Increase the appropriation for the Teacher Corps by $2.5 million.

- Increase the appropriation for special youth programs administered by the Employment and Training Administration of the Department of Labor by $500 million if the unemployment rate rises sharply in 1980, allocating the additional funds for civil service apprenticeships and public service employment.
- Adopt a long-run policy under which gradually rising proportions of funds for special youth programs would be used for in-school rather than out-of-school youths, thereby adjusting to a changing situation in which fewer youths will drop out or graduate with deficient basic skills if our policies are adopted.
- Enact legislation that would exempt youths under age 20 from social security coverage.
- Pursue policies designed to involve the private, for-profit sector more extensively in employment and training programs for disadvantaged youth, with emphasis on training subsidies and with limitation of wage subsidies to modest, experimental programs.
- Allocate CETA funds in such a way as to stimulate expansion of apprenticeship programs in the civil service and the military services, in community colleges, in industries that have not traditionally had apprenticeships, and in programs for high school students, encouraging policies now followed by the Department of Labor.
- Provide for a program of premilitary training conducted by the Department of Defense in cooperation with the Department of Labor.
- While placing increased emphasis on programs serving all youth or large segments of youth, rather than heavily targeted toward the disadvantaged, continue to support selected programs, such as the Job Corps and the Career Intern Program, that are specifically designed for severely disadvantaged or deprived youth.
- Establish a National Youth Service Foundation to coordinate and fund youth service projects initiated by local communities, state agencies, institutions of higher education, and other organizations. Appropriate $600 million for the first year of

the new program (1980-81), with a provision that one-half of the funds require 50 percent matching by groups submitting project proposals. Gradually increase the appropriation in future years on the basis of experience and evaluation rather than on the basis of a predetermined formula.

* Establish a National Education Fund to administer educational credits resulting from federal contributions on behalf of youths in civilian or military service, savings of youths on their own behalf, employer contributions on behalf of employees, savings by employees themselves, and contributions by parents on behalf of their children.

The Administration

* Emphasize interagency coordination of programs for youth, especially by the Department of Labor and the Department of Health, Education, and Welfare.
* Change the name of the bureau within the Office of Education that is currently charged with administering the Vocational Education Act to the Bureau of Occupational Skills and Student Services and pursue policies within Office of Education designed to ensure that the bureau reforms vocational education along the lines recommended in this report.
* Give greater priority to the problems of secondary schools in the administration of the Elementary and Secondary Education Act, not only in connection with allocation of the additional $500 million that we recommend but also through continuous evaluations of programs to stimulate innovation in secondary schools.
* Within the Department of Labor, continue to seek out new ways of encouraging apprenticeships, more effective coordination of CETA programs with school programs for disadvantaged youth at the local level, and such programs as the regularizing of odd jobs and bonuses for youth who stay on the job.

The States

* Provide the matching funds for the proposed work-study program and for the reoriented $300 million of vocational education funds.

- Review policies of state aid to local school districts to determine whether additional funds are needed for secondary schools, perhaps by revising state average daily attendance (ADA) formulas to give greater weight to secondary school pupils, without reducing funds for elementary schools.
- Provide continuous encouragement and support for changes in school structure in local school districts along the lines recommended in Section 8.
- Develop policies under which state agencies design and administer youth service programs, within the general framework of the National Youth Service Foundation program.
- Give strong state support to reform of teacher training and provision for in-service training programs for teachers.
- More generally, take advantage of declining school populations to increase support for innovative programs, especially in states in which the percentage of personal income expended on the schools is below the national average.

School Districts

- Consider seriously changes in school structure where these have not already been carried out.
- Make certain that the work-experience programs, revamped vocational education programs, and other related changes proposed in this report are adopted and effectively administered.
- Make certain that cooperation with CETA in planning and administering employment and training programs for disadvantaged youth is effective and that a work-education council is established in the community if one does not already exist.
- Pay particular attention to the development of more effective programs for reducing absenteeism, including establishing closer contact with parents of chronic truants.

Mayors and City Councils

- Make certain that adequate attention is being given to well-designed programs for youth under CETA, that effective cooperation between CETA and school officials is achieved, and that employers and unions become actively involved in work-education councils and other aspects of local efforts to improve employment and training opportunities for youth.

Colleges and Universities

• Seek out participation in pairing plans with community high schools along the lines of the Boston plan.
• Community colleges, in particular, (1) cooperate with CETA and school authorities in the development of training and work-experience programs, (2) experiment with admitting students at age 16 and with the development of middle colleges, (3) provide opportunities for high school students to participate in occupational programs of the college, (4) and develop more opportunities for cooperative education and apprenticeship for both secondary and postsecondary students.
• Coordinate participation of students in community service by establishing offices of community service, and coordinate the work of such offices, through consortia, with other institutions of higher education in the region to develop youth service projects on a broad regional basis.
• Take decisive steps to reform teacher education to meet the changing needs of the 1980s.
• Give special attention to improvements in the training of school administrators.
• Develop interdiscplinary programs at the master's level for the training of community coordinators of programs for youth.

Foundations

• Give high priority to projects supporting innovation in secondary schools.
• Give support, in particular, to programs designed for deprived youth.
• Provide grants to assist in financing youth service projects.

Appendix A

Lessons from Other Industrial Countries

As we note in the Preface, the Council has sponsored the preparation of a series of essays on *Youth Education and Employment in Contemporary Societies,* and some of the policies discussed by the authors of those essays have been mentioned at various points in this report. We summarize here the most promising labor market and education policies identified in these essays. We also draw on other sources of information, especially in the case of certain countries, such as Canada and France, which were not included in the country essays. (We do not include policies in Mexico and South Asia, covered in one of the country volumes, because they are more relevant for less-developed countries.) In addition, there is a brief summary of recent developments in the relationship between youth education and work in the People's Republic of China (Kerr, 1978).

Labor Market Policies

Belgium

- Occupational Orientation Centers

    Belgium has long had a network of centers for retraining the unemployed, in which subsistence costs are covered by unemployment insurance. However, it gradually became apparent that unemployed young people needed more individualized care and guidance than unemployed adults. Accordingly, in 1974, the National Office of Employment created special centers for the "observation and orientation of the young unemployed." At these centers the first step is testing the skills and aspirations of the young and attempting to adapt these to job opportunities with a minimal cost in time and effort. The second step consists of measures designed to increase motivation. If these measures prove insufficient, the youngster proceeds to the third step, which determines the specific program of studies and training that the individual should follow in a regular vocational center. At this stage, also, the possibility of probationary employment in a private firm or in public service is investigated.

France

· Employers are exempt from social security taxes for newly hired persons under age 25.

Great Britain

· Community Industry (CI)

Initially sponsored by the National Association of Youth Clubs, this was the largest of a number of voluntary programs for youth to emerge in the early 1970s. It operates a network of enterprises throughout the country that provides various goods and services that are of value to the community but that are not normally supplied by private enterprise. Young people working in the project are paid and are expected to turn out work that meets the quality criteria of the users, who are mainly local authorities and community groups. Those accepted for the projects must be under 18 years of age, and they normally spend a year or more with the program. Some of the youngsters are assigned to craft or educational courses during their employment.

· Careers Service

The Careers Service, which was established in 1974 as a successor to the former Youth Employment Service, is entirely responsible for the placement of school-leavers below the age of 18 and, in general, handles those in older age groups for the first two years after they leave full-time education. The service is legally required to maintain a school-leaver unemployment register, to receive notification of vacancies, and to handle placement. In addition, the career departments are involved in a wide range of functions in the youth employment field, including guidance and referrals to manpower programs.

· Youth Opportunities Program

In 1977 the British government committed itself to a unified, comprehensive youth opportunities program. This program is designed to reach approximately one-half of all unemployed youth under age 19 and provides training, work experience, and education options. The details of the actual projects are planned by local committees representing community, educational, management, and trade union interests. The guaranteed uniform compensation rate (of £18 a week) is intended to eliminate any financial advantage of one program over another, which might affect the young person's choice. Yet it could induce young people to leave school, because this sum is considerably more than the educational maintenance allowances offered, though infrequently, by educational authorities to children from poor families who remain in school or college beyond the age of 16.

· Work-Experience Program

This program (WEP) is of particular interest because it has no precise parallel in other countries (to the best of our knowledge) and is regarded in Great Britain as relatively successful. The government pays the total compensation of the young people, who are unemployed workers, aged 16 to 18. They are placed in private firms or public agencies for six months or more in order to gain experience. They are not considered employees nor trainees in the usual sense, but the need for a planned, supervised program of induction and subsequent training is emphasized. The training includes, whenever possible, formal instruction in general skills, either by day release for further education or through existing in-company and industrial training board facilities.

Japan

• Training in Industry

Among the industrial nations included in the Carnegie Council series, Japan stands out as the only country that does not have a significant youth unemployment problem. However, a particularly interesting trend in vocational training in Japan is the establishment and maintenance of training facilities by private industries. By 1975, 365 such institutions were authorized by prefectural governors. These programs combine high school education and skills training on a residential basis to carefully selected youths. Part of the attraction is that all the education and subsistence costs of the participants are covered by the company. Employment for those who complete the program satisfactorily is guaranteed. In addition, in some programs, after a minimum of three years work, those who are given a high evaluation by their supervisors can go on to more advanced, full-time educational programs while receiving a regular salary from the company.

• An exceptionally effective youth placement service, with much of the responsibility carried by high school principals.

Sweden

• Vocational Guidance and Counseling

Sweden has long emphasized vocational guidance and counseling in the school system. Full-time officers for student and vocational orientation are employed in all educational institutions. Vocational counselors are required to have had one year of special training and at least six months of work experience other than teaching. Counseling begins around age 13 and is supplemented by practical work orientation, along the lines advocated by proponents of "career education" in the United States.

In the eighth grade, about a week is allocated for group visits to factories and offices, while in the ninth (or last grade of compulsory school), pupils spend two weeks in various places of work. Starting in fall 1977, pupils in the ninth grade were to be doing much more actual work in various enterprises—from six to ten weeks in 60 pilot municipalities.

- Local Community Councils

    Local planning councils for youths have recently been made obligatory for the nearly 300 municipalities throughout the country. The local school authorities are given the responsibility of leading these work-education councils, which also include representatives of the municipal authorities, the employment service, and employer and union representatives. The schools, in cooperation with these planning councils, also have the responsibility for following, advising, and guiding all young people for two years after the end of compulsory school.
- Other Labor Market Policies

    Sweden has a wide variety of programs providing work training, work relief, public service employment, moving allowances, and employer subsidies for hiring youth. While Swedish labor policies are not greatly different from those of other countries, they are more comprehensive and involve a larger percentage of the unemployed and of the total labor force.

Federal Republic of Germany

- Policies to reverse the decline in the number of apprenticeships

    Apprenticeship has been the predominant means of providing vocational education to the large proportion of German youth who leave school after completing compulsory education. Measures to combat youth unemployment have tended to center around vocational education in general and the apprenticeship system in particular. Recently, firms engaged in training have agreed to add more training positions, while the federal and state public agencies have also increased the number of their training positions.

Education

Canada

- Cooperative education programs in most provinces intended for the less successful pupils in secondary schools, under which students alternate study and work.

Denmark and Sweden

- Short courses for unemployed youth in upper secondary schools.

    In Sweden, if those who seek work after compulsory school have difficulty getting jobs, the employment service and vocational counselors help them return to school, even in the middle of a term. By having certain courses start continuously throughout the year, the secondary schools are encouraging a return to school.

- Sweden has taken another major step toward a more open and egalitarian educational system through recent reforms in its higher education system. Eligibility for entrance to institutions of higher education has been extended to those who have at least a two-year upper secondary school certificate, as well as to persons who have reached the age of 25 and have had at least four years of work experience, provided that they are competent in Swedish and English and have a basic knowledge of the subject to be studied.

- Denmark has also carried out some experiments involving both work and education that have succeeded in creating motivation and interest among disadvantaged youth on a scale hitherto unknown. At the Aabaek Continuation School, for example, the students and teachers do all the necessary work connected with housekeeping and with all of the other functions carried on at the school, including farming, fishing, repairing furniture, building boats, and repairing automobiles. The guiding principle is that the students must produce things that are necessary for survival. Many youngsters who were quite incapable of adapting to a regular school have flourished at Aabaek, and the contact between the school and the community has helped greatly in having the students placed in jobs in the neighborhood.

France

- Manual and technical training for all pupils in the "core curriculum" in the four years of secondary education.
- A new policy of providing entrance examinations for admission to institutions of higher education for candidates who

have acquired an occupational qualification in secondary education. Some 70 institutions of higher education will be open to such candidates.

Great Britain

• In postsecondary education there has been a trend toward more egalitarianism in recent decades. The development of the nonuniversity sector of higher education was a major phenomenon between 1963 and 1972. It involved the expansion of both the colleges of education and the colleges of further education, as well as the designation of some of the latter institutions as "polytechnics." In addition, a few sixth-form colleges were developed for the 16- to 19-year-old age group, with open admissions policies and academic and vocational options resembling those of community colleges in the United States.

In higher education, some alternatives to full-time attendance have been developed. One type, most frequently found in technically oriented universities and polytechnics, centers on "sandwich" courses that alternate school attendance with work or on-the-job training on a three- or six-month basis. Another distinctive development of the 1970s in Britain is the Open University (OU), in which adults may earn credits toward a university degree through an educational program that combines tutorial instruction in regional centers around the country, television programs, correspondence courses, and a short residential summer program. The OU's current enrollment is about 56,000 and thus far 21,230 students have earned degrees. Its high-quality instructional materials have been widely admired and used in other countries where similar programs have been developed. Although the students are mostly teachers and other white-collar workers, many of them are of working-class origin.

Federal Republic of Germany

• The federal and state governments have approved the expansion of vocational/technical schools at the upper secondary level for those aged 15 to 18 who do not go to full-time schools. In addition, a full-time vocational school year for those who have completed basic school is being seriously considered. There is much interest in the innovative program in the upper secondary schools of North Rhine-Westphalia, in which students can obtain both a vocational and an academic qualification, regardless of whether they are enrolled in primarily academic or primarily vocational programs. In these schools, education in any subject includes the whole spectrum of related academic disciplines.

Poland

· Among those going on to secondary school, the percentage of students enrolling in vocational schools has increased dramatically since 1960. Those from either general or vocational secondary schools who pass the final graduation examination are eligible for admission to all types of institutions of higher education. There are also postsecondary two-year schools that train general secondary school-leavers for professional work. About 20 percent of those who enter institutions of higher education have come from vocational schools. Thus, there are opportunities for graduates of both academic and vocational programs in secondary schools to be admitted to institutions of higher education.

China

China's educational policies are discussed in Section 5, and additional details are provided here. The "Four Modernizations" in agriculture, industry, national defense, and science and technology are the great new themes for national effort. One great necessity for modernization is skilled personnel: scientists, technicians, teachers, and the like. China must create as rapidly as possible vast numbers of such skilled personnel, and it is making great new efforts to find and develop talent throughout Chinese society.

· The current policy emphasizes:
    Teaching attitudes favorable to the dignity of all useful work and of working hard.

Having students visit factories and communes to see people at work, including their parents, and to have shops and gardens inside their schools wherever possible.

Having students work 15 percent of the time in the schools or in an outside factory or agricultural commune. Work includes mental as well as manual labor. Some of this work is during the vacation period.

Having many students (perhaps 70 percent to 80 percent) employed between secondary and higher education; about 20 to 30 percent of those admitted to college now go directly from middle school (the rough equivalent of the high school in the United States).

Operating substantial educational programs in factories and communes to enable workers to improve their general knowledge and upgrade their technical skills.

- Nontraditional approaches to education

Currently, there is an all-out effort at training on and off the job in many forms: apprenticeship programs, part-time and full-time schools in the factories, evening schools, three-day schools (where students can attend school three days and then work three days while another group goes to school), radio and television programs, and correspondence courses.

- Postsecondary education is being expanded rapidly, but capacity is limited, and only a small proportion of applicants can be admitted. There is intense continuing debate over educational policy, particularly over the rules governing entrance into universities. Talent is sought, and the best students go to "key" schools and universities that receive special support as models of academic excellence.

Appendix B

List of Carnegie Council Volumes on Education and Youth Employment

A Series of Special Studies

BELGIUM
Henri Janne

JAPAN
Hidetoshi Kato

POLAND
Barbara Liberska

GREAT BRITAIN
Stuart Maclure

MEXICO AND SOUTH ASIA
Alberto Hernández Medina and Carlos Muñoz Izquierdo/
Manzoor Ahmed

SWEDEN AND DENMARK
Gösta Rehn and K. Helveg Petersen

FEDERAL REPUBLIC OF GERMANY
Klaus von Dohnanyi

YOUTH EDUCATION AND UNEMPLOYMENT PROBLEMS:
AN INTERNATIONAL PERSPECTIVE
Margaret S. Gordon, with a chapter by Martin Trow

Appendix C

Participants and Observers of International Symposia, 1976 and 1977

The Ditchley Foundation Conference on Young People
in Contemporary Industrial Society
in Association with
The Carnegie Corporation of New York
October 28-31, 1976

Participants

Jocelyn Barrow
Great Britain

Richard W. Boone
United States

Ernest L. Boyer
United States

Frederick Dainton
Great Britain

Alec Dickson
Great Britain

Donald J. Eberly
United States

Peter B. Edelman
United States

John R. Ewen
Great Britain

Marcia Freedman
United States

Margaret S. Gordon
United States

Rahmat Haghdan
Iran

Henri Janne
Belgium

Clark Kerr
United States

Stuart Maclure
Great Britain

Peter Mandelson
Great Britain

David Metcalf
Great Britain

John Monks
Great Britain

David Moore
Great Britain

Sara A. Morrison
Great Britain

Richard O'Brien
Great Britain

James A. Perkins
United States

Alan Pifer
United States

Gösta Rehn
Sweden

Wilson Riles
United States

Edward A. Robie
United States

Justine Farr Rodriguez
United States

Cyril Smith
Great Britain

Margery Tabankin
United States

Martin Trow
United States

Klaus von Dohnanyi
Federal Republic of Germany

Anthony G. Watts
Great Britain

Gareth L. Williams
Great Britain

Shirley Williams
Great Britain

Willard Wirtz
United States

Lord Wolfenden, Chair
Great Britain

Observers

Mr. and Mrs. Hoyt Ammidon
United States

Michael Murphy
Great Britain

Sir Patrick and Lady Dean
Great Britain

Mr. and Mrs. H. D. H. Wills
Great Britain

Simon May
Great Britain

International Symposium on
Youth, Education, and Employment
Fère-en-Tardenois, France
April 27-30, 1977

Participants

Ladislav Cerych
France

Hywel C. Jones
Belgium

Paola Coppola Pignatelli
Italy

Clark Kerr
United States

Peter B. Edelman
United States

Barbara Liberska
Poland

Marian Edelman
United States

Stuart Maclure
Great Britain

L. J. Emmerij
The Netherlands

Olav Magnussen
Norway

John Flower
Belgium

Peter Melvyn
Switzerland

Henri Janne
Belgium

Dieter Mertens
Federal Republic of Germany

Alberto Moncada
Spain

David Moore
Great Britain

James A. Perkins
United States

Alan Pifer
United States

Gösta Rehn
Sweden

Anthony G. Watts
Great Britain

Willard Wirtz
United States

Observers

Didier Jeanperrin
France

Terry N. Saario
United States

Secretariat

Madeleine Bouillet
France

Mary McGurn
United States

Appendix D

List of Experts on Aspects of Youth Problems

The following experts on the problems of youth education and employment provided assistance and counsel in the preparation of this report.

Curtis Aller
Director
Center for Applied Manpower
    Research
Berkeley, California

Bernard E. Anderson
Director
Social Sciences
The Rockefeller Foundation

Stephen K. Bailey
Professor of Education and
    Social Policy
Harvard University

Letitia Chambers
U.S. Senate Committee on
    Labor and Human Resources

David Cohen
Director of Program
    Development
Mayor's Office of Employment
    and Training, Chicago

Henry David
Team Leader
Vocational Education Study
    Team
National Institute of Education

Donald J. Eberly
Executive Director
National Service Secretariat

Peter B. Edelman
Attorney
Foley, Lardner, Hollabaugh
    & Jacobs
Washington, D.C.

Ilona Hancock
West Coast Regional Director
ACTION

Robert J. Havighurst
Professor of Human
    Development and
    Education
The University of Chicago

Leslie Koltai
Chancellor
Los Angeles Community
    College District

Sar Levitan
Chairman
National Commission on
    Employment and
    Unemployment Statistics

Beverly R. Maimoni
Director
Instructional Services
Berkeley Unified School
    District, California

John R. Porter
Superintendent of Public
    Instruction
Department of Education,
    Michigan

Beatrice Reubens
Senior Research Associate
Conservation of Human
    Resources
Columbia University

Terry Tinson Saario
Program Officer
Division of Education and
    Research
The Ford Foundation

Isabel V. Sawhill
Director
National Commission for
    Manpower Policy

Vivien Stewart
Program Officer
Carnegie Corporation of
    New York

Mitchell Sviridoff
Vice-President
The Ford Foundation

Scott Thompson
Deputy Executive Director
National Association of
    Secondary School Principals

Michael Timpane
Deputy Director
National Institute of Education

Richard Ungerer
Director
Work-Education Consortium
    Project
National Manpower Institute

Donald Vial
Director
California Department of
    Industrial Relations

Roger Yarrington
Vice-President
American Association of
    Community and Junior
    Colleges

Barbara Yoder
Director
Office of Community and
    Employment Programs
City of Berkeley, California

References

ACTION. Interim progress report of the National Youth Community Service Demonstration Project for the period, July-December 1978. Washington, D.C.: 1979.

"Administration Proposes Revamped Higher Education Programs." *Higher Education Daily,* Supplement, July 30, 1979.

Ahmed, M. "South Asia." In *Education and Youth Employment in Less Developed Countries.* Berkeley, Calif.: Carnegie Council on Policy Studies in Higher Education, 1978.

American Association of Community and Junior Colleges. *The Project for Service-Learning.* Final report. Washington, D.C.: 1975.

American Association of Community and Junior Colleges. *Community and Junior Colleges and the Comprehensive Employment and Training Act; Participation and Recommendations for Improvement.* Washington, D.C.: 1977.

America's Volunteers: A Report on the All-Volunteer Armed Forces. Washington, D.C.: Manpower Reserve Affairs and Logistics, Office of the Assistant Secretary of Defense, 1978.

Armbruster, F., with contributions by P. J. Bracken and the assistance of J. Lind. *The U.S. Primary and Secondary Educational Process.* Croton-on-Hudson, N.Y.: Hudson Institute, 1975.

Arthur D. Little, Inc. *Cost and Service Impacts of Deinstitutionalization of Status Offenders in Ten States: "Responses to Angry Youth."* Washington, D.C.: 1977.

Bachman, J. G., Green, S., and Wirtanen, I. D. *Youth in Transition.* Vol. 3: *Dropping Out—Problem or Symptom?* Ann Arbor: Institute for Social Research, University of Michigan, 1971.

Bailey, S. *The Purposes of Education.* Bloomington, Ind.: Phi Delta Kappa Educational Foundation, 1976.

Barr, R. D., Colston, B., and Parrett, W. H. *Viewpoints* (bulletin of the School of Education, Indiana University), 1977, *53* (4), 1-30.

Barton, P. *Juvenile Delinquency, Work, and Education.* Unpublished report prepared for the U.S. Department of Health, Education, and Welfare. Washington, D.C.: National Manpower Institute, 1976.

Bass, G. V. *A Study of Alternatives in American Education.* Vol. 1: *District Policies and the Implementation of Change.* Prepared for the National Institute of Education. Santa Monica, Calif.: The Rand Corporation, 1978.

Becker, B. E., and Hills, S. M. "Today's Teenage Unemployed—Tomorrow's Working Poor?" *Monthly Labor Review,* Jan. 1979, pp. 69-71.

Berman, P., and others. *Federal Programs Supporting Educational Change.* Vol. 5: *Executive Summary.* Santa Monica, Calif.: The Rand Corporation, 1975.

"Birth of Budget Item." *San Francisco Chronicle,* Jan. 24, 1978.

Boston Public High Schools: A Guide for Parents and Students. Prepared by the Citywide Educational Coalition. Boston: Boston School Department, 1979.

Bowles, S. "Towards Equality of Educational Opportunity." *Harvard Educational Review,* Winter 1968, *38,* 89-99.

Bowles, S., and Levin, H. M. "The Determinants of Scholastic Achievement—An Appraisal of Some Recent Evidence." *Journal of Human Resources,* Winter 1968, *3,* 3-24.

Boyer, E. L. "Commissioner's Model for the 1980s." *New York Times,* Jan. 7, 1979, p. 14.

The Budget of the United States Government, Fiscal Year 1980. Appendix. Washington, D.C.: U.S. Government Printing Office, 1979.

Bullock, P. *Aspirations vs. Opportunity: "Careers" in the Inner City.* Ann Arbor: Institute of Labor and Industrial Relations, University of Michigan-Wayne State University, 1973.

Bushnell, D. S. *Cooperation in Vocational Education: Executive Summary of the Joint Study by the American Association of Community and Junior Colleges and the American Vocational Association.* Washington, D.C.: 1978.

"Califano Refuses to Back Away from Attack on Voc Ed." *Manpower and Vocational Education Weekly,* Dec. 7, 1978, p. 4.

Campbell, R. C. "Child Welfare and Attendance Services." *Thrust for Education Leadership,* 1973, *2* (14), 14-16.

Card, J. J., and Wise, L. L. "Teenage Mothers and Teenage Fathers: The Impact of Early Childbearing on the Parent's Personal and Professional Lives." *Family Planning Perspectives,* 1978, *10* (4), 199-205.

Carnegie Commission on Higher Education. *Quality and Equality: New Levels of Federal Responsibility for Higher Education.* New York: McGraw-Hill, 1968.

Carnegie Commission on Higher Education. *Continuity and Discontinuity: Higher Education and the Schools.* New York: McGraw-Hill, 1973a.

Carnegie Commission on Higher Education. *Opportunities for Women in Higher Education: Their Current Participation, Prospects for the Future, and Recommendations for Action.* New York: McGraw-Hill, 1973b.

Carnegie Commission on Higher Education. *Toward a Learning Society: Alternatives to Life, Work, and Service.* New York: McGraw-Hill, 1973c.

Carnegie Council on Policy Studies in Higher Education. *The Federal Role in Postsecondary Education: Unfinished Business, 1975-1980.* San Francisco: Jossey-Bass, 1975.

Carnegie Council on Policy Studies in Higher Education. *Next Steps for the 1980s in Student Financial Aid: A Fourth Alternative.* San Francisco: Jossey-Bass, 1979.

Carnegie Council on Policy Studies in Higher Education. *Education and Youth Employment.* A series of country studies. Berkeley, Calif., 1978, 1979, and forthcoming.

Chamber of Commerce of the United States of America. *Employee Benefits, 1975.* Washington, D.C.: 1976.

Children's Defense Fund. *Children Out of School in America.* Cambridge, Mass.: 1974.

Chilman, C. "Possible Factors Associated with Higher Out-of-Marriage Births Among Adolescents." Paper presented at the annual meeting of American Psychological Association, Washington, D.C., 1976.

Clorfene, L. "Giving Students a Chance: The Story of Evanston Township High School." *Integrated Education,* Sept.-Oct. 1977, pp. 18-21.

Coleman, J. S. "The University and Society's Demands upon It." In C. Kaysen (Ed.), *Content and Context: Essays on College Education.* New York: McGraw-Hill, 1973.

Coleman, J. S., and others. *Equality of Educational Opportunity.* (2 vols.) Washington, D.C.: U.S. Government Printing Office, 1966.

College Entrance Examination Board. *On Further Examination: Report of the Advisory Panel on the Scholastic Aptitude Test Score Decline.* New York: 1977.

Committee for Economic Development. *Jobs for the Hard-to-Employ: New Directions for a Public-Private Partnership.* New York: 1978.

"Community Colleges Offer over 1,200 Apprenticeship Programs." *Higher Education Daily,* Sept. 12, 1977, p. 4.

A Compilation of Federal Education Laws, as Amended Through December 31, 1974. Prepared for House Committee on Education and Labor and Senate Committee on Labor and Public Welfare. 94th Cong., 1st sess. Washington, D.C.: U.S. Government Printing Office, 1975.

Comptroller General of the United States. *Assessment of the Teacher Corps Program.* Washington, D.C.: U.S. Government Printing Office, 1972.

Comptroller General of the United States. *Additional Cost of the All-Volunteer Force.* Washington, D.C.: U.S. Government Printing Office, 1978.

Conant, J. B. *The American High School Today: A First Report to Interested Citizens.* New York: McGraw-Hill, 1959.

Conant, J. B. *Slums and Suburbs: A Commentary on Schools in Metropolitan Areas.* New York: McGraw-Hill, 1961.

Conant, J. B. *The Education of American Teachers.* New York: McGraw-Hill, 1963.

Conant, J. B. *The Comprehensive High School: A Second Report to Interested Citizens.* New York: McGraw-Hill, 1967.

Congressional Budget Office. *Budget Options for the Youth Employment Problem.* Washington, D.C.: U.S. Government Printing Office, 1977.

Congressional Budget Office. *National Service Programs and Their Effects on Military Manpower and Civilian Youth Problems.* Washington, D.C.: U.S. Government Printing Office, 1978.

"Construction Union Apprenticeships Key to Steadier Jobs." *Manpower and Vocational Education Weekly,* Sept. 10, 1975, p. 9.

Control Systems Research, Inc. *The Program for Local Service.* A preliminary research report prepared for ACTION. Seattle, Wash.: 1973.

Cooper, R. V. L. *Military Manpower and the All-Volunteer Force.* A report prepared for Defense Advanced Research Projects Agency. Santa Monica, Calif.: The Rand Corporation, 1977.

Corwin, R. G. *Reform and Organizational Survival: The Teacher Corps as an Instrument of Educational Change.* New York: Wiley, 1973.

Crain, R. L., Mahard, R. E., and Narot, R. E. *Making Desegregation Work: How Schools Create Social Climates.* Santa Monica, Calif.: The Rand Corporation, forthcoming.

"DOL to Test Feasibility of Consolidation of Youth Programs." *Manpower and Vocational Education Weekly,* Feb. 8, 1979, p. 6.

Dryfoos, J. G., and Heisler, T. "Contraceptive Services for Adolescents: An Overview." *Family Planning Perspectives,* 1978, *10* (4), 223-233.

Eberly, D. J. "Universal Youth Service Milestones, 1945-1975." Paper prepared for the universal youth service conference sponsored by the Eleanor Roosevelt Institute, Hyde Park, N.Y., 1976.

Echternacht, G. J. *A Comparative Study of Secondary Schools with Different Score Patterns.* Princeton, N.J.: College Entrance Examination Board, 1977.

Economic Development Council of New York City. *Truancy in New York City's Public Schools: Its Nature, Costs, and Implications for the Future.* New York: Oct. 1977. (Duplicated.)

The Education of Adolescents: The Final Report and Recommendations of the National Panel on High School and Adolescent Education. (John H. Martin, Chairman and Director.) Washington, D.C.: U.S. Office of Education, 1976.

Employment and Earnings, Jan. 1979.

Federal Bureau of Investigation. *Crime in the United States, 1977.* Washington, D.C.: U.S. Government Printing Office, 1978.

"Feds Plan 1.7 Million Jobs for Youth." *Manpower and Vocational Education Weekly,* May 17, 1979, p. 10.

Feldstein, M. "The Economics of the New Unemployment." *The Public Interest,* Fall 1973, *33,* 3-42.

Feldstein, M., and Ellwood, D. "Teenage Unemployment: What Is the Problem?" Paper presented at a conference on youth unemployment sponsored by the National Bureau of Economic Research, Airlie, Va., May 1979.

Fernandez, C., Espinosa, R. S., and Dornbusch, S. M. *Factors Perpetuating the Low Academic Status of Chicano High School Students.* Stanford, Calif.: Stanford Center for Research and Development in Teaching, Stanford University, 1975.

Ferrin, R. I., and Arbeiter, S. *Bridging the Gap: A Selection of Education-to-Work Linkages.* Supplemental report of the State-Level Study in

Career Education. New York: College Entrance Examination Board, 1975.

Freeman, R. B. *Why Is There a Youth Labor Market Problem?* Working Paper no. 365. Cambridge, Mass.: National Bureau of Economic Research, 1979.

Friedlander, S. L. *Unemployment in the Urban Core: An Analysis of Thirty Cities with Policy Recommendations.* New York: Praeger, 1972.

Friedman, M. *Capitalism and Freedom.* Chicago: University of Chicago Press, 1962.

Fund for the Improvement of Postsecondary Education. *Unemployed Youth: A Postsecondary Response.* Washington, D.C.: Education Division, U.S. Department of Health, Education, and Welfare, 1979.

Furstenberg, F. F., Jr. *Unplanned Parenthood.* New York: Macmillan, 1976.

Furstenberg, F. F., Jr., and Crawford, A. G. "Family Support: Helping Teenage Mothers to Cope." *Family Planning Perspectives,* 1978, *10* (6), 322-333.

Galbraith, J. K. "Let Us Begin: An Invitation to Action on Poverty." *Harper's,* March 1964, p. *228.*

Gavett, T., and others. *Youth Unemployment and Minimum Wages.* Washington, D.C.: U.S. Bureau of Labor Statistics, 1970.

Gibboney, R. A., Associates, Inc. *The Career Intern Program: Final Report.* Vol. 1: *An Experiment in Career Education that Worked.* Washington, D.C.: U.S. National Institute of Education, 1977.

Gordon, D. M. *Theories of Poverty and Underemployment: Orthodox, Radical, and Dual Labor Market Perspectives.* Lexington, Mass.: Heath, 1972.

Gordon, D. M. (Ed.). *Problems in Political Economy: An Urban Perspective.* (2nd ed.) Lexington, Mass.: Heath, 1977.

Gordon, M. S. *Retraining and Labor Market Adjustment in Western Europe.* Washington, D.C.: U.S. Office of Manpower, Automation, and Training, 1965.

Gordon, M. S. "Youth Unemployment in Western Industrial Countries." In M. S. Gordon with a chapter by M. Trow, *Youth Education and Unemployment Problems: An International Perspective.* Berkeley, Calif.: Carnegie Council on Policy Studies in Higher Education, forthcoming.

Grasso, J. T., and Shea, J. R. *Vocational Education and Training: Impact on Youth.* Berkeley, Calif.: Carnegie Council on Policy Studies in Higher Education, 1979.

Green, E. G. "Apprenticeship: A Potential Weapon Against Minority Youth Unemployment." In *From School to Work: Improving the Transition.* Papers prepared for the National Commission on Manpower Policy. Washington, D.C.: 1976.

"Hartford, Connecticut: Schools as Entrepreneurs." *Manpower and Vocational Education Weekly,* May 18, 1978, pp. 6-7.

Havighurst, R. J., Graham, R. A., and Eberly, D. "American Youth in the Mid-Seventies." *Bulletin of the National Association of Secondary School Principals,* 1972, *56* (367), 1-13.

Hesburgh, T. M. Unpublished paper on the Peace Corps, 1965.

Hoffman, L. W., and Nye, F. I. *Working Mothers: An Evaluative Review of the Consequences for Wife, Husband, and Child.* San Francisco: Jossey-Bass, 1974.

Hoyt, R. G. "Learning a Lesson from the Catholic Schools." *New York,* Sept. 1977, pp. 48-55.

Humphrey, H. H. "American Youth Service Milestones, 1945-75." *Congressional Record,* Sept. 23, 1976, S 16501-16504.

Husèn, T. *Changing Attitudes to Education and Work Among Youth in the Achievement-Oriented Society.* Prepared for the High Level Conference on Youth Unemployment, meeting of the preparatory group, Oct. 20-21, 1977. Paris: Organization for Economic Cooperation and Development, 1977. (Duplicated.)

Husèn, T. *The School in Question: A Comparative Study of School and Its Future in Western Societies.* Cambridge, England: Oxford University Press, 1979.

James, W. "The Moral Equivalent of War." *International Conciliation,* No. 27. New York: Carnegie Endowment for International Peace, 1910.

Janne, H. *Education and Youth Employment in Belgium.* Berkeley, Calif.: Carnegie Council on Policy Studies in Higher Education, 1979.

Jencks, C., and Brown, M. D. "Effects of High Schools on Their Students." *Harvard Educational Review,* 1975, *45* (3), 273-324.

Jencks, C., and others. *Inequality: A Reassessment of the Effect of Family and Schooling in America.* New York: Basic Books, 1972.

Kato, H. *Education and Youth Employment in Japan.* Berkeley, Calif.: Carnegie Council on Policy Studies in Higher Education, 1978.

Kerr, C. "Education and the World of Work: An Analytical Sketch." In J. A. Perkins and B. B. Burn (Eds.), *Access, Systems, Youth, and Employment.* New York: International Council for Educational Development, 1977.

Kerr, C. *Observations on the Relations Between Education and Work in the People's Republic of China: Report of a Study Group.* Berkeley, Calif.: Carnegie Council on Policy Studies in Higher Education, 1978.

Killingsworth, C. C. "Discussion." In R. A. and M. S. Gordon (Eds.), *Prosperity and Unemployment.* New York: Wiley, 1966.

Klerman, L. V., and Jekel, J. F. *School-Age Mothers: Problems, Programs, and Policy.* Hamden, Conn.: Shoe String Press, 1973.

Knowles, A. S., and Associates. *Handbook of Cooperative Education.* San Francisco: Jossey-Bass, 1971.

Kohler, M. C., and Dollar, B. "Youth Service Work: An Antidote to Alienation." In R. W. Tyler (Ed.), *From Youth to Constructive Adult Life: The Role of the Public School.* Berkeley, Calif.: McCutchan, 1978.

La Noue, G. R. *Educational Vouchers: Concepts and Controversies.* New York: Teachers College Press, 1972.

Larson, M. A. *Federal Policy for Preschool Services: Assumptions and Evidence.* (Rev. version.) Research memorandum prepared for Office of the Assistant Secretary for Education, U.S. Department of Health, Education, and Welfare. Menlo Park, Calif.: Stanford Research Institute, June 1979.

Larson, M. A., and others. *Better Basic Skills for Youth: Four Proposals for Federal Policy*. Prepared for the U.S. National Institute of Education. Menlo Park, Calif.: Stanford Research Institute, 1977.

Levin, H. M. "A Decade of Policy Developments in Improving Education and Training for Low-Income Populations." In *A Decade of Federal Antipoverty Programs: Achievements, Failures, and Lessons*. Madison: Institute for Research on Poverty, University of Wisconsin, 1977.

Levine, D. U., and Havighurst, R. J. *The Future of Big-City Schools: Desegregation Policies and Magnet Alternatives*. Berkeley, Calif.: McCutchan, 1977.

Levitan, S. A., and Johnston, B. H. *The Job Corps: A Social Experiment That Works*. Baltimore: Johns Hopkins University Press, 1975.

Liberska, B. *Education and Youth Employment in Poland*. Berkeley, Calif.: Carnegie Council on Policy Studies in Higher Education, 1979.

McCloskey, P. N., Jr. "National Youth Service System." *Congressional Record*, 1979, *125* (30), pp. E 1070-1071.

Maclure, S. *Education and Youth Employment in Great Britain*. Berkeley, Calif.: Carnegie Council on Policy Studies in Higher Education, 1979.

McCurdy, J., and Speich, D. "Drop in Student Skills Unequaled in History." *Los Angeles Times*, Aug. 15, 1976a.

McCurdy, J., and Speich, D. "School Standards Also Decline." *Los Angeles Times*, Aug. 16, 1976b.

McCurdy, J., and Speich, D. "Answers to Decline of Student Skills Unsought." *Los Angeles Times*, Aug. 17, 1976c.

McGurn, G., and Davis, W. "Occupational Education in the United States." In *Between School and Work*. Paris: Institute of Education, European Cultural Foundation, 1976.

Mangum, G., and Walsh, J. *Employment and Training Programs for Youth: What Works Best for Whom?* Report to the Office of Youth Programs, U.S. Employment and Training Administration, from the National Council on Employment Policy. Washington, D.C.: U.S. Employment and Training Administration, 1978.

Manpower Demonstration Research Corporation. *Analysis of Nine-Month Interviews for Supported Work: Results of an Early Sample*. New York: 1977a.

Manpower Demonstration Research Corporation. *Analysis of Nine-Month Interviews for Supported Work: Results of an Early AFDC Sample*. New York: 1977b.

Manpower Demonstration Research Corporation. *The Youth Entitlement Demonstration Program: A Summary Report on the Start-Up Period of the Youth Incentive Entitlement Pilot Projects*. New York: 1979a.

Manpower Demonstration Research Corporation. *The Youth Entitlement Demonstration: An Interim Report on Program Implementation*. New York: 1979b.

Manpower Demonstration Research Corporation. *The National Supported Work Demonstration: Effects During the First 18 Months After Enrollment*. Prepared by Mathematica Policy Research, Inc. Princeton, N.J.: 1979c.

"Many School Officials Approve of Contracting Voc Ed to Private Industry." *Manpower and Vocational Education Weekly*, Nov. 16, 1978, p. 4.

Marland, S. P., Jr. *Career Education: A Program for Reform.* New York: McGraw-Hill, 1974.

Marshall, F. R., and Briggs, V. M., Jr. *The Negro and Apprenticeship.* Baltimore, Md.: Johns Hopkins University Press, 1967.

Massey, G. C., Scott, M. V., and Dornbusch, S. M. "Racism Without Racists: Institutional Racism in Urban Schools." *The Black Scholar,* Nov. 1975, pp. 10-19.

Matters of Choice: A Ford Foundation Report on Alternative Schools. New York: Ford Foundation, 1974.

Mayor's Office of Manpower Resources, Baltimore. *Toward a Local Manpower Delivery System: An Annual Report of Services of the Baltimore Metropolitan Manpower Consortium, Fiscal Year 1977.* Baltimore, Md.: 1977.

Mead, M. *Coming of Age in Samoa.* (3rd ed.) New York: Morrow, 1961.

Mead, M. "A National Service System as a Solution to a Variety of National Problems." In S. Tax (Ed.), *The Draft: A Handbook of Facts and Alternatives.* Chicago: University of Chicago Press, 1967.

Medina, A. H., and Izquierdo, C. M. "Mexico." In *Education and Youth Employment in Less Developed Countries.* Berkeley, Calif.: Carnegie Council on Policy Studies in Higher Education, 1978.

Michael, L. S. "Alternative Modes of Organizing Secondary Schools." In *Humanizing the Secondary School.* Washington, D.C.: Association for Supervision and Curriculum Development, National Education Association, 1969.

Moore, K. A. "Teenage Childbirth and Welfare Dependency." *Family Planning Perspectives,* 1978, *10* (4), 233-235.

Moore, K. A., and Caldwell, S. B. "The Effect of Government Policies on Out-of-Wedlock Sex and Pregnancy." *Family Planning Perspectives,* 1977, *9* (4), 164-169.

Moskowitz, R. D. "School 'Voucher Plan' Revived." *San Francisco Chronicle,* Jan. 9, 1979, p. 5.

Moynihan, D. P. "Why Private Schools Merit Public Aid: The Constitutional Case for Tuition Tax Credits." *Washington Post,* March 5, 1978, pp. C-1 and C-4.

National Advisory Council on Education Professions Development. *Teacher Corps: Past or Prologue? A Report with Recommendations to the President and the Congress.* Washington, D.C.: 1975.

National Association of Secondary School Principals. *25 Action-Learning Schools.* Reston, Va.: 1974.

National Association of Secondary School Principals. *This We Believe: Secondary Schools in a Changing Society.* Reston, Va.: 1975.

National Association of Secondary School Principals. *Guidelines for Improving SAT Scores.* Reston, Va.: 1978.

National Child Labor Committee and National Urban League. *Toward a National Youth Development Policy (A Call to Action).* New York: 1978.

National Commission for Manpower Policy. *An Employment Strategy for the United States: Next Steps.* Second annual report to The President and the Congress. Washington, D.C.: 1976.

National Commission for Manpower Policy. *An Enlarged Role for the Private Sector in Federal Employment and Training Programs.* Fourth annual report to The President and the Congress. Washington, D.C.: 1978.

National Commission on Employment and Unemployment Statistics. *Counting the Labor Force: Preliminary Draft Report, Prepared for Public Comment.* Washington, D.C.: Jan. 1979.

National Committee on Employment of Youth. *The Transition from School to Work: A Study of Laws, Regulations, and Practices Restricting Work Experience and Employment Opportunities for Youth.* New York: 1975.

National Council on Crime and Delinquency. *Prisons: The Price We Pay.* Hackensack, N.J.: 1978.

National League of Cities and United States Conference of Mayors. *CETA and Youth: Programs for Cities: Baltimore: Harbor City Learning Program.* Washington, D.C.: n.d.

National Manpower Institute. *Work-Education Councils: Profiles of 21 Collaborative Efforts.* Washington, D.C.: 1977.

National Manpower Institute. *Job Placement Services for Youth.* Washington, D.C.: 1978.

Organization for Economic Cooperation and Development. *Education and Working Life in Modern Society.* Report of the secretary-general's ad hoc group on the relations between education and employment; (Clark Kerr, Chairman.) Paris: 1975.

Organization for Economic Cooperation and Development. *Beyond Compulsory Schooling: Options and Changes in Upper Secondary Education.* Paris: 1976.

Organization for Economic Cooperation and Development. *Policies for Apprenticeship.* Paris: 1979.

Perrella, V. C., and Bogan, F. A. "Special Labor Force Report: Out-of-School Youth, February 1963." *Monthly Labor Review,* 1964, *87* (11), 1260-1268, table A-3.

Pifer, A. "The Responsibility for Reform in Higher Education." Report of the president in *Annual Report for 1971.* New York: Carnegie Corporation, 1971, p. 4.

Pifer, A., and others. *Systems of Higher Education: United States.* New York: International Council for Educational Development, 1978.

Pollard, V. "Berkeley Project: Programming Kids for the Job Race." *San Francisco Chronicle,* April 2, 1979, p. 17.

Potomac Institute. *Youth and the Needs of the Nation.* Report of the Committee for the Study of National Service. Washington, D.C.: 1979.

Radner, R., and Miller, L. S. *Demand and Supply in U.S. Higher Education.* New York: McGraw-Hill, 1975.

Rains, P. *Becoming an Unwed Mother.* Chicago: Aldine, 1971.

Rawlins, V. L. *Government-Sponsored Programs for the Disadvantaged Youth as a Part of Efficient Long-Run Manpower Policy.* Unpublished doctoral dissertation, Department of Economics, University of California, Berkeley, 1969.

The Reform of Secondary Education: A Report of the National Commis-

sion on the Reform of Secondary Education. (B. Frank Brown, Chairman; Commission established by the Charles F. Kettering Foundation.) New York: McGraw-Hill, 1973.

Rehn, G., and Petersen, H. *Education and Youth Employment in Sweden and Denmark.* Berkeley, Calif.: Carnegie Council on Policy Studies in Higher Education (forthcoming).

Reischauer, R. D., and Hartman, R. W., with the assistance of D. J. Sullivan. *Reforming School Finance.* Washington, D.C.: Brookings Institution, 1973.

Reubens, B. G. "Vocational Education for *All* in High School?" In J. O'Toole (Ed.), *Work and the Quality of Life: Resource Papers for Work in America.* Cambridge, Mass.: M.I.T. Press, 1974.

Reubens, B. G. *Bridges to Work: International Comparisons of Transition Services.* New York: Universe Books; Montclair, N.J.: Allenheld and Osmun, 1977.

Rice, P. D., and others. *Year-Round Schools: Models and Issues.* Report prepared for the Office of Assistant Secretary for Planning and Evaluation, U.S. Department of Health, Education, and Welfare. Washington, D.C.: 1975.

Robison, D. *Training and Jobs Programs in Action.* New York: Committee for Economic Development in cooperation with Work in America Institute, 1978.

Rockefeller Foundation. *Youth Unemployment.* Working Paper. New York: 1977.

Schneider, E. "Programs for Transition to Adulthood in the Portland Public Schools." In R. W. Tyler (Ed.), *From Youth to Constructive Adult Life: The Role of the Public School.* Berkeley, Calif.: McCutchan, 1978.

Schorr, A. *Poor Kids.* New York: Basic Books, 1966.

Shepard, M. A., and others. *Year-Round Schools: The Importance of Year-Round Schools.* Cambridge, Mass.: Abt Associates, 1975.

Sheppard, N., Jr. "The No-Nonsense' High School." *San Francisco Sunday Examiner and Chronicle: This World,* June 18, 1978, p. 31.

Silberman, C. E. *Crisis in the Classroom: The Remaking of American Education.* New York: Random House, 1970.

Silberman, C. E. *Criminal Violence, Criminal Justice.* New York: Random House, 1978.

Simpson, J. E., and Van Arsdol, M. D., Jr. "Residential History and Educational Status of Delinquents and Nondelinquents." *Social Problems,* 1967, *15* (7), 25-40.

Sizer, T. R. *Places for Learning, Places for Joy: Speculations on American School Reform.* Cambridge, Mass.: Harvard University Press, 1973.

Smith, V. H. *Alternative Schools: The Development of Options in Public Education.* Lincoln, Neb.: Professional Educators Publications, 1974.

Stadtman, V. A. "Alternatives and Equivalence in Secondary Education." Unpublished paper prepared for a seminar sponsored by the American Council on Education, the Council of Chief State School Officers, and the National Association of Secondary School Principals. Berkeley, Calif.: Carnegie Council on Policy Studies in Higher Education, 1977.

Taussig, M. K. "An Economic Analysis of Vocational Education in New York City High Schools." *Journal of Human Resources,* Summer 1968.

Teacher Education in the United States: The Responsibility Gap. Report by the Study Commission on Undergraduate Education and the Education of Teachers. Lincoln, Neb.: University of Nebraska Press, 1976.

Teachers for a School in Transition. A summary of viewpoints and proposals presented by the 1974 Swedish Commission on Teacher Education (LUT 74). Uddevalla, Sweden: Bohusläningens AB, 1979.

The President. *Manpower Report of the President, 1972.* Washington, D.C.: U.S. Government Printing Office, 1972.

The President. *Manpower Report of the President, 1974.* Washington, D.C.: U.S. Government Printing Office, 1974.

The President. *Employment and Training Report of the President, 1977.* Washington, D.C.: U.S. Government Printing Office, 1977.

The President. *Employment and Training Report of the President, 1978.* Washington, D.C.: U.S. Government Printing Office, 1978.

The President. *Economic Report of the President, 1979.* Washington, D.C.: U.S. Government Printing Office, 1979.

"39 Congressmen Warn Against Draft Renewal." *San Francisco Chronicle,* April 10, 1979, p. 9.

Timpane, M. "Some Notions on the Performance of Secondary Schools in the United States." Unpublished paper. Washington, D.C.: U.S. National Institute of Education, 1978.

Timpane, M., and others. *Youth Policy in Transition.* Prepared for the Office of the Assistant Secretary for Planning and Evaluation, U.S. Department of Health, Education, and Welfare. Santa Monica, Calif.: The Rand Corporation, 1976.

Trow, M. "Reflections on Youth Problems and Policies in the United States." In M. S. Gordon, *Youth Education and Unemployment Problems: An International Perspective.* Berkeley, Calif.: Carnegie Council on Policy Studies in Higher Education, forthcoming.

Tyler, R. W. "The Federal Role in Education." *The Public Interest,* Winter 1974, *34,* 164-187.

"Umana School Shows Citywide Popularity." *Tech Talk* (Massachusetts Institute of Technology), June 28, 1978, pp. 1, 8.

U.S. Bureau of the Census. "Estimates of the Population of the United States, by Single Years of Age, Color, and Sex, 1900 to 1959." *Current Population Reports.* Series P-25, no. 311. Washington, D.C.: U.S. Government Printing Office, 1965.

U.S. Bureau of the Census. "Projections of the Population of the United States, by Age and Sex: 1970 to 2020." *Current Population Reports.* Series P-25, no. 470. Washington, D.C.: U.S. Government Printing Office, 1971.

U.S. Bureau of the Census. "Estimates of the Population of the United States, by Age, Sex, and Race: April 1, 1960 to July 1, 1973." *Current Population Reports,* Series P-25, no. 519. Washington, D.C.: U.S. Government Printing Office, 1974.

U.S. Bureau of the Census. *Historical Statistics of the United States: Colonial Times to 1970.* (2 vols.) Washington, D.C.: U.S. Government Printing Office, 1975.

U.S. Bureau of the Census. "Estimates of the Population of the United States by Age, Sex, and Race: 1970 to 1977." *Current Population Reports.* Series P-25, no. 721. Washington, D.C.: U.S. Government Printing Office, 1978.

U.S. Bureau of the Census. "Marital Status and Living Arrangements." *Current Population Reports.* Series P-20, no. 338. Washington, D.C.: U.S. Government Printing Office, 1979a.

U.S. Bureau of the Census. "School Enrollment—Social and Economic Characteristics of Students: October 1977." *Current Population Reports.* Series P-20, no. 333. Washington, D.C.: U.S. Government Printing Office, 1979b.

U.S. Bureau of the Census. "Estimates of the Population of the United States, by Age, Sex, and Race: 1976 to 1978." *Current Population Reports.* Series P-25, no. 800. Washington, D.C.: U.S. Government Printing Office, 1979c.

U.S. Bureau of Labor Statistics. *News,* Oct. 5, 1977.

U.S. Bureau of Labor Statistics. "Students, Graduates, and Dropouts in the Labor Market, October 1977." *Special Labor Force Report 215.* Washington, D.C.: U.S. Government Printing Office, 1978.

U.S. Bureau of Labor Statistics. "Employment and Unemployment During 1978: An Analysis." *Special Labor Force Report 218.* Washington, D.C.: U.S. Government Printing Office, 1979.

U.S. Department of Labor. *News.* Office of Information. April 19, 1978, pp. 1-2.

U.S. Employment and Training Administration. *Youth Initiatives.* Washington, D.C.: U.S. Government Printing Office, March 1978.

U.S. Manpower Administration. *Low-Income Labor Markets and Urban Manpower Programs: A Critical Assessment.* Washington, D.C.: U.S. Government Printing Office, 1972.

U.S. National Center for Education Statistics. *Digest of Education Statistics, 1977-1978.* Washington, D.C.: U.S. Government Printing Office, 1978a.

U.S. National Center for Education Statistics. *Projections of Education Statistics to 1986-87.* Washington, D.C.: U.S. Government Printing Office, 1978b.

U.S. National Center for Education Statistics. *The Condition of Education: 1978 Edition.* Washington, D.C.: U.S. Government Printing Office, 1978c.

U.S. National Center for Education Statistics. *The Condition of Education: 1979 Edition.* Washington, D.C.: U.S. Government Printing Office, 1979.

U.S. National Center for Health Statistics. *Monthly Vital Statistics Report,* Supplement, March 29, 1978, *26* (12).

U.S. National Institute of Education. *The Community Is the Teacher.* Washington, D.C.: U.S. Government Printing Office, 1976.

U.S. National Institute of Education. *A Plan for the Study of Vocational Education.* Transmitted to the Congress, Dec. 30, 1977. Washington, D.C.: U.S. Government Printing Office, 1977a.

U.S. National Institute of Education. *Violent Schools—Safe Schools: The*

Safe School Study Report to Congress: Executive Summary. Washington, D.C.: U.S. Government Printing Office, 1977b.

U.S. Social Security Administration. *Social Security Bulletin: Annual Statistical Supplement, 1975.* Washington, D.C.: U.S. Government Printing Office, 1977.

Vial, D. "A State View." Paper presented at the 1978 spring meeting of the Industrial Relations Research Association. *Labor Law Journal,* Aug. 1978, pp. 527-530.

Vocational Foundation, Inc. *Our Turn to Listen: A White Paper on Unemployment, Education and Crime Based on Extensive Interviews with New York City Dropouts.* New York, n.d.

"Voc Ed Group Calls for $1 Billion Education Program in Youth Employment Bill." *Manpower and Vocational Education Weekly,* June 28, 1979, p. 3.

von Dohnanyi, K. *Education and Youth Employment in the Federal Republic of Germany.* Berkeley, Calif.: Carnegie Council on Policy Studies in Higher Education, 1978.

Wallace, P. A. *Pathways to Work: Unemployment Among Black Teenage Females.* Lexington, Mass.: Lexington Books, 1974.

Weiler, D., with the collaboration of others. *A Public School Voucher Demonstration: The First Year at Alum Rock, Summary and Conclusions.* Prepared for the U.S. National Institute of Education. Santa Monica, Calif.: The Rand Corporation, 1974.

Whitehead, A. N. *The Aims of Education and Other Essays.* New York: Free Press, 1929.

Wilson, S. R., and Wise, L. L. *The American Citizen: 11 Years After High School.* Vol. 1. Palo Alto, Calif.: American Institutes for Research, 1975.

Winer, E. N., and Hochman, R. M. *Report on Massachusetts Secondary School Work Experience Program.* Boston, Mass.: Massachusetts State Department of Education, 1976.

Winkler, K. J. "Desegregation in Boston: Colleges, Schools Pair Off." *Chronicle of Higher Education,* Nov. 17, 1975, pp. 3-4.

Wirtz, W., and the National Manpower Institute. *The Boundless Resource: A Prospectus for an Education/Work Policy.* Washington, D.C.: New Republic Books, 1975.

"Wisconsin Schools and the Job Service Team Up to Prepare Youths for Work." *Manpower and Vocational Education Weekly,* Sept. 22, 1977, p. 9.

Wolfgang, M. E., Figlio, R. M., and Sellin, T. *Delinquency in a Birth Cohort.* Chicago: University of Chicago Press, 1972.

Work in America Institute, Inc. *World of Work Report,* 1978, *3* (4).

Work in America Institute, Inc. *Job Strategies for Urban Youth: Sixteen Pilot Programs for Action.* Scarsdale, N.Y.: 1979.

"Yielding to Pressure, White House Approves Voc Ed Funds at FY1979 Levels." *Manpower and Vocational Education Weekly,* Jan. 11, 1979, p. 1.

Young, A. Testimony Before the Joint Economic Committee, U.S. Congress. *Congressional Record,* Sept. 24, 1976, S 16609-16612.

Youth: Transition to Adulthood. Report of the Panel on Youth of the President's Science Advisory Committee. (James S. Coleman, Chairman.) Washington, D.C.: Office of Science and Technology, Executive Office of The President, 1973.

Zelnick, M., and Kantner, J. F. "Contraceptive Patterns and Premarital Pregnancy Among Women Aged 15-19 in 1976." *Family Planning Perspectives,* 1978, *10* (3), 135-142.

Zelnick, M., Kim, Y. J., and Kantner, J. F. "Probabilities of Intercourse and Conception Among U.S. Teenage Women, 1971 and 1976." *Family Planning Perspectives,* 1979, *11* (3), 177-183.

Index